D0876442

BOOKS BY

Rose Macaulay

LAST LETTERS TO A FRIEND (editor, Constance Babington-Smith) 1963
LETTERS TO A FRIEND (editor, Constance Babington-Smith) 1962
THE TOWERS OF TREBIZOND 1957
FABLED SHORE 1951
THE WORLD MY WILDERNESS 1950
AND NO MAN'S WIT 1940
THE WRITINGS OF E. M. FORSTER 1938
I WOULD BE PRIVATE 1937
PERSONAL PLEASURES 1935
THE MINOR PLEASURES OF LIFE (editor) 1935
JOHN MILTON 1935
GOING ABROAD 1934
THEY WERE DEFEATED (*American title*, THE SHADOW FLIES) 1932
CAROLINE 1932
SOME RELIGIOUS ELEMENTS IN ENGLISH LITERATURE 1931
STAYING WITH RELATIONS 1930
DAISY AND DAPHNE 1928
A CASUAL COMMENTARY (*essays*) 1926
CREWE TRAIN 1926
ORPHAN ISLAND 1925
TOLD BY AN IDIOT 1924
MYSTERY AT GENEVA 1923
DANGEROUS AGES 1921
POTTERISM 1920
THREE DAYS (*poetry*) 1920
LEE SHORE 1913
VIEWS AND VAGABONDS 1912

BOOKS BY

Constance Babington-Smith

LAST LETTERS TO A FRIEND (*editor*) 1963
LETTERS TO A FRIEND (*editor*) 1962
TESTING TIME 1961
The Story of British Test Pilots and Their Aircraft
AIR SPY 1957
The Story of Photo Intelligence in World War II

Rose Macaulay

LAST LETTERS TO A FRIEND

1952–1958

Rose Macaulay in Venice: photographed by Roloff Beny in 1957

Rose Macaulay

LAST
LETTERS TO A FRIEND
1952-1958

Edited by Constance Babington-Smith

Atheneum : New York

1963

Contents

Preface

These letters were written by Dame Rose Macaulay to her cousin, the Rev. John Hamilton Cowper Johnson, of the Society of St John the Evangelist (commonly known as the Cowley Fathers) between 1952 and her death in 1958. They are a continuation of the series which has already been published in *Letters to a Friend*. The entire correspondence began in 1950 when Father Johnson, who had not seen Rose Macaulay since he left England for America in 1916, wrote to congratulate her on her book *They Were Defeated*. The letters of the first two years, 1950 to 1952, covered the time of her return to the Anglican Church, helped by his guidance, after a lapse of thirty years: those of the next six show the renewed spiritual vigour and the many activities of the final period of her life.

After Dame Rose's death Father Johnson was anxious that the letters he had received from her should be put into safe keeping. He believed that if they could be published (after careful editing) they would be of help to many. He had met me once, through the introduction of Dame Rose, who was my third cousin, when I was in America in 1956, and it was this personal link which led him to arrange for the letters to be dispatched to England early in 1959 and entrusted to me.

No literary executors had been appointed, and the copyright of the letters had devolved upon Miss Jean Macaulay, Dame Rose's sister—the only surviving member of this branch of the Macaulay family. Miss Macaulay was therefore consulted, as well as others concerned, and it was decided that the letters should be prepared for publication without delay. One of the main reasons for this was that Dame Rose's religious position, in the context of her whole life, had been widely misunderstood; her letters to Father Johnson would clarify the situation with unique authoritativeness. I was asked to undertake the editing, and when I accepted this responsibility Miss Macaulay decided to transfer the copyright to me. Since then I have frequently discussed the project with her and she has given it her whole-hearted approval. She has also recently completed the sorting of the many letters from Dame Rose to herself. These letters, forming an important record of the loving friendship between the two sisters, and showing the variety of their common interests, are to be published in a later volume.

For over a year I corresponded with Father Johnson, and he gave me much helpful advice before his health failed, during the year preceding his death in March 1961. (His superior, the Rev. G. Mercer Williams, s. s. j. e., was kept informed of the planning as it progressed.) Throughout this time his enthusiasm was a continual encouragement to me, and his belief in my abilities a continual surprise. Discussing the editing of the letters he wrote: "I think you are the only person in whom I should feel confidence for a safe choosing and pruning and presenting of them. You knew her real mind, and about the extreme seriousness and centrality of her religion, and you perfectly understand the nature of the intimacy between her and me, what it was, and what it wasn't."

No question arose of publishing the "other half" of the correspondence, namely the replies from Father Johnson, because they had been among the vast quantities of private letters addressed to Dame Rose which were destroyed a few weeks after her death, according to informal written instructions she had left with her sister as to the disposal of the belongings in her flat. Miss Macaulay had promised her sister she would carry out these instructions, and with much regret she personally burnt all the private letters concerned. Dame

Rose did not, however, leave instructions of any kind banning the publication of letters written by herself.

The Introduction to this book is intended to give such background as is needed for an understanding of the letters. A more detailed account of Rose Macaulay's life and further biographical facts concerning Father Johnson have been given in the Introduction to *Letters to a Friend*. A genealogy of Rose Macaulay and a diagram showing the family relationship between her and Father Johnson are also included in the earlier book.

In editing the letters I have omitted passages which might cause embarrassment to living persons; the only other omissions are passages which appear to be unintentionally repetitive. In order to distinguish such omissions from ambiguous cases where ". . . " appears in the original I have added [*sic*] in these latter instances. As in *Letters to a Friend* I have identified the letters which were air-mailed by the symbol † placed alongside the date.

Some of the original letters are typed but many are handwritten, and in the deciphering of these I was ably assisted by Miss M. F. McKnight. In the hand-written letters there are frequent contractions; as in *Letters to a Friend* I have extended most of these, and I have also corrected occasional typing errors, apparently unintentional mis-spellings, and punctuation which might be misleading. In general, however, I have not amended quotations, book titles, etc., where they are written incorrectly or in contracted form.

My deepest debt of gratitude is to Miss Jean Macaulay for her warm co-operation, and for the lively interest she has taken in every aspect of the work on the letters. I am also greatly indebted to several of Dame Rose's friends, and of my own, whose understanding and support have counted for more than I can say, and to those members of the Society of St John the Evangelist who have repeatedly given me their help and encouragement. I am again extremely grateful to Miss

Dorothea Conybeare, Dame Rose's first cousin, for her invaluable advice on matters of family history, as well as to Mr A. F. Scholfield, who has helped me in translating the Latin quotations, besides advising on many other points, as he did in the case of *Letters to a Friend*. I would also like to thank Professor Bruce Dickins for his continued interest, and Dr F. J. E. Raby, whom I again consulted about some of the footnotes. I discussed quite a number of passages and footnotes with Mr Christopher Hollis, and many others with Miss Doreen Berry; this was most helpful and I am very grateful to both of them. I would also like to express my thanks to all those who kindly assisted me in various other editing matters (mainly in supplying information for footnotes), especially to the following: Mr James Babington Smith, the Rev. Michael Dean, the Rt. Rev. S. A. Eley, Mr Eric Gillett, Miss M. E. A. Hancock, the Rev. Gerard Irvine, Mr Julian Jebb, Miss Mary Barham Johnson, Lord Kinross, Dr R. D. Ladborough, Fr Lothian, S.S.F., Mrs Frank C. Paine, Miss Emily Smith, and the Rev. Cyril Tomkinson. To Mr T. S. Eliot I am indebted for permission to quote from *Ash Wednesday* and I would like to thank Mr Roloff Beny for permission to reproduce his photograph of Dame Rose at Venice.

Constance Babington-Smith

Cambridge, 1962

Introduction

The last years of Rose Macaulay's life were extremely active. In March 1955, when she was nearly seventy-four, she wrote to her sister Jean, " I have an intuition that I shall die in three years, i.e. in 1958, so I must bustle about and do a lot of things in the time." A month later she was immersed in *The Towers of Trebizond*. Her last novel, with its light-hearted blend of satire and fantasy, was entirely characteristic of Rose, as she was then and as she had always been. Its serious theme— the conflict between the torments and the joys of a guilty love —reflected the tragic secret in her own past (many guessed this when they read the book). But its underlying message—the living hell of not really *wanting* to journey towards the City of God, in spite of an unforgettable longing for it—was not (as some believed it to be) a representation of her own state of mind at the time she wrote it. For by then, thanks in the first place to her correspondence with Father Johnson, she had already found the way out of her "wilderness" and had attained to serenity of heart and spirit.

In those last six years before her death in 1958 Rose was at her gayest. But it was a new kind of gaiety, with roots in renewed Christian faith: spiritually she had come home. Home to the grace of Divine forgiveness within the Anglican Church she had always loved, to a closer intimacy than ever before within her own family, to the revivified enjoyment of her friendships, her writing, her travels, her reading, her multitudinous doings and interests.

In her earlier letters to Father Johnson—those in *Letters to a*

Friend—Rose told him much about her family and a certain amount about her own personal life. The following account is therefore given to elucidate various references, some direct and some implicit, in the letters which are now published.

On both sides of Rose's ancestry there were innumerable connections with the Church. Her Macaulay grandfather and great-grandfather were both Anglican parsons, and before that several of the line had been Presbyterian ministers. On her mother's side a great many of the Conybeares, including her grandfather, had been parsons, and one of them (in the eighteenth century) a Bishop. She was also connected with other ecclesiastical clans, notably the Roses, after whom she herself was named. It was through the Roses that she and Father Johnson were related; a chance mention of the reason for her name led to the discovery of their cousinship. Both sides of Rose's ancestry also included eminent scholars. Lord Macaulay was her grandfather's first cousin, and the Macaulays were related to the Trevelyans, while among the Conybeares were distinguished scientists, linguists, and writers. The tradition of scholarship first touched Rose's life through her father George Macaulay. A classic at Eton and Cambridge, he later specialised in English studies, and in the course of a steady but unspectacular career gained a lasting reputation as a translator and editor. His logical mind and scholarly thoroughness, as well as his gentleness and reticence, were beloved ideals of Rose's youth. Temperamentally her mother was a great contrast to her father. Grace Conybeare, the lovely younger cousin whom George Macaulay had married, was imaginative, emotionally volatile, and guided by intuition rather than reason.

For the first nine years of their marriage they lived at Rugby, where George Macaulay was an assistant master. Rose (or rather Emilie Rose) their second daughter, was born there on 1st August 1881. Their eldest child Margaret and four younger children, Jean, Aulay, Will, and Eleanor, were also born while they were at Rugby. Here too began the friendship between the Macaulays and the family of Rupert Brooke; his father, like George Macaulay, was a Rugby master.

When Rose was six years old the family moved to Italy, in the interests of her mother's health, and they took a house at Varazze on the Ligurian coast. George Macaulay worked at translations but could barely scrape a living, so the family had to live very simply. The children were taught mostly by their parents, but for a short time the three elder girls went to a local convent school. Rose's memories of this school were lastingly unfavourable. On walks when men were encountered the little girls were ordered by the nuns to lower their eyes, the "little heretics" were not allowed to pray with the other children, and the religious instruction, compared with their mother's " Sunday school " teaching, seemed inferior indeed. Grace Macaulay was a gifted story-teller; her renderings of the Bible stories made an indelible impression, and her teaching based on the Collects was equally inspiring. To the Macaulay children, however, especially to the eldest five who were inseparable, the eight years at Varazze were chiefly memorable for the joyful freedom of their outdoor playtime. Rose's lifelong passion for bathing dated from the amphibious adventures of the Varazze shore.

The family's next move was back to England in 1894. They lived for a time in Oxford, where Margaret, Rose, and Jean were sent to the High School. Desperately shy, the Macaulay girls made a pact to stick together as much as possible so as to avoid painful contacts with strangers. Rose was the prettiest of the three as well as the gayest, and a tomboy in her tastes and ways. She was not, as a girl, particularly inclined to religion; at fourteen she submitted to confirmation merely to avoid making a fuss. Then when she was nineteen a magnanimous godfather, her uncle Regi Macaulay, gave her the unexpected chance of going to the university. The Macaulays were a Cambridge family (Rose was enchanted when later in life she was awarded a Cambridge doctorate) but they were still living in Oxford, and it was decided she should go to Somerville. There she read History and lost her heart to the seventeenth century. She also found her feet socially and her shyness fell away. The intellectual company at Somerville was very congenial, and she missed it greatly when afterwards she lived at home near Aberystwyth, where her father was then teaching. But she soon found consolation in writing. Ever since childhood she had delighted in writing poetry; now she also tried her hand at novels; her first, *Abbots Verney*, was published in 1906. Originally it ended unhappily, but Rose's publisher demanded "a gleam of light" in the form of an engagement, so with set teeth she manufactured one.

In 1906 Rose's father was appointed to a Lectureship in English at Cambridge, and the family moved once more. They settled at Great Shelford, within easy reach (by bicycle) of the Brookes at Grantchester and the Conybeare cousins in Cambridge. It was while the Macaulays were at Great Shelford, in February 1909, that they all received a severe shock which for Rose was to have far-reaching repercussions. Her brother Aulay, who had joined the Royal Engineers and gone to India, was murdered by native thieves on the North-West Frontier. For the first time Rose found herself impelled towards religious faith and towards the High Church practice in which her mother had been brought up. Meanwhile she was being considerably influenced by the brilliant preaching of Father Waggett, the Cowley Father, who was then in Cambridge. Soon she began making her confessions regularly at the Cowley Fathers' House in Westminster. Just before the first war she was often in London; already she was being recognised as a promising novelist, and to her great delight was meeting some of the leading writers of the day.

It was shortly after this, at the beginning of the first war, that Rose came into touch with Father Hamilton Johnson. Her confessor, Father Lucius Cary, often had to be absent from London, and when he was away Father Johnson deputised for him. He was then thirty-seven, having taken holy orders ten years previously (following the tradition of his family—he was one of the Norfolk Johnsons, for generations a well-known family of clergy) and had already been a Cowley Father for five years. He heard Rose's confessions about half a dozen times, and she attended one Retreat conducted by him. Their only meetings were these "professional" ones, and the only letters they exchanged were notes to arrange appointments. Then in November 1916 he was transferred to the Cowley Fathers' community in Boston, Massachusetts, and he and Rose never met again.

The year 1917, Rose's thirty-sixth year, was a crucial one for her. Before this, though she prized her independence, her family had been the axis of her life. But after her father's death early in the war she took a job at the War Office and soon came to regard London as her home. And in wartime London she fell deeply in love with a man who, she later learnt, was already married. For some years she struggled to combine their friendship with her now habitual religious practice. In the early twenties, however, their secret attachment deepened and eventually she broke away from the sacramental life of the Church. Her attachment became known to her sisters and to her mother (who died in 1925) and among her intimate friends in London it was tacitly accepted, but otherwise nothing was known of it.

The novels with which Rose is most often identified— *Potterism, Dangerous Ages, Told by an Idiot, Orphan Island, Crewe Train, Keeping up Appearances*—were written during the twenties. These gaily satirical novels, in which she skated with such zest and finesse over the surface of contemporary life, won for her an adoring public and a high place in the literary world. Her lightly mocking commentary upon the hypocrisy and lack of logic of her fellow-men was delightfully refreshing during the years between the wars. Many of her novels were also published in America and Father Johnson often read them. He specially enjoyed the references to religion that Rose so often introduced.

As Rose reached her fifties her work acquired a new maturity and she wrote fewer novels. *Some Religious Elements in English Literature* was followed by *They Were Defeated*, the historical novel of seventeenth-century Cambridge and Devonshire which she herself regarded as the best of her books. After this came her short life of Milton, her book of essays *Personal Pleasures*, and her study of the writings of E. M. Forster. During the second world war and for several years after it, she wrote no novels at all. Death and disaster came close to her and numbed her. The man she loved fell fatally ill; her sister Margaret died a painful death; when her flat was bombed she lost most of her library. She herself was ill for a time, then for some years suffered periods of acute depression. In sombre mood she wrote *The World my Wilderness*, the book which in Father Johnson's view (so he later told me) betrayed her "longing to be back." Still obsessed by the theme of disintegration she then buried herself in research for her massive history of ruins. At this point, in August 1950, she received the sudden letter from Father Johnson, in praise of *They Were Defeated*, which was to spark off their momentous correspondence.

The earlier part of their exchange of letters, of which Rose's side has been published as *Letters to a Friend*, was the providential means towards escape from her spiritual "ruins." It was also the beginning of an intimate friendship between two people with a remarkable coincidence of tastes. Obscure Latin collects, the latest novels and biographies, fine points of semantics, intricacies of ecclesiastical history—Rose and Father Johnson both enormously enjoyed discussing topics such as these, as well as the doings of their numerous friends and relations (among them his cousin John Cowper Powys). Their transatlantic

dialogue continued steadily, despite illnesses and other contre-
temps, at a rate of about a letter a week in each direction for
more than two years. And for Rose, along with the light-
hearted exchange of learning and gossip, went the seeking and
the finding that was gradually to lead her through the door that
for thirty years she had not approached.

By mid-1952, however, she was reaching a new stage of
spiritual development. She no longer depended upon Father
Johnson's guidance as she had during the first stage of their
letter-writing, when he was giving her what he described as
"the little push back to where she belonged, *inside* the church
door, instead of standing in the porch." When they first
corresponded Father Johnson could hardly keep up with Rose's
letters and she eagerly awaited his replies; later on she often
found herself replying to several at once. Nevertheless she
still attached great importance to his opinions, her gratitude
for his help was profound and lasting, and their fourth
cousinship, which they had discovered with such joy early
in 1952, provided a continuing bond of affection. The
demands of work and play encroached more and more on
Rose's letter-writing, but she still loved to keep closely in
touch with "dear Hamilton," commenting in detail on his
news and views and regaling him with her own.

At the time when she was writing the first of the letters in
this book the Grosvenor Chapel in South Audley Street held
a central place in Rose's religious life. It was conveniently
accessible from her flat in Hinde Street, off Manchester Square,
and every morning just before eight-fifteen she sped there in
her small car. Her attachment to "my chapel," as she called
it, was heartfelt. The restrained elegance of its architecture and
the "dignity without fuss" of its liturgy seemed to provide the
perfect setting for her worship. Rose's devotional life was
centred on the Eucharist, and she was a daily communicant.
For her the Feast of Corpus Christi was one of the highlights
of the Church's year. And in her private devotions the

recurrent theme was the Divine Light, "the Light that lighteth every man." The prayers and texts—some in Latin, some in English—which she inscribed in her *Preces Privatae* echoed this again and again. *O Sapientia*, the Advent invocation to the Holy Wisdom that illumines both mind and heart, was one of her constant favourites.

Just as regular and as unobtrusive as her daily worship were her weekly visits to her sister Jean at Romford. One afternoon and evening every week Rose kept jealously free from engagements so that she could be with her "darling twin" (they had been born within a year). Jean was the only person in the world with whom Rose, in her seventies, could share mutual memories of the Macaulay family life. After their sister Eleanor, who was a missionary, died in India in 1952, they were the only ones left out of the family of seven. And there was no younger generation at all—not one of the brothers or sisters had married. Both their parents had been dead for many years, and their uncles and aunts were all dead too, except for one, Mary Macaulay, who in her old age was sadly incapable.

Rose's return to the Church, which "Jeanie" had never left, brought the sisters very closely together. During the time of Rose's estrangement they were never entirely at one. They had always corresponded, however, and met as often as possible, though Jean's work as a nurse had tended to cut her off from the family. She was one of the pioneers of District Nursing, and was awarded the M.B.E. for her fine record when she retired. Jean's last nursing appointment brought her to Romford in 1939. After her retirement in 1956 she stayed on there, sharing a small house with her lifelong friend Nancy Willetts, also a District Nurse. The three of them spent several holidays together on the Isle of Wight, and Rose made a great point of being with them for Christmas.

Even after Jean settled at Romford, and Rose was seeing her every week, they were continually exchanging letters. Like many of the Conybeare family they both doted on lively debates, particularly on questions of moral theology; they also relished discussions about books, broadcasts, friends, and family matters, as well as the general news of the day. Another interest they shared was in the practices of the various Christian churches and sects. Rose was an enthusiast for inter-communion, and although the austerity of Nonconformist places of worship did not appeal to her, she made a point, on principle, of attending their services occasionally as a communicant. Until her death, however, she clung stubbornly to her prejudices against Roman Catholicism.

In September 1952, when the earliest letters in this book were written, Rose was suffering from persistent attacks of undulant fever and at the same time striving to finish her book *Pleasure of Ruins*. Her health was remarkably good for her age but it was a worry to her sister, as well as to her friends, that she lived alone and insisted on "looking after herself." During serious illnesses such as the undulant fever, Jean and Nancy Willetts used to come up every day in turn from Romford to look after her. This is never mentioned or even hinted at in the letters to Father Johnson, and Jean comments that Rose cherished the illusion that she could look after herself when ill. Another such illusion—well known to many of her friends—was that she was a good driver, and that people were not nervous when she gave them lifts in her "darling car."

By the spring of 1953 she had delivered her manuscript, thrown off her illness, and was enjoying a blissful holiday in Cyprus, Syria, and Israel. The following summer too she went abroad, to Turkey—the trip that foreshadowed *The Towers of Trebizond*. That summer of 1954 was also the time when there came a new development in her church-going. She had always been attracted by good preaching, even during the time of her thirty-year lapse, and it was partly because she had heard warmly favourable reports of the preaching at St

Paul's, Knightsbridge, where Jock Henderson was vicar, that she started going there occasionally. Gradually she became more and more fond of St Paul's—"it is beautiful, rather dark, very ungarish"—and towards the end of her life she divided her regular attendance almost equally between Knightsbridge and Grosvenor Chapel. (My own "religious companionship" with Rose, as Father Johnson called it, began when we discovered that we were both in the habit of attending St Paul's. Thereafter we often went there together, and also to Grosvenor Chapel. Although she and I were cousins we had never got to know one another before this.)

For some time the *épanouissement* of Rose's inner life had been bringing her to share her faith with others. She began, for example, to think seriously about her responsibilities as a godmother, and this led her to start taking one of her god-daughters to children's services at St Mary Abbots; she also corresponded regularly with another god-daughter in America. She loved the company of Anglicans of her own "high but broad" persuasion, and each autumn during her final years she attended a Retreat at Pleshey in Essex. She also enjoyed the personal friendship of quite a number of clergy. And one of the companionships she valued most was with Susan Lister, a fellow-worshipper at Grosvenor Chapel, to whom she dedicated *The Towers of Trebizond*.

The publication of *The Towers of Trebizond* dominated 1956. Beforehand she wrote to Father Johnson to prepare him for some of her jokes about the Church; but Father Johnson was not at all shocked, at least not by the jokes. The thing that did shock him, later on, was the way in which some people missed the point of the book. " Oh yes, *The Towers* has been greatly misunderstood," he wrote to me after Rose's death. " The amusing beginning about Fr Chantry-Pigg and his church, which is only a clever and good-natured caricature of a state of affairs which we all deplore but are unable to cure, is thought to be a repudiation of all that Rose actually held most dear.

And then the Reviewer in *The Times Lit. Sup.* (of all papers!)
writes of: 'on the one hand a cheerful and courageous acceptance of life's possibilities as well as its problems, and on the
other a deep, often moving, and apparently ineradicable
spiritual anguish'! Why the whole book is to show that it is
not ineradicable, but that it is eradicable only by those 'who
desire to enter that strange bright city on the hill more
strongly than they desire all other cities.' Do the people who
are amused by Fr Hugh Chantry-Pigg and think him merely
absurd, do they think he was absurd, or that Rose meant him
to be thought absurd, in Chapter 7, when he spoke the word
of God to Laurie on that Whit Sunday morning on the Black
Sea?"

But even if *The Towers* was misunderstood it was an
extremely successful book, both in England and in America.
It brought Rose the best press she had ever had, as well as some
touching private appreciations which moved her profoundly.
When she showed these tributes to her sister she told her that
never in her life had she been so happy. It was Rose's greatest
desire to help others by means of her own most poignant
experience.

The last of the letters to Father Johnson was written on
12th June 1958. Rose had not written to him for more than
six months and had much to tell him. In February she had gone
to Buckingham Palace to be "damed" (in the New Year's
Honours list she had been created a Dame Commander of the
British Empire) but she was far from well at the time so she
went afterwards to Dorset to convalesce. After her return she
had a fall and broke a hip and a wrist, and was in hospital for
six weeks. Now she was back at home desperately trying to
catch up and planning to go on a cruise to the Black Sea in
August.

Venice, the Greek Islands, Istanbul, her dear Trebizond. . .
In October she was in London again with her usual busy round.

She was looking forward to the peace of a Retreat at Pleshey in November. The opening chapter of her new novel was on paper: Venice, the city she loved perhaps more than any other, was to be the setting for part of her story. She was toying with ideas for a title: *Venice Besieged*, perhaps, or *Venice Regained*. During the last week of October an attack of bronchitis began to give her trouble and her doctor advised her to stay in bed for a couple of days. She stayed in bed for one day, then was up and about once more, shopping and party-going and writing letters. On the morning of 30th October there was a sudden relapse and she suffered a coronary thrombosis. Death came with merciful swiftness.

A week later, at a Requiem Mass at Grosvenor Chapel, George Herbert's soaring hymn of praise was sung.

> King of Glory, King of Peace,
>   I will love thee;
> And that love may never cease
>   I will move thee.
>
> Thou hast granted my request
>   Thou hast heard me;
> Thou didst note my working breast
>   Thou hast spared me.
>
> Wherefore with my utmost art
>   I will sing thee
> And the cream of all my heart,
>   I will bring thee.
>
> Though my sins against me cried,
>   Thou didst clear me;
> And alone, when they replied,
>   Thou didst hear me.

Seven whole days, not one in seven,
  I will praise thee;
In my heart, though not in heaven
  I can raise thee.

Small it is, in this poor sort,
  To enrol thee;
E'en eternity's too short
  To extol thee.

The poetry of Rose Macaulay's beloved seventeenth century provided for her a fitting epitaph.

Constance Babington-Smith

1952

20, *Hinde House, Hinde St., W.*1
16th *September*, 1952†

My dear Hamilton,

Thank you for two air papers (posted 8th and 11th), one of which I got just before going off [to Oxford] . . . on Thursday, the other last night on my return. . . . I drove home yesterday by devious ways, through the lovely Oxfordshire country—Godstow, Witham, Hinksey, Abingdon, Dorchester, Warborough—where I called on my old cousin W. J. Conybeare and his delightful wife. James had my fever some years ago, and lay in bed for *six months*, and for some 2 years afterwards had these come-backs that I get.[1] However, he is now quite over it; and digs gaily in his garden, in corduroy trousers, at the age of nearly 80. He was Provost of Southwell but now only does some helping in the churches round Warborough. He said he brought my sister Eleanor into a sermon the other day—I think he preached about lives of devoted service.[2]

I read in the C[*hurch*] *Times* about your great Convention.[3] It sounds most impressive. I'm glad too much burden and toil doesn't fall on you from your guests.

I am glad *Letters to a Layman* is to have a new edition.[4] I expect *The Words of the Missal* will come my way in Duckett's good time; I hope so.[5] It must be an illuminating companion

---

[1] R. M. had been suffering from recurrent attacks of undulant fever.

[2] Eleanor Macaulay, who died on 7th August, 1952, had been a missionary in India.

[3] A General Convention of the Episcopal Church in America.

[4] Dom Gregory Dix, *The Question of Anglican Orders* (1944); usually known by the sub-title *Letters to a Layman*.

[5] R.M. had ordered C. C. Martindale's *The Words of the Missal* (1932) from the bookseller Duckett.

to the Missal. I looked up that Paschal Prophecy you quoted. What a service that must be! I *must* go to it (All Saints', I think) next Easter. With only one priest, such affairs are beyond the scope of Grosvenor.[1] The *Exultet*, sung round the candle, must be very splendid,[2] "*Ut qui me, non meis meritis, intra Levitarum numerum dignatus est aggregare; luminis sui claritatem infundens. . . .*"[3] I wonder why a candle is so much better than an electric light, for religious purposes. Old association, no doubt.

The Church in the Markets—I am noting that to read.[4] And the Holy Week Book. What a lot of good literature you point out to me; books, and bits of Breviary and Missal. I am now, I hope, about to get from the library Evelyn Waugh's *Men at Arms,* and Harold Nicolson's *George V* — I expect both have already been published over your side of the trough. How do you get on with *Noughts and Crosses* by the way?[5] . . .

"Justification by Faith"—I have never grasped it. What *can* they mean? [Justification] by *Works* one can understand (see St James).[6] But what a lot the other has meant to people ever since Augustine! My sister's Requiem Mass is on Thursday. I shall of course go to it, well or not so well. But I shall be well.

Much love,

R. M.

[1] Although the Grosvenor Chapel in South Audley Street was R. M.'s regular place of worship, she liked to go to All Saints', Margaret Street, on certain feast days.

[2] In the Western liturgy the *Exultet* or " Paschal Praise " is sung at the blessing of the Paschal Candle on Holy Saturday.

[3] ". . . *infundens (cerei hujus laudem implere perficiat).*" " That he, who hath been pleased, for no merit of mine, to admit me into the number of his Levites, may pour on me the brightness of his light, and make me meet to proclaim the praises of this candle."

[4] B. Ifor Evans, *The Church in the Markets* (1948).

[5] J. Hichens, *Noughts and Crosses* (1952).

[6] James 2. 14-26.

20, *Hinde House, Hinde St., W.*1
25th September, 1952†

My dear Hamilton,

Your letter posted 22nd followed quickly your a[ir] p[aper] of 20th; one came yesterday, the other to-day. What a lot of interesting things in both (the 2nd particularly rich in them). Too many to answer in an a.p., though it is less than moral of me to write a longer letter, pressed about as I am with work not done—still, for once I will fall. When I wrote to you last, I was *in undulationibus*; that was Tuesday. By Thursday morning (thank you for remembering the day) I was able to go to Tufton St. for the Requiem Mass.[1] I was very glad, for it was a v.g. service, and after it we had breakfast, and I talked to several people who knew Eleanor in India, including an extremely pleasant Father Davey[2], who was a great friend of hers. It was all very consoling and good. I wish the Bp of Chota Nagpur[3] could have been there; but I shall see him before long.

Translated prayers—oh yes, they are *not* satisfactory, on the whole. Of course English can't be so *brief*, being an uninflected language and requiring therefore so many prepositions, besides all the *the*'s and *a*'s (though this does prevent the confusion one sometimes finds in one's understanding of Latin, between *the* and *a*) and other words. That prayer "*Adjuva* [*nos Deus salutaris noster*]," in 17 words. In English I can't do it (can you?) in less than 24 [*sic*]: "Help us, God of our Salvation, and let us come rejoicing to the *recolenda* (reflection ?? consideration?) of the kindnesses by which thou hast deigned to redeem us."[4] But

[1] The service for R. M.'s sister Eleanor was held in the chapel of the Society for the Propagation of the Gospel in Tufton Street, Westminster. Eleanor Macaulay had worked as a missionary for the S.P.G.

[2] Rev. L. W. Davey.

[3] Rt. Rev. G. N. L. Hall (1891-1962).

[4] See the Roman Missal, *Oratio super populum* ("Prayer over the people"), post-communion prayer for Monday in Holy Week.

31

that "praises of this column" is awful! I like your interpretation
—or could one translate *novimus* "renew"? " Now we renew
the proclaiming (setting forth) of this column, which that
shining fire lights to the honour of God."[1] I have now trans-
scribed the prayer *"ut qui me . . . intra Viatorum numerum . . ."*[2]

Yes, that Jewish-Christian continuity is a wonderful thought.
So, though more obscurely, is the *non*-Jewish and Christian
continuity—the *Lux Vera quae illuminat omnem hominem
venientem in hunc mundum.*[3] The Covenant there is with the
spirit and conscience of man, that it shan't be left in darkness
ever, and that the light of reason shall lead it. The progressive
lighting of conscience; as you say, we shall be given the desire
and will and power to follow it, and how much better that
is than living by rules handed out. (By the way, you say " if
they can't afford children, I know what they ought to do, and
if they ask me I can tell them." What should they do? Birth
control, or abstain from intercourse—but this would be no real
marriage and could come to no good, I suppose—or just have
the children and trust to God to see to them? What *would* you
advise them, if they asked you?) This leads to *Noughts and
Crosses.* I'm so glad you like it. You ask about the author.
She is about 35 now, I think; a very nice, gay, bright young
woman; *not* her own heroine, she says . . . I liked her outbreak
against the un-Christianity of refusing to join with other
Christians in worship; I always feel that myself . . . If I was
reviewing the book, I would say it was amusing, full of real
people, poses a problem clearly and solves it well. I think it
was rather well reviewed (tho' I am sure *not* in the *Tablet*!).
The dialogue is very true to life, I think. Yes, I'm sure the
social relationships of men and women have changed a lot. Not

[1] " This column " means the Paschal Candle (see above p. 30*n*), and the
context is quoted from the *Exultet*: " *Sed jam columnae hujus praeconia
novimus, quam in honorem Dei rutilans ignis accendit.*"

[2] " Since thou (hast admitted) me into the number of Travellers."

[3] " The true light, which lighteth every man that cometh into the
world." John 1. 9.

that I and my sisters didn't go about quite freely with young men on walking tours, bicycling, bathing together, days out, games (hockey and tennis), river, etc., etc. (I think Norfolk must have been more sparsely peopled with young people than the University towns I resided in.) Yes, we certainly did go about together; and stayed with our young men friends in their homes, and went expeditions alone with them, or with other friends. (For that matter I believe my mother did this too, though less). But there is probably more of it now. You must find that your younger American friends do it all the time. *And* "neck" too, and "pet", as they call it. Oh what social joys! I used to go bathing at Grantchester with Rupert Brooke (a family friend from our childhoods). So, I mean, friendships and outings with young men were common form. What *has* increased out of all knowledge is the further intimacies, which we (in my generation and class) never even conceived of, so far as I know. We should have thought such a notion excessively "low". There is a refreshing absence of these in this novel. . . . The author was at Downe [House] school (of which I knew many ex-pupils) and (I believe) Oxford (L. M. H.)[1]. She occasionally turns up at the Grosvenor [Chapel], though she lives outside London.

Sept. 26th. Good news from Duckett this morning—they have got me *The Words of the Missal*, which I narrowly missed before. A second-hand copy, 5/-. I will collect it this afternoon. I looked up the prayers you mentioned in *The Mind*[2] . . . [*sic*] but haven't so far identified our Prayer for the whole Church, which the *American P. B.* (Shepherd)[3] says Cranmer " newly composed," though " the sequence of the petitions follows the traditional pattern of the intercessions in the Daily Offices, the Bidding Prayer, and the Litany."

[1] Somerville College, not Lady Margaret Hall.

[2] C. C. Martindale, *The Mind of the Missal* (1929).

[3] Massey H. Shepherd, Jr., *The Oxford American Prayer Book Commentary* (2nd printing, 1951).

But everywhere one finds in the P.B. echoes of older prayers, which is partly what makes the liturgical prayers so fascinating to read. . . .

How *very* disingenuous the R.C. church is about many things, including St Mary Magdalene. I see that it was Gregory the Great who first confused her with (a) the woman who was a sinner (b) Mary of Bethany: the Greek Fathers, and every good modern commentary, including Gore's,[1] say there is no evidence whatever for identification—and all the internal evidence seems against it—but the Latin Fathers (guided by Gregory the Great) came along and confused all three women, and now they are hopelessly entangled in Church commemorations, and the *Catholic Encyclopaedia* upholds this (it has to) and says how "probable" it is. But how *im*probable that the people at supper at Bethany would have said "Can he know what kind of woman it is that is anointing his feet?" if it was the well-known Bethany Mary, a friend of Our Lord's, and highly respected in the town—what nonsense. As to Mary of Magdala, all *she* had, so far as we know, was "seven devils," probably fits of some kind and infirmities, of which she was healed. However, I suppose now that she has for over 1,000 years been the great type of penitence, she will never be extricated; all the Homes for Fallen Women would have to be re-named.

I have now been to Duckett and got my *Words of Missal*, which I am delighted to have. By the way, thank you so much for those magazines (packet *and* roll)—most interesting. *Too* interesting actually, as if I am tempted to read more than a little of them yet, I shall be completely sunk. I wish you knew how deplorable is my state, how *minus* my time, and how I could do with a 48-hour day, and still not get done. And soon those tiresome BBC "Critics," on which I am for 6

[1] *A New Commentary on Holy Scripture, edited by C. Gore, H. L. Goudge and A. Guillaume* (1928).

weeks, will start; I promised to join them in the summer, when I thought my book[1] would be finished before now. And lo, it is far from finished, and how much time I do waste. *Ora pro me.* I need it. And now (7.30 p.m.) must set to work, leaving you my love and thanks. Have you read Simone Weil? She is good.

20, *Hinde House, Hinde St., W.*1
6th October, 1952†

My dear Hamilton,

To hand, your splendid long letter of Sept. 27-9, and (to-day) air paper, also splendid but less long, of 30th. The trouble is, they inspire so much to say, but there is no time for more than an a.p., so I will do what I can in that. I am interested in what you say about the place of R[oman] C[atholic]ism in your parts. I suppose it is because of the great number of immigrants, Irish and European. Someone (I think Archbp Mathew) was saying to me the other day that the Church in [the] U.S. had suffered detriment, he thought, from the great infusion of Irish, with their rather puritanical and philistine version of the faith (we were both comparing the present Irish Church with its glorious early past). All the same, these American R.C. magazines do seem excellent; *Common-weal* in particular. I found a lot that interested me in those you sent. I am also reading with much interest *The Words of the Missal* . . . I have looked up his trans[lation] of *veneranda commercia* (pp. 82 and 133) but can't think why he has to say "transaction" (or you "commercial transactions") for what I should have thought better translated as "inter-course," or "commerce" in its old sense (now not quite

---

[1] R. M.'s *Pleasure of Ruins.*

obsolete, surely?) of intercourse or converse.[1] In the 16th, 17th, and even 18th centuries, it was very common, and often used for converse with heaven. "The commerce between God and us" (Hooker). "A commerce of letters", "the commerce of wits", "in commerce with the muses", and, in the *Penseroso*, "With looks commercing with the skies, Thy rapt soul sitting in thine eyes", etc., etc. Looking up *commercium* in Cassell, I see it does give "intercourse" as one meaning. "Commerce" in English also had a special meaning of intercourse between the sexes. But *very* commonly with God, or the saints. So why not translate the collect, "God, who by the honourable" (see *Te Deum* for this use of it)[2] "commerce of this sacrifice dost make us partakers", etc. Wouldn't this do? I like it better than bringing in the idea of barter, tho' of course it *could* mean that, and it *is* a kind of barter—"here we offer and present", etc. Well, I don't know. If one calls it "commerce" it can bear either sense, according to one's feeling at the moment. Yes, I suppose Coleridge's phrase "partaker of" *would* shock the Evangelicals of his day, and Lamb, who was a Unitarian, too.[3] Also he [Lamb] disliked mysticism, and thought C. quite too off the earth. He [Coleridge] was a rather sublime preacher; he preached so well and so mystically that people couldn't afterwards quote anything he had said, but just had felt transported into heaven, commercing with the skies. I have got the Revised Standard Bible (American), just published here. It seems very good, and wanted doing. I've only looked up a few bits so far. I see it puts "Behold a young woman" instead of "virgin" (Isaiah) which is accurate, isn't

[1] See *The Words of the Missal*, p. 82: "O God . . . who through the most worshipful transaction of this Sacrifice has caused us to be participators in one supreme Divinity . . ." (*Secreta* for 4th Sunday after Easter).

[2] "Thine honourable, true, and only Son."

[3] In 1796 Coleridge wrote to Lamb, in a letter of condolence: "You are a temporary sharer in human misery, that you may be an eternal partaker of the Divine nature." See E. K. Chambers' *Samuel Taylor Coleridge* (1938).

it? The word is *amala*, I think.[1] I am also reading a small book on the Fathers of the Western Church[2] . . . which gives very lively pictures of them. How very disagreeable Jerome was! As Milman wrote, he had "an almost unrivalled faculty of awakening hatred".[3] And how he hated marriage, and the continuance (therefore) of the human race. What you say about marriage interests me. I am sure you are right that *celibacy* need be no hardship; abstinence within marriage is different, of course. Take a couple who had had already (say) three or four children, and felt they could not rightly afford more; they might be still quite young, and to ask them not to live together normally would be asking a frustration (anyhow to the man; women do feel differently about it, I think) which might starve and poison their relations together. That act of love eases intercourse, heals quarrels, fulfils affection; I don't think it should be given up except for some very weighty reason. Of course there are the so-called "safe" periods; but they are not really safe. If they are not to exercise some kind of birth control, they will either be swamped with children (too many) or starved of normal marriage. I can never quite see why birth control is wrong, as the Catholic church holds it to be. On C. S. Lewis's "other planet" married abstinence is all right because the people are less sense-bound (I haven't read that book,[4] but shall) but here, as human nature is . . . [*sic*] However, I do agree that many people have gone to the other extreme in their theories about the huge part sex must play in life. The psycho-analysts have encouraged this, unfortunately, and it needed no encouragement. I feel sure that anything you said to people consulting you would help them to a sane view of it all, and to a higher view of what they could achieve, whatever they decided to do. You see, you would be learned

[1] Hebrew *'almāh* (a marriageable young woman). See Isa. 7. 14.
[2] Robert Payne, *The Fathers of the Western Church* (1952).
[3] See H. H. Milman's *History of Christianity from the Birth of Christ to the Abolition of Paganism in the Roman Empire* (1840), Vol. III.
[4] C. S. Lewis, *Out of the Silent Planet* (1938).

and witty; and without any assistance from any Doctor of Letters. Of course that Prior found you so, and I'm glad he appreciated it. To escape from the bedlam of prelates and find you to talk to would indeed be refreshing. Talking of prelates, the Bishop of Chota Nagpur came to tea the other day; he was my sister's bishop in Ranchi, and very fond of her. I like him very much; a spare, lean, perambulating bishop, covering vast miles of diocese on foot, and very enthusiastic. We discussed the expenditure of the legacy she left me, which I am giving to the mission, as they are badly in need of funds. Eleanor will be terribly missed there; they all valued her so much, and loved her. After reading all the letters about her, I feel she was far more than we knew, tho' we knew she was doing admirable work.

That verb seems to be *undo*; *hodie non undo*,[1] nor yesterday, nor, I hope, to-morrow. If I only do it for a day or two about once a month, I shan't complain; and it should get less as the months go by. The last time was 5 days ago, when I had to cancel a lunch, but was able to receive Archbp Mathew for tea. Sometimes it makes me very sick; sometimes only feverish. And always quite stupid. A queer illness.

Valedico, and much love,

R. M.

20, Hinde House, Hinde St., W.1

12th October, 1952†

My dear Hamilton,

Thank you so much for a[ir] p[aper] posted Oct. 5th. To pursue the subject of Mary Magdalene, what Gore's Commentary says is " In no case is there the least ground for accepting Gregory the Great's identification of the woman who was a sinner, or Mary of Bethany, with Mary of Magdala.

---

[1] " To-day I do not undulate," i.e. suffer from undulant fever.

Plainly Luke does not identify them. They appear to be three distinct women. Gregory's view has been rejected by many later R.C. scholars, especially in France". St John, of course, relates how Mary of Bethany anointed Our Lord at supper, and how the disciples said the money should have been given to the poor instead of wasting precious ointment like that. It was, apparently, a common Eastern greeting. When the woman of the town who was a sinner did it they said "if this man were a prophet he would know what kind of woman is touching him"[1]—surely an impossible remark if the woman had been Mary of Bethany, already known to be, with her brother and sister, a friend of His, and no doubt known to everyone in Bethany. There really seems no identification of the sinning woman with either Mary. Gregory the Great was, it seems, the first to identify them, and the Church adopted the theory and has held it since (the Roman Church, I mean). What Fr Williams[2] said about Protestant criticism of it is in the *Catholic Encyclopaedia*, which is obviously trying to make a case for the tradition, and I think makes a very weak one, since the rejection of the theory is purely on the evidence in the Gospels, and I am sure has nothing to do with any Protestant angle on sin. I think Protestants would *prefer* Gregory's idea, it is more interesting than having just an anonymous woman as a type of the forgiven sinner. After all, they dropped out many other saints from the 1552 P[rayer] B[ook] too. I have seen the identification denied in all commentaries I have come across, except the R.C. Encyc[lopaedia], and I dare say even that may climb down presently, in fresh editions, for that Church does seem to be becoming a little more scholarly and critical in its approach. I see that St John doesn't relate the story about the woman who was a sinner at all, only that of Mary of Bethany and the spikenard. R. A. K[nox] in his notes makes no identifying comment.[3]

[1] John 12. 3-8.   [2] Rev. G. Mercer Williams, s.s.j.e.
[3] R. A. Knox, *The New Testament: A New Translation* (1945).

13th. I am in bed this morning with what feels more like a feverish cold than U[ndulant] F[ever], so will finish this in my best copperplate. Apropos "partakers in the Divine Nature" (which so shocked Lamb) it is the chief thesis in William Law's spiritual writings. You know how much I get from him, and it occurs to me to send you the *Pocket* edition[1], which I possess as well as a larger and fuller one.[2] Of course there is some skip, and some views we no longer hold; but most of it is excellent and inspiring stuff, and especially when he gets on to God's nature in us, growing like a seed, our only cause of response to God outside us. Lamb should have read it. Anyhow, if I can get a copy I will send it you. And for myself I will order from the library C. S. Lewis and Karl Stern.[3] . . . I have . . . lent [a friend of mine] . . . a delightful book I have been reviewing, *Period Piece*: *A Cambridge Childhood*, by Gwen Raverat, who was a Darwin. It is really charming: so are her illustrations to it. Do get it if you can, when it is out in your parts. The Darwins are the salt of the earth. She is very funny about them, and about those who have "inadvertently married Darwins." The drawings are charming. I think her American mother was rather behind the times as regards children's clothes and upbringing. There were much more comfortable fashions than those which Gwen and her sister had to endure. Mrs Darwin didn't share the usual Cambridge dowdiness and indifference about clothes. *We* were dressed comfortably both as children and grown-up girls, as were most girls I knew. Also, they had governesses, whereas most Cambridge children went to the Perse School; my Conybeare cousins[4] did. *We*, of course, were not living in Cambridge till later.

. . . [A Roman Catholic friend] . . . to whom I gave *Noughts and Crosses* writes "a very natural account of the

[1] *The Pocket William Law, edited by A. W. Hopkinson 1950.*
[2] *Selected Mystical Writings of William Law, edited by S. Hobhouse (1938).*
[3] Probably Karl Stern's *The Pillar of Fire* (1951).
[4] Alison and Dorothea Conybeare.

reactions of someone who approaches the Church prematurely, and not for the primary reason." I suppose the primary reason is that one believes it to be God's wish that everyone should join it, and that He deplores all the other churches. A strange point of view, but no doubt it obtains . . .

Much love and no more room,

R. M.

20, Hinde House, Hinde Street, W.1
24th October, 1952†
Feast of Raphael & Tobias & his Dog

My dear Hamilton,

I am ashamed to say that I have *three* air papers from you since I wrote last; the fact is that I have been, and am, almost too busy to do anything. What with the BBC Critics (which entails seeing a play, a film, an art exhibition, read a book, and hear a radio programme each week, besides actual recording, which takes a whole afternoon), and what with having to do two longish reviews (one is of Dr Joad's new book, *The Recovery of Faith*,[1] the other *Period Piece* . . .) and what with *Ruins* . . . [*sic*] I might add, what with a bad cold, which I had when last I wrote, and still have a little, but nearly well now. Yes, I much liked *The Man on a Donkey*, which I read when I was ill in the summer; an excellent bed book except physically; it is heavy to hold. I liked the early part best; I, and others, found it dragged a little later on. I think it is a great achievement, that huge canvas and sweep, and the characters emerge very vividly, and the period.[2] She doesn't, of course, attempt the language; but manages

[1] C. E. M. Joad, *The Recovery of Belief: a Restatement of Christian Philosophy* (1952).

[2] H. F. M. Prescott's *The Man on a Donkey* (1952) is a long historical novel of 16th century England, in the form of a chronicle, which tells the story of the Pilgrimage of Grace.

without being aggressively modern; one just doesn't notice the speech, only its content. I wonder what you will think of the Pilgrimage of Grace, later on. She is a very able Oxford woman (Lady Margaret Hall) of, I suppose, about 50, and has written other novels, but this is the best. What a work it must have been! She is not R.C., by the way. I like what you say about "the primary reason." Of course it is true. The Ch[urch] Times printed today the first chapter of Why I am not a Rom[an] Cath[olic], by Fr Ross of All Saints'. It is an interesting piece; I expect you see the Ch[urch] T[imes], and will possibly see the book—except that America is sometimes frightened of publishing anything their Romans might not like. He is very courteous; but says " We have so long been a target for R.C. abuse . . ." He seemed to me to put it very lucidly and firmly. I shall read the book when it appears. Dr Joad's book is interesting, though the philosophical parts are rather stiff going —they will use such jargon. But mostly it is lucid; he relates the intellectual reasons which have led him to the Church, from a life of almost militant anti-religion, as well as of a good deal of moral error. Poor man, I am afraid he is dying, within the year, of cancer. He chose the C. of E. rather than the R.C. because he liked it; he likes the country churches, the liturgy, the tolerance, the beauty. Yes; how much nicer we are than they are. I agree with Sir Leoline Jenkins about that.[1] Anyhow, I imagine Dr Joad has too rational a mind to swallow the R.C. myths; though he says he thinks that our greater modernity of outlook probably loses us some popularity compared with Rome; I wonder if he is right. I think he meant among rather simple people, who like to be told firmly what to think, and don't mind its being improbable. Oh how good our Church is! I love it more and more, as I get more

[1] Sir Leoline Jenkins (1623-1685), High Church lawyer, wrote of the Anglican liturgy, " Neither Rome nor Muscovy . . . have anything in the public services that can enter into comparison with it." See Letters to a Friend, p. 249.

deeply dug in—well in, as you say. And being free to use any prayers from any other P[rayer] B[ook] when we like; the R.C.s can't do that, poor things. *We* can honour the *venerandum commercium* in two languages.[1] I like these brief prayers you insert into your letters. You seem to have been so clever about binding that poetry of mine, that I don't in the least understand, for all your detailed account, what you have done. It does sound good—a convex ball! I feel you have missed your vocation, and should have been a professional binder; I keep wanting books re-bound, and can never get them done. It is really medieval, isn't it, for Religious to practise handicrafts. All the self-bound booklets you have sent me are admirable, and very charming. At Mass this morning was Noel Chota Nagpur, celebrating. . . . After Mass, when [I] left, he followed me to the church door and wished me goodbye, for he sails for India again next week. I am glad to have seen him. I have handed over Eleanor's legacy to me to the Ranchi mission, for their hospital, schools, and whatever other needs they like. They need money badly. They have offered to name a bed after her in the hospital, with an inscription in Hindi and English. She would have liked that. I apologise to many million Americans for calling them "immigrants", but I suppose they were. Many of them have families in Italy (especially Sicily) to whom they return; and the Irish still talk of "the ould country". As you say, we are all immigrants; but those of Norman blood have been here 900 years, which is enough to dig themselves well in. We Macaulays are immigrants from Denmark (Olaf, who came over to the Scotch islands about 900), the Oliviers (who married into Conybeares) were French Huguenot refugees, like your Livii. So far as I know, the Roses and the Conybeares were indigenous. Yes, I know the " Micks " police the U.S. cities; and I fear also have made politics the corrupt business they are. I like the Irish, but they are certainly rather immoral. The Irish quarter

[1] See above p. 35.

43

of Liverpool is a criminal byword; so are the Glasgow Irish. . . . I shall certainly get hold of that Planet book in the end.[1] Also of the *Pocket Law* for you, as I'd like to know what you think of it. You won't like it as I do, I think, quite; Law is my very particular cup of tea. J. C. Powys is right about Cambs. But Oxon is better country, much; I think almost the loveliest county—that part round Hinksey and Godstow and on to Abingdon. I have to go to Oxford on Nov. 12th to address the University Literary Society on Men's women and Women's men, in literature. Not an un-fruitful subject. Against the niminy-piminy Amelia, and Scott's heroines, set Rochester in *Jane Eyre*, etc. Which are worse? And so to bed.

Much love,

R. M.

20, *Hinde House, Hinde St., W.*1
All Hallows, 1952†
[*Postmark:* 1 *Nov.,* 1952]

My dear Hamilton,

Your letter posted 27th was very nice, as usual. I'm glad you got mine of 25th (which seems miraculous) in time to reply on Surface 5.[2] And now here we are in Hallow-tide. This morning Mass was very glorious and moving (to me)—one somehow felt the dim, candled chapel was full of the hallows, listening and joining. I do so love that introit "Rejoice we all in the Lord, keeping holy-day in honour of all the hallows, in whose solemnity the angels rejoice, and glorify the Son of God."[3] I like it better, really, than in Latin—perhaps because

[1] Probably *Out of the Silent Planet.*
[2] Father Johnson habitually numbered the five "writing surfaces" of his "air papers."
[3] Introit for the Feast of All Saints.

44

of that lovely old English word "hallows," which comes with its associations of poetry and ancient prose: "the blessed company of hallows", "Christ shall come, with all his hallows". I even like the oath "by all the hallows". A pity it is gone out, except in All Hallows, Hallow E'en, Hallow-tide, etc. I think I shall swear "by the Hallows" occasionally. Did you know that "halibut" means "holy flat-fish", because eaten on holy days ("butt" = flat-fish)? Well, anyhow, I like our version of that introit even better than the Latin *"sanctorum omnium"*[1], though here you won't agree, I fancy. If we met, it would be interesting to go through a great number of the ancient Latin prayers and English translations, comparing the merits of each one. I think honours are about even; but I know you don't, being a more inveterate Latinist, and possibly less devoted to the 16th and 17th [century] vagaries and beauties of English? I don't mean you're *not*—only that I believe I have a very special doting on our language and its old modes, as you on Latin. But I give you the Latin often. I like your *"Tui nos . . . transire consortium"*[2] *better* than our English. And *"Per signum crucis de inimicis . . ."*[3] which, at your suggestion, I often use. We are fortunate to have all these lovely choices. And, thanks to you, fresh Latin prayers continually come into my ken, and get adopted by me among my *sacrosancta commercia*[4]. Oh yes, how they build up, as you say, into one whole—"a whole world of truth and light."

I'm glad poor Dr Joad has groped his way into it; from nothing. Did I tell you I have just been reviewing his book *The Recovery of Belief* for to-morrow's *Sunday Times*. It is an interesting book, with perhaps too much (for the ordinary person) about the various philosophies he weighed and

[1] "Of all the saints [or 'hallows']."

[2] These few words do not show the meaning of the quotation.

[3] " By the sign of the Cross, (deliver us) from our enemies . . . " See the Roman Missal, Mass for May 3rd (Feast of the Finding of the Holy Cross).

[4] "Sacred exchanges" i.e. her private devotions.

examined (he is a lecturer in philosophy)[1] before opting for
a) Theism, b) Christianity, c) *Anglicanism*, I'm delighted to say.
The same *Sunday Times* is, it seems, referring to the BBC
"Critics", on which I have been (as Radio Critic) for the last
few weeks (it is a weekly programme, where *five* people
discuss a play, a film, a book, an art exhibition, and a radio
programme). Last week I selected "Six Talks on the 7 Deadly
Sins" for us to criticize[2]—the editor of the *Sunday Times*
thought this a good topic for the little Sunday sermon they
print... [It discusses] the Critics' (and others') attitude towards
Sin, which I myself thought rather negative and odd, all except
mine and those of a Papist, Desmond FitzGerald. The Anglican
and the Papist believed in the validity, to-day, of those 7
sins: the others, being heathen creatures (as *Piers Plowman*
puts it) apparently didn't. Seems odd to me. What *do* they
make of Sloth, Anger, Envy, Lust, etc.? Surely they must
own them wrong. Perhaps I'll send you ... [the] sermon-
ette! ...

How much I require *you in this flat!* It is littered with
defective fountain pens, effete Biros, broken-backed books,
paper that would make note-books in your hands. A week's
work from you, and I should be well set up with such com-
modities and my room would be integrated, restored, made
coherent and seemly; then, when you had done all this, you
would run through my Roman Missal and Breviaries, marking
all the prayers I might profitably use, filling in the gaps in our
epistolary *commercium gratum*.[3]

If you *don't* see the Ch[urch] *Times*, tell me, and I'll send
you the 2nd of Fr Ross's articles on why he is not R.C. This
one deals with the dogmatizing of the Assumption, and is very
learned, good and thorough. (What, I wonder, *is* the R.C.

[1] A Reader in Philosophy at London University.
[2] A BBC series of seven talks on *The Seven Deadly Sins and the Contemporary World.*
[3] "Pleasant intercourse."

answer to such evidence?) I would like you to read it, and say what you think of it, so let me know if you don't see it. The *Ch. T[imes]* is not, on the whole, much worth while. Have you got on with *Man on Donkey*, I wonder? It *does* weigh too much, doesn't it. Now I go out to visit the sick—my friend Raymond Mortimer in a Nursing Home after an operation, my aunt[1] in Westbourne Grove (85). I must hurry, if I'm to get in both.

My love to my best cousin and only pen-maker.

R. M.

20, *Hinde House, Hinde Street, W.*1
8th November, 1952

My dear Hamilton,

Behold an ocean letter, to enclose (a) my *S[unday] T[imes]* review of Dr Joad, (b) . . . little piece about the Critics on the 7 Deadlies, (c) an infuriate R.C. letter to me abusing me for upholding our Liturgy (of course the words he takes exception to, "our incomparable liturgy", are not mine, but such a familiar 17th c. quotation that you would think even an infuriate R.C. would know it;[2] but their fury that an eminent philosopher should have turned to *Anglicanism* upsets their balance), and (d) Fr Ross's "Why I am not R.C.", (no. 2), in case you didn't see it.

Well, very many thanks for a[ir] p[aper] of All Hallows, posted (on 3rd) before you had got *mine* of the same Hallows. I am very sorry indeed about the sad Paine news.[3] Yes, how

[1] Mary Macaulay.

[2] In R. M.'s *Sunday Times* review of *The Recovery of Belief* she quotes from Sir Leoline Jenkins (see above p. 42*n*) and then comments "to have arrived at the incomparable liturgy in the village church from atheism is to have travelled far."

[3] The death of Frank C. Paine, husband of Virginia Paine (friend and former penitent of Fr Johnson).

wonderful of Frankie[1] to fly back and forth, baby in arms, like that! I hope it wasn't bad for her, *and* that she'll be able to stay a while with her mother. *Surely* Mrs P. will "stay in the C. of E."? You told me it meant so much to her—and in bereavement I suppose one would cling still more to it. Or did you mean she might be moved to turn elsewhere? I hope not. I expect by now you'll have seen her.

Thank you for remembering my sister on All Souls. We had a most lovely Requiem Mass at 8.15, also at 7.30. . . .

Here we (most of my friends and I) are vexed about the U.S. election. Surely the good Ike is very unsuitable for anything but guiding armies, whereas Stevenson is a liberal, cultured, apparently very educated man, far-seeing and intelligent. But our Tories are pleased, so is an American lady I met at lunch (well, *moderately* pleased: she is *on the whole* Republican, but no bigot, and likes Stevenson). What do the people round you feel about it, I wonder? This sea letter throws our *commercia* all skewy; I must write an a.p. soon.

Meanwhile, my love,

R. M.

[*Postmark*: *London, W.*1]
10*th November,* 1952†

My dear Hamilton,

Yours of the 6th came to-day, thank you so much. I sent you a sea letter the other day, to enclose my review of Dr Joad and . . . [a] little piece about the Critics and Sin, from the *Sunday Times,* and a furious letter I had from an irate R.C., who objected to my having quoted in my review (from Sir Leoline Jenkins, C.17) praise of the P[rayer] B[ook] Liturgy, which, my correspondent bitterly complained, we had stolen from the Roman missal and breviaries, as we had stolen their

[1] The Paines' daughter.

cathedrals, churches and schools. I never answer these angry letters, though I do answer the courteous ones. When you will get my sea letter, I don't know. I have also bidden Mowbray to send you the *Pocket William Law*, which I like so much. It is very much concerned with the inward light, Christ dwelling in us—I suppose rather Quakerish in some ways, though he is also an ardent and devoted sacramentalist. I like what he says about salvation—that, though we all think we want Christ for our Saviour, we don't always remember that the only mode of salvation is letting Him save us from our sins, and this we by no means always want. There is some skip in the book, but I like it nearly all, and find it full of "the riches of eternity" (his phrase). I wish someone would write a detailed history of those Non-Jurors; they are very interesting. Many of them must be among the Hallows.

Oh yes, I am happy, and pretty well. I was not being sly and crafty in my All Hallows letter; I do often write, not type. Sometimes, when one feels tired or lazy, sitting up at the table to type a letter seems the last straw; one can *write* it in one's lolling-chair; but I know this is hard on those who have to read it. Yes indeed: two years ago I didn't feel jolly; I was in a state of darkness and tension and struggle. But you stepped in with the remedy for that; and now I am jolly, even though much too busy, sometimes too tired, and sometimes undulant. And how often immersed in "the vanity of time", and forgetful of the state to which I am called. But there it is all the time, and I am in it whether or no, and can't always quite believe my good fortune.

Did you see Fr Martindale's trans[lation] of that Advent 3 *Secreta*? " May the Sacrifice of our devotion not only carry through the Holy Mystery as ordained, but marvellously produce in us Thy Salvation" (*Words of Missal*, p. 106). It seems rather abbreviated, and omits "*jugiter*"[1]. But he obviously takes it, as you do, as the Sacrifice, with capital S. That little

[1] "Continually."

49

book is very good and elucidating, and I like to have it by me.
11*th*. (*Beatus vir, sanctus Martinus, urbis Turonis Episcopus*).[1]
A nice bright day, but cool: I dare say it was pretty cold that
day in Tours when St Martin cut his cloak in two. I always
thought it would have been a still nicer deed to have given the
whole cloak; but there was perhaps something in the sym-
bolism of sharing.

You ask about my Oxford visit. It is tomorrow, and I am
only going for one day; in the evening I give an address to
the University Lit[erary] Society on the creation of men by
women, women by men, in fiction, drama and poetry. I think
both sexes have tended to make their heroes and heroines rather
their ideals of what they would like a man or a woman to be,
whereas their own sex they often draw more from within, and
achieve more realism. Not, of course, always. Anyhow, I shall,
I suppose, be able to cough up something, when the time
arrives. Enough to set them talking, I hope. I am glad to say
my sessions with the BBC Critics are ending after this week,
so I shall get more time to finish *Ruins*; I have had to neglect
them shamefully this last month. They (BBC) have asked me
to give a New Year's Eve talk on "Changing Manners (or
Morals, or both)" from the earliest time on to now, which
would have been amusing, and rather my cup (if you know
that phrase), but I had to say no, as I simply shan't have the
time to prepare it; I *must* stick to my *Ruins* now till done. I
was surprised at the last Critics discussion, by the way, that my
4 colleagues all agreed that Browning is no more read to-day,
either by young or old. I was the only dissentient; "a forth-
right minority" again, as on Sin. In fact, the others never seem
to have read him much at all. I was brought up on him, and
read him still. He seems due for rediscovery. How odd these
fashions are. Poets go down out of sight, and after some years
up again (sometimes, that is; some founder for good). I have
this morning a note of agreement with me from Fr Patrick

[1] "That blessed man, Saint Martin, Bishop of the City of Tours."

McLaughlin, vicar of St Thomas's, Regent Street, where Gerard Irvine also ministers; he says " How can ANY observant critic of to-day suppose that Browning is at the bottom of the trough of post-mortem obscurity! My own circumscribed observation has convinced me that Browning is now engaging more and more interest, and is being recognized as a precursor of the complex writers of to-day." He is an intelligent, civilized priest, much addicted to Basilican rites; but, since the St Thomasian services clash with the Grosvenor, I don't see much of them, tho' I sometimes go to discussion meetings, etc., at St Anne's House,[1] whereof Patrick McLaughlin is a warden; I like them all there. Dear me, what a number of talkable-to clergy I know in these days; two years ago, how few! In fact, actually none, well (except a few relations). . . .

I think the *Catholic Mind*[2] is right about modern historians, on the whole. In spite of Hugh Ross Williamson (Anglican near-Roman priest) who said in a BBC discussion lately that Jesuits all deplored the Gunpowder Plot at the time. He should read some of their contemporary reactions and see Consul Hugh Lee's letters from Lisbon on Fr Floyd's reactions to the Great Powder Action—there were others too; but no more space, as you see!

My love,
R. M.

---

[1] St Anne's House, Soho; "a kind of centre of discussions, lectures, etc., connected with St Thomas's church and run by the clergy there." (See *Letters to a Friend*, p. 161.)

[2] Roman Catholic journal published in New York.

My dear Hamilton,

Thank you so much for a[ir] p[aper] of 15th-17th, which arrived this morning. I am not writing supine, as you counselled, but seated erect on my sofa and tapping away with energy, if not precision. Outside my windows it is a drizzling, snow-like, dark day; November at its worst. I like your scraps of liturgy that broke into it this morning—and also our lit reserved chapel,[1] to which I drove Canon Hood for the 8.15 (which sounds like a train, but isn't). . . .

I like "ponder on reasonable things", (though "ever" may be excessive for such an exercise). *O Sapientia!* "Spiritual" seems quite off it. But what a good prayer. We none of us ponder enough on *rationabilia.* I have been pondering on Phil[ippians] 2 (did I raise this before?), whether we are to bow *at* or *in* the name.[2] Greek *en*, Latin *in nomine*, Knox "before", Gore's Commentary "in". I prefer "in" myself; it is wider and less mechanical than the idea of bowing "at" the name. What do you think? Did you see—or shall you see—a sermon by the Bishop of Monmouth in the *Church Times*, about the Coronation Oath?[3] Tell me what you think of it. He asserts, I suppose truly, that the word " Protestant " is nowhere used in *any* C. of E. formularies, Prayer-Book or other, and therefore should not be in the Oath, which promises to maintain the Protestant Reformed Church as established in the United Kingdom, covering thus both England and Scotland, whose churches are not in communion. He also gives a rather partisan account of the Reformation, leaving out Henry VIII altogether, saying that the Church merely decided to improve

[1] R. M. means the Lady Chapel at Grosvenor Chapel (then lighted up), where the Holy Sacrament is reserved.

[2] " That at the name of Jesus every knee should bow," Phil. 2. 10.

[3] A sermon preached in Westminster Abbey by Rt. Rev. A. E. Morris, and reported in the *Church Times* of 21st November, 1952.

itself, as Roman errors had grown up; and have, he adds, now increased a lot in the past century. What with "Roman errors" and "Nonconformist defects", I should think the sermon would give some offence; but I have seen no reactions so far. Well, I hope the C. of E. will go on keeping its variety, and provide something for all minds, as it now does. Next Tuesday Gerard Irvine from St Thomas's is taking our Mass. . . . I think he will be careful. I went to his birthday lunch the other day; I am really very fond of this gay and extreme young man, and it is quite fun to know him. . . .

You ask about Oxford. I went there by train, to give myself a chance to make a few notes of what to say, as I hadn't had really time to prepare a speech. They were a nice lively audience, full of comments and questions after I had finished. I left them at it and caught the last train home, as I had to get back that night. I am glad that engagement is now cleared out of the way. I am now settling again to *Ruins*, and work at them as much as I can. I have refused an invitation from the BBC to give a talk at the end of the year on "Changes in Morals and Manners", so they now say will I give one on Morals later, when I have time, and someone else is doing Manners on New Year's Eve. The interesting changes in morals have been among people who mean well, of course. The disappearance of the practices of slavery, torture, various kinds of barbarous punishments which were universally thought right, etc. Then there is sex morality, the treatment of women, of children—all kinds of things. Whether I shall ever really give this talk, I don't know, I am feeling at the moment that I shall never have time, or be free from my load of work; I wish I could be. Now I think I must go to bed, in order to rise early (earlier than usual) and fetch Canon Hood to Mass.

22nd. Actually Stir-up Sunday[1] to-morrow—I wasn't expecting

[1] 25th Sunday after Trinity.

it so soon. I read the collect at Mass to myself; then looked it up in the Latin. Our translation is certainly rather poor; not accurate, and not nearly so good.[1] I don't like the substitution of "reward" for "remedies"; nor the rendering of *exsequentes* by "bringing forth". Should it not be "following after the fruits of thy divine working"? (Or perhaps "seeking"?) And could it be translated "the more willingly they pursue the fruits of thy divine works,' the more they may, by thy mercy, receive thy remedies (or healing)"? I mean, could it be a dependent clause like that? (I don't think dependent is the right grammatical term here, but you know what I mean.) Anyhow, the P.B. version seems weak. But I prefer "stir up" to *excita*. I see it ends with our old friend *percipiant*.[2] Well, anyhow, Advent is, in all senses, coming. One could do with a longer year—so much to do, so little done, alas.

Much love,

R. M.

Tell me when you "perceive" the little *Wm Law* from Mowbrays.

5th December, 1952[†]
Train from Romford

My dear Hamilton,

Cold fog envelops me, as I sit in this evening train back to Bond Street from Romford, my first visit there for nearly a month[3]; first I had a long cold (or flue) then my sister did and all the time she was too terribly overworked to take any half-days (she is entitled to two a week, but seldom now gets one, as they are so understaffed in her district, and half the time she is doing another nurse's work besides her own. So then I don't

---

[1] " Stir up, we beseech thee, O Lord, the wills of thy faithful people; that they, plenteously bringing forth the fruit of good works, may of thee be plenteously rewarded . . ."

[2] Literally "that they may receive." See *Letters to a Friend*, p. 147.

[3] R. M. usually visited her sister Jean at Romford once a week.

go there). This afternoon was foggy—in London thick—and bad for travelling.

6th. (*St Nicholas*) I got home latish, and to-day drove out at 8 into a fog that grew so dense round Grosvenor Square that I left my car (lights on) in the square, and searched on foot for the Chapel in S[outh] Audley Street, which eventually I found, and was able to honour St Nicholas by attendance at the post-Gospel part of his Mass. Fog has continued all day, getting thicker. Fortunately this evening I am at home and haven't got to brave the indecipherable roads and the fog which totally comprehends all lights.

Thank you for two good letters, 22nd and 26th.

I think I must get *The Man on Donkey* from the library again, and read it now I am stronger in body and mind than I was in the summer. I was interested in it then, but not really feeling much up to close and attentive reading of so large and copious and many-threaded a book. I'm sure I should get more from it now. I am glad the best American papers were appreciative; anyhow the R.C. ones. I feel it may be among the scriptures written for our learning that we pray to-morrow to mark and inwardly digest.[1] I never confine this prayer wholly to the Bible having been told as a child that it included all profitable literature. Oh dear, how can Ronald Knox publish such cheap, sneering stuff as this new book I see reviewed in yesterday's *Church Times*? The bits quoted are really vulgar and insolent—as that it will be no use arriving for Judgment without "R.C." on one's identity disc, even if one may get a little good from a Buchmanite meeting or early services at Pusey House; and other rude sneers at Protestants.[2] Those who know him now say he has ceased to think, which

[1] See Collect for 2nd Sunday in Advent.
[2] See R. A. Knox's *The Hidden Stream* (1952), p. 132. This collection of addresses to Roman Catholic undergraduates at Oxford was reviewed in the *Church Times* of 5th December, 1952, under the heading "Unworthy of Monsignor Knox."

seems tragic for his influence in his own Church and will surely put off possible converts who read and hear him, besides all Anglicans and probably all Dominicans! I can imagine the dislike the brothers Mathew must feel for his latest utterances. (By the way, should not *one* new cardinal have been chosen from England?) I was taken over Lambeth Palace the other day. . . . I hadn't been there since long before it was bombed and the chapel so badly . . . It is a haunted place; I felt the spirits of all that line of archbishops whispering about, muttering comments on the actions of the Church to-day—a cloud of probably rather critical, but interested and friendly, witnesses. No doubt all pleased by the coronation service and its ceremonies; though its expense must seem to them wildly excessive, as indeed it does to me, when money is so badly needed for our old and only barely subsisting poor people, and so many other things. It's all wrong, and humanity is not sane or just on this matter of expenditure. Surely they must know it more important that almost destitute people, here and in other lands, should have some relief than that the Queen's coronation robe should be woven from the best velvet, costing about a hundred pounds an inch. Oh dear, what a crazy race human beings are. What a chance for a strong-minded and right-minded young queen to take a more thoughtful and intelligent line, and how it would increase her popularity! . . . And how could there be an Advent (apart from incursions into individual souls) into a world such as we make it? What a shock it would be, to us so sunk in the vanity of time, so remote from the riches of eternity. . . . Under 3 weeks to Christmas. For me, the second Xmas in which I have joined. I shall stay here for the midnight Mass, and go to Romford on Xmas morning. . . . Tell me *how you are*. You say too little of this. I am well.

Much love,
R. M.

20, *Hinde House, Hinde St., W.*1
13*th December*, 1952†

My dear Hamilton,

I have just done up my Christmas card to send you by surface mail, but I fear too late to reach you by 25th. This a[ir] p[aper] is, on the other hand, too early, but it brings my love for Christmas; I am beginning it now, while staying indoors on this dark cold afternoon and trying to get some of the chores of the season done—lists, etc.—and this letter is a break in this dreary labour. Thank you so much for yours posted 5th, with account of your day at Wayland,[1] mention of *Understanding Europe*[2] (which I will get from the L[ondon] L[ibrary]) acknowledgment of *William Law*, on which I shall hope sometime to hear your views, and other interesting matters. I am at present awaiting Dr R. W. Chapman, of the Oxford [University] Press, who is looking [in] for a drink. I shall like to see him; he is so very bibliophile and erudite, as well as very pleasant.

I met another nice person the other day—the Rev. Ulrich Simon, a clever young Austrian refugee Jew, who lectures on Hebrew and Theology in King's Coll[ege], London, and has now taken Anglican orders and has the cure of some Bedfordshire village.[3] I had him to lunch to meet Victor Gollancz, which pleased and stimulated him greatly. He wrote to me afterwards of [how] much he had enjoyed it, adding, " I am in no sense a Liberal, and don't often come across, theologically, the liberal point of view, which I feel that both you and V. G. so well represent; I like to hear what I don't altogether agree with well expressed". I don't quite know what he was

---

[1] The Paine family home: Greenways, Wayland, Mass.

[2] Christopher Dawson, *Understanding Europe* (1952).

[3] Dr Ulrich Simon came from Germany in 1933, was ordained priest in 1939 and is the author of several books.

referring to; I don't think we discussed theology, but V. G. of course does represent a quite individual point of view; he was brought up in strict orthodox Judaism, from which he broke completely away (tho' even now his *stomach* can't take to oysters or pig), thought at one time of being baptized, but receded from that, and is now a very religious-minded, God-believing crusader for all good causes, without adopting any church belief. A very generous-minded courageous man, so egotistical that he shocks some people, so unreticent in what he prints about himself that he embarrasses others; and so entertaining as company that he makes any gathering a roaring success. A unique character; I am very fond of him. He charmed Ulrich Simon completely.

I am glad you had that afternoon at Mrs Paine's, and saw also B—— and son. And how good that she is happy (the girl, I mean) after all the beginning part of it. How well it has worked out. Poor Mrs Paine; I hope she will be happy after the first shock and loneliness. If ever it comes in unobtrusively, do give her my sympathy; or perhaps I asked you to do that before.

More and more, I can't imagine any other church one *could* belong to with content besides ours. Certainly not the Roman; certainly no form of Protestantism but ours; in fact, certainly nothing. I think all these very Romanizing churches make a great mistake, throwing away the specific Anglican beauty and distinction for something a little artificial and tawdry. Still, it does seem to suit some minds. We kept Dec. 8th at Mass calling it the Feast of the Conception of the B.V.M. (as I suppose our Missal[1] does); at St Thomas's Regent Street they kept the Feast of the *Immaculate* C[onception], as no doubt whatever missal they use there does. To me this seems so *superfluous*. What do we gain by such a theory? No warrant in Scripture, Gerard Irvine admits (I drove him this

[1] The Altar Missal at Grosvenor Chapel.

58

morning up to Hampstead to communicate Dr Joad)[1], but to him it seems to have a certain logic. To me, none. Not that it matters one way or another; except that to pile miracle on miracle makes unreason and unreality and more stumbling-blocks. Anyhow, are we to believe that any human being has ever been perfect?

[We had] . . . such a good Advent sermon [at Grosvenor Chapel] about our personal relation to the coming of Christ, and what it might mean to us as a re-creating process (I mean the *second* coming). How badly we shall need that! The hell we make for ourselves, the heaven we so little make—no struggling can ever make enough heaven in our minds to make us heaven-worthy. I get nightmares in which I seem to hear Him say, " Depart, I don't know you", and then an end of all prayer, all communion, all being guided and cared for by Him, only darkness and aloneness, and a door shut for ever because we wouldn't open it while we could. *Timor mortis conturbat me.*[2] However, there is, we hope, purgation-time; only the " Depart " is, I suppose, uttered *after* all that, if we haven't even then made the grade. Can you really believe it could happen, that we could be shut, or allowed to shut our-selves, right out of God's love for ever? I don't really believe it could. The Romans think it is a formal and technical thing —either you die in Grace or you don't. Those mechanical views seem to me ridiculous as well as immoral; but they must bring a certain relief and peace to those who hold them. I suppose what they picture as being said is, " Depart, you died not in grace", with no reference to character or conduct. Beautifully easy. Or else terribly distressing, for those who die outside the means of grace. Well, we will not brood on these sad matters—I don't know how I got on to them. Advent

[1] This was during Dr. Joad's fatal illness; see foreword to his *Folly Farm* (1954).

[2] "The fear of death confoundeth me," the refrain in William Dunbar's *Lament for the Makers*. See *Letters to a Friend*, p. 47.

Thoughts, I suppose, as the little books at Mowbrays call them.

Yes: what a happy come-back of Religious Orders in Britain. Were there really none before Fr Benson made the S.S.J.E.?[1] It seems odd that the High Churchmen of the 17th and 18th centuries never thought of it—or anyhow did it (apart from Little Gidding, a faint shadow of it). Law would have approved; so would Jeremy Taylor, I think. And Dr Cosin; and, surely, Laud? (Only he was too near the Dissolution and Reformation; the others had got right away.) My Yule love: I may write again, nearer the Day.

R. M.

20, *Hinde House, Hinde St., W.*1
16*th December,* 1952†

My dear Hamilton,

I want to send another word to catch Christmas, which this, posted early to-morrow, should about do, with the tardy Christmas posts. I hope you won't mind handwriting—I have had such a day of shopping and chores, and feel dead to the world.

Your letters of 10th and 11th came together yesterday; thank you so much for them—bright beams in the mist of Christmas cards and letters that assault one and must be coped with. I have been coping most of to-day, despatching my private card, a few others to those who wouldn't understand my card (I sent it to you by surface, and no doubt you'll get it sometime), and slopping about in the slushy snow trying to shop. Odd weather: alternate frost and snow and thaw and rain. I fetched Canon Hood this morning and we glissaded gently down melting snow streets. But oh yes, I *am* living well

[1] The Society of St John the Evangelist (the "Cowley Fathers"), founded in 1865 by R. M. Benson, is the oldest Anglican society for men religious.

within my strength and velocity. Jeanie isn't, alas, but I am. A nice warm flat, nice sedentary work, a nice car—and, what do you think, now two sweet little stoves in chapel, one on either side of the altar, giving a perceptible warmth, tho' no torrid heat.

I'm afraid Royal Extravagance is an impregnable mountain to assault. I don't think it ever dawns on royal minds not to practise it. William IV tried, but was brought into line. The only hope would be in an archbishop who had revolutionary views on money (perhaps Temple might, if he was here) and an influence over the sovereign. . . . We have indeed got beyond "to every man a damsel or two", but not beyond the vulgarity of great riches. Well, one mustn't be censorious.

Did I tell you I hope to keep the Coronation in Cyprus; mid-May to mid-June, as I had planned (or else Italy) this summer, but undulated instead.[1] I hope to find Abroad almost empty of my compatriots! (But they *may* all think of Cyprus too.) Speaking of the holy scriptures written for our learning, . . . [I have been] given . . . for Christmas such a good scholarly collection of 14th and 15th century religious writings, taken largely from MSS, by a very scholarly woman called Kirchberger.[2] There is a lot of v.g. stuff in it. I like that Erasmus letter you quote. And that is a v. interesting question you raise as to what the Papacy lost—usually people only consider what *we* lost (and gained). One could pursue this further. But here is the end; I send much love for Christmas. How *good* to know that you are there. Much more to say but no space, and no time. What about *hell*??

Yours always with love and Christmas wishes.

R. M.

---

[1] See *Letters to a Friend*, p. 318

[2] *The Coasts of the Country; An Anthology of Prayer drawn from the Early English Spiritual Writers*, edited by Clare Kirchberger (1952).

My dear Hamilton,

Here I am in *dom: sororis* in the p.m. of *Fest: Nat: Dom:*, very slothful and rather drowsy, surrounded by Christmas accessories—cards, holly, crib, sister, sister's friend,[1] presents, etc., etc. I came down this morning, so have had no Christmas services since midnight Mass in the Chapel, which was very beautiful. I had a full Christmas Eve. Last minute cards all the morning, then a friend to lunch, then the King's Coll: Christmas Eve carol service on the radio in the afternoon, then to the Chapel to be shriven, then out to dinner with Arthur Koestler (do you know his books?) where my two fellow-guests, great friends of mine, were going off to Brompton Oratory for the M[idnight] M[ass] there, they being of that way of thinking, and trying to make me accompany them. But I, remarking firmly " Hell roast the Pope", turned my back on them and departed for my Anglican chapel. Then had a lovely long sleep till I rose and came down here.

Epistolam tuam 17 *Dec*: *accepi et non antea rescripsi, tam libenter legi*.[2] Cicero seems to say *antea* for "already" but I suppose *jam* would be all right, wouldn't it? Anyhow, I allude to your *epistolam aeream* lately received: I love what you say about your telling the just-returned Fr Palmer (who always sounds so likeable)[3] about the Latin Collects and *The M[an] on a D[onkey]* and Erasmus on Fisher and Colet, about which last he uttered definite opinions. I'm glad you have him back to converse and discuss with. One does need someone at hand who takes an interest in the same things and likes to talk about

---

[1] Nancy Willetts.

[2] "I received your letter of the 17th Dec., and I did not reply before; but I read it with such great pleasure."

[3] Rev. R. F. Palmer, s.s.j.e.

them, and if views differ, so much the better, it stimulates the mind. My sister and I like to discuss the same things, and differ quite a lot. We were discussing just now the Quaker habit of never saying Sunday, Monday, Tuesday, etc., but always "the first, second, third day of the week", to avoid using the names of heathen gods. Certainly the Q.s are faddy people, but they do know what they think is right and stick to it, tho' *why* they think it wrong to use the ordinary names for days and months (months, of course, are equally suspect) puzzles non-Quakers. Well, they are an excellent people, and perhaps the most logical of Christians. No sacraments, no liturgy, no church, no creed. To do so much upon so little argues great will-power and faith.

Oh yes, how veiled they are, those figures of the past. And how glorious it would be to see those first Christian decades clearly. I think no historian can do that for us, ever. . . . My view [is] that in many respects the Evangelists (writing long afterwards from memory) must have got much of His actual words wrong, and imparted into them some Jewish bias or tradition. . . . [For instance] our Lord's reported words about hell—"Depart, I never knew you" etc.[1]—which imply God's final abandonment of the souls he has tried so hard, in life, to guide and redeem, but who, perhaps, refuse salvation. Is that ultimate darkness and rejection (even tho' self-inflicted) possible? Those words seem so unlike Him. . . . If only we had a shorthand transcript—or a Boswell! (Which reminds me of your question about Dr Johnson. What he said was about women preaching: it was like a dog walking on his hind legs, not done *well*, but wonderful that it should be done at all.)[2] Tell me sometime how you react to Wm Law. I like the parts about Christ in the soul, and the perpetual choice between heaven and hell, and the power of the "working will" in us. I hope you got my last *epistola* in time for Christmas. This you

[1] See Matt. 7. 23.
[2] See Boswell's *Life of Johnson*, Vol. 1, p. 463. (Ed. G. B. Hill.)

will get before next year. All my love and good wishes for it. S. V. B.[1] this wintry weather. One of our congregation—a girl—was killed in that Austrian avalanche; very shocking for her people.

Your devoted
R. M.

20, Hinde House, Hinde St., W.1
New Year's Eve, 1952†

My dear Hamilton,

I've no business to be taking time off to write to you (instead of about the ruins of the Knights Hospitaller at Rhodes)[2] this morning; but I have two enchanting letters from you since Christmas, and feel moved to write on this last day of 1952 (for me a happy year, for which I am thankful). First, I'm sorry about the way my printers bungled my card. As you noticed, they dropped out *nisi*, and I dropped out (at the last minute) the opening clause that put the sentence into the accusative and subjunctive, forgetting that the rest of the sentence needed it. This was to save space, trying to get it all into two lines, and mere Christmas-rush carelessness and oblivion. The dropping of *nisi* was the printer's fault (I fear no Latinist) and mine too for not reading it carefully before it was too late. I ought to have pointed out to you these defects, which have vexed me rather.[3] I had a puzzled letter from

---

[1] *Si vales bene est.* ("If you are flourishing, good.")

[2] See R. M.'s *Pleasure of Ruins,* p. 448.

[3] R. M.'s Christmas card included a quotation from Cornelius à Lapide (Cornelis Cornelissen van den Steen, s. j., 1567-1637): "*Hemerobaptistae censerent hominem non posse vivere, nisi singulis diebus in aqua mergeretur, ac ita ablueretur et sanctificaretur ab omni culpa. Verum haec est anatum potius et piscium vita, quam hominum.*" ("The Hemerobaptists believe that man cannot live unless on every day he plunge into the water and be washed clean and be sanctified from every sin. Nay, but this is rather the life of ducks and fishes than of human beings.") See *Letters to a Friend,* p. 352.

64

E. V. Knox about it; he ends, "However, it is a beautiful thought". I particularly like myself the "life rather for ducks and fishes than for men". Fr Cornelius s. j. would have considered me much too much of a duck or fish.

No, I didn't draw the picture, tho' I composed the verse,[1] and drew a design for the picture, to be copied by someone who can draw, which I can't, alas. Even the *Adeste* in the balloon would have come out in crooked and uneven lettering, had I done it. But I suggested the fishes, the sea-horse, etc.—and of course the ruined church. I like to muse on such submarine scenes, very much; they mean a lot in my life.

How good are both your letters! . . . About *Timor Mortis*. . . . I do [think] those words reported in the Gospels uncharacteristic,[2] and that one has to allow for a margin of error and misreporting by reporters writing at second hand years afterwards, and inclined to colour their records with their traditional Jewish feelings, often exclusive and intolerant. I have always thought this. . . . I looked at that third Exhortation[3] (first in the American P[rayer] B[ook], which omits, I see, the sentence about eating and drinking to our damnation) and it reminded me once more of that "great and endless comfort" which has come to me—I mean, I have come to it—during the last two years, and that surely, while we cling to it, won't ever repudiate us, however poor our efforts. Yes; I wish the P.B. had kept "*concede, quaesumus . . .*"[4], also "*da nobis . . . fulget in mente*"[5] and "*Hujus nos, Domine*".[6] But Cranmer did very

[1] And they who swim on Christmas Day may hear the thin sigh
    Of faint bells, of sunk bells, and drowned quires cry.
  "*Adeste, natatores,*" and down the swimmers come,
    Singing "*Adoremus dominum.*"
[2] "Depart from me . . ." See above p. 59.
[3] The Third Exhortation to Holy Communion in the Book of Common Prayer.
[4] "Grant, we beseech thee . . ."
[5] "Give us . . . shines in our hearts."
[6] These few words do not show the meaning of the quotation.

well; one could scarcely have better. I feel better about *Mortis* now, thank you very much, dear Father.

I feel that you and Fr Palmer might have found a more stimulating and comforting "little something" on a December afternoon (and Christmas at that) than milk and cold coffee. At Romford we were better comforted than that; also so was I at my Boxing-Night dinner at Hampstead, with charming friends, where also was . . . the Rector of —— (I forget his name) he was nice and genial, and believed in anointing, both for body and soul. My sister says it has had little effect on those of his parishioners who have now been settled on a new housing estate in ——, and are so wicked that the nurses rather shudder at visiting them after dark; their . . . rector says he isn't surprised, from what he knows of them. He should anoint them more earnestly and assiduously.

Why doesn't St Paul's have a midnight Mass on Xmas Eve? I can't think. Nor why, since they do have a watch-night service,[1] they don't make it a Mass. But above all, why neglect Xmas Eve as they do? I shall ask the good Dean sometime.[2] So many churches, town and country, do have it now; surely our great cathedral should. The Abbey is lost to everything but the Coronation; it has shut up most of itself, to fix seats, etc. Really it is a disgrace, 6 months of this nonsense.[3] Such a *fuss*. I shall be glad to be out of it, in a better country. I shall write to you from Cyprus, tho' difficult for you to write to me, as I shall be on the move. Unless you indite one letter, and send it to Poste Restante, Famagusta, Cyprus, sometime—but I'll send you that address nearer the time. Did I tell you of the hymn I found about that blessed island? Oh it will be most beautiful. I shall aim at sending you a birthday greeting from it.

I think I will go to St Paul's to-night. There is something very noble and impressive about those vast echoing halls swelling with hymn and prayer, and the great bell booming

---

[1] On New Year's Eve.   [2] Very Rev. W. R. Matthews.
[3] The Coronation of Queen Elizabeth II took place on 2nd June, 1953.

out the year's close, and the chimes of all the churches ringing in the next. And it is a time for furbishing up resolutions and aspirations and giving thanks: *gratias agere*, indeed. I wonder how you will be spending it. And why don't High Churches have a watch-night? I suppose because it's not done at Rome: but again, why not? It is interesting to track out these mysteries of different usages, how far they spring from differences inherent in different communions and parties, how far they have developed by chance, more or less.

Do you read Jeremy Taylor? I see there is a new edition of the *Golden Grove* just out, which I must get hold of. I am very partial to him myself. A reviewer says he didn't believe in the Real Presence. I must look and see. I don't feel sure that this reviewer knows quite what the R.P. is; but he *may* be right about Jeremy, tho' I should be surprised. He did believe in Confession; John Evelyn was one of his penitents. And he wrote the most exquisite prose. I do wish you such a good new year, such a very good one indeed. And pray you may have it, and so many more. You have my love for all of them; how good to know I have yours!

Your loving
R. M.

1953

*20, Hinde House, Hinde Street, W.*1
8th January, 1953†

My dear Hamilton,

I daren't disturb the sheets now in my typewriter half typed, so must try this by pen—I hope you won't be defeated by it. Your letter posted New Year's Eve came two days ago, thank you so much. I must get *View-review*[1], in spite of its odd and discouraging name. It sounds worth reading. Did it perhaps review *Man on Donkey* in an earlier number? The reviews here have been good. I suppose the *popular* American reviews wouldn't think it quite on the level of their readers— too long and difficult. I am glad you are so seized of it, apprehended and comprehended by it. I have been thinking that the author would surely be pleased if you should *write* to her about it; [though] not *quite* as pleased as I was when you wrote to me in August 1950 about *They Were Defeated,* because she won't have the memory of you that I had, that made it so delightful to hear from you. But she couldn't but be pleased, and you might have an interesting and pleasant correspondence about it. Do put this in hand, *instanter,* and let me know how it goes. All you have said about that book to me would be of immense interest to her, of course.

We had a lovely Epiphany Mass—I do like this feast. *Stella ista sicut flamma coruscat*[2]. . . .

Why is it that Christ as *light* means more to me than any other aspect? The light that lighteth every man. . . .

Someone showed me yesterday *The Month,* which has a very waspish article on Charles Williams, whom it called an Anglican idol.[3] There were some other articles I want

[1] A quarterly "guide to Christian reading and teaching", published by the S.P.C.K.

[2] "That star sparkles like a flame."

[3] H. D. Hanshell, "A Heresy Hunt," *The Month,* January 1953.

to read, too. It's Dominican, isn't it?[1] I am reading Sean O'Faolain's *Newman's Way* in bed at night. It interests me; there is a lot about his family, his brothers and sisters and parents. One brother very dotty; another (Francis) very Calvinist, and went off to convert savages to Plymouth Brotherhood.

The Oxford part is good. We see John Henry as a gauche, silent, very devout young Fellow of Oriel, nervously conscious of his dim social background, using the wrong implements at the Fellows' Table, so that the Provost said, "Mr Newman, we do not serve sweetbreads with a spoon", and he felt terribly inferior. Gradually, I suppose, he expanded, socially and intellectually. I must look again at *Young Mr Newman*.[2] O'Faolain is a sympathetic and entertaining writer, Irish R.C. of course, but pretty critical of the Church, and certainly no bigot. On the other hand, I doubt if he knows anything *from the inside* about the Anglican Church—indeed, how could he?

What naïvely simple beliefs Newman, and most of his generation (pre-Darwin, of course) held. It is difficult now to understand how good intelligences could accept all those fundamentalist theories about the earth, for instance. Or about the Church and the Papacy. As O'Faolain remarks: "Savonarola, swinging on a rope above a fire, by order of Alexander VI, would not have agreed with this". But how *good* John Henry was: how unselfish, how compassionate, how generous! A refreshment to read, after the life of the vulgar worldling Arnold Bennett.[3]

Did I tell you Gerard Irvine is going to be in charge of Cranford Mission Church, Middlesex? There is also an old church there, where Fuller was once vicar, and Bp Wilkins.

[1] *The Month* is edited by Jesuits, not by Dominicans.
[2] Maisie Ward, *Young Mr Newman* (1948).
[3] R. Pound, *Arnold Bennett; a Biography* (1952).

It will be good for Gerard to have a church to run, and a parish of 10,000 people to serve.[1]

Much love, and do act on my epistolary suggestion.

R. M.

20, *Hinde House, Hinde Street*, W.1
18th *January*, 1953

My dear Hamilton,

An ocean letter this time to enclose a rather good little cutting from the *Sunday Times.* . . . It is Christian Unity week here, or about to be. I can't go to any meetings about it, as I have to work all day and all night till end of month. But I like this about bridging our differences. I . . . rather like the differences . . . they keep up a wholesome subversiveness against unthinking uniformity. If only the Romans would come off their high pole and stop being so stuck up and drop a little of their "tribal patriotism" and stupid contempt, the rest of us could soon get together—I mean worship together, in spite of differences. William Temple would have worked it, if he had lived. And the R.C.'s really *are* getting rather better, the last few years, though still stuck-up and contemptuous and untruthful. There was an offensive and stupid attack on the Marian martyrs in a R.C. paper lately—I'm glad *we* never attack the Elizabethan ones. Well, we must pray for them, that they may have a larger charity and understanding.

Thank you for your v.g. letter of Epiphany. I haven't, literally, had a moment in which it would have been right to give the time to answer it. I oughtn't to be doing so now really, but felt I wanted to. You are probably right about a midnight Mass at St Paul's. I put it to the Dean the other day,

[1] The Church of the Holy Angels, Cranford, serves a London Diocesan Home Mission district with an estimated population of over 10,000. The mother church, St Dunstan's, Cranford, is where Thomas Fuller was Rector 1658-61. Bp John Wilkins followed him in 1661.

meeting him. He said they wouldn't grasp it or like it, or even (some of them) behave seemly at it. So I suppose he is right. I have been thinking of you at your Retreat, 5th—10th; I hope it was good. I like Benedictions as a rule, both Anglican and Roman.

I hope you acted on my suggestion and wrote to Miss Prescott. I am sure she would like it. You have so wonderfully and richly grasped and appreciated her book,[1] marked and inwardly digested it. When I am out of this jungle, I shall read it again. Do you think, but for the form our Reformation took, the English influence would have helped to steady and sanify the Church? Save it, I mean, from some emotional excesses and faults of taste? And possibly from some intolerance—tho' God knows we were *all* intolerant enough once. There is a book Miss Prescott could write: an imaginary story of an English unreformed Church. Do suggest it to her. I must stop. So much love.

R. M.

20, *Hinde House, Hinde Street, W.*1
23*rd January,* 1953†

My dear Hamilton,

I am knocking off my admirable discursion on the Bantu ruins in Southern Rhodesia (not built well, but marvellous that Bantu negroes should have built in stone at all) in order to send you an air letter, as my last (what date? I forget) was surface mail, in order to enclose something (what? I forget) and you won't get it quite yet. Since I wrote it, your a[ir] l[etter] of 13th has arrived, and deserves a better answer than this can be. Well, I'm sorry you think you won't write to the Woman Behind the Man on the Donkey, but I do see your point of view, which is entirely my own where letters are concerned,

[1] *The Man on a Donkey.*

74

and I can think of few things more disastrous than starting a new correspondence with any one. Letters are a burden indeed ... they seem often the last straw that breaks the back ... you should see the piles of those that I *must* answer that litter and weight my writing table. Which disposes of your notion that I should ever write to Miss Prescott. Perish the thought! Uninterrupted equanimity, indeed! If I could only get half an hour of this. All I do get is $\frac{3}{4}$ hour at Mass each morning; what I should do without that ... [*sic*] I expect my mind would altogether go to pieces. Of course when I have this book done, it will be quite different, and I hope that in Cyprus my equanimity will be only interrupted by the ravishing spectacles of medieval monasteries and castles on mountain heights, medieval cities on the sea, ancient cities dedicated to the cult of Aphrodite, etc., as well as by bathing in that heavenly sea and driving a hired Ford up and down the mountains. Not that these enjoyments will make me anything but equanimous. So we'll neither of us write to Miss Prescott; who is, I believe, an Anglican, by the way, but probably not a cousin or an old penitent, but none the less would be highly gratified and interested to hear from you. One likes interesting and understanding letters about one's books. I had one yesterday from a daughter of old Hilaire Belloc, about my *Wilderness* —so entirely understanding all I meant to say in it, and so appreciative, that I was really pleased.[1] She says we met in 1920, when I defended her from someone's snub, but I quite forget that.

Yes, I like that *Coelesti lumine*[2] collect very much. You'd be surprised at the number of prayers, passages, and psalms about light that are collected in my *Preces Privatae*. I use them at Mass. Just now, sitting rather wearily among my rocky ruins, I sometimes repeat to myself at Mass those lines from Eliot's *Ash Wednesday*; do you know it? The lines are:

[1] Elizabeth Belloc had written to R. M. about *The World my Wilderness*.
[2] "Heavenly light."

> " Teach us to sit still
> Even among these rocks,
> Our peace in His will;
> And even among these rocks
> Suffer me not to be separated,
> And let my cry come unto Thee."

No light there, but peace. Then I have *O Oriens, splendor lucis aeternae . . . veni illumina*,[1] etc., and *Emitte lucem tuam*,[2] and *Et mentis nostrae tenebras . . . illustra*,[3] and "Grant that the splendour of Thy brightness may shine forth upon us, and that the light of Thy light . . ." and *Lucerna pedibus meis*,[4] and "by the guiding radiance of Thy compassion" (Gothic Missal), and other lights, that I must add to, come Candlemas. We always went on a picnic on Candlemas Day, and it is still one of my favourite feasts—I wrote about it in *Personal Pleasures*, I think. But there can be no such Candlemasses here and now, without sunshine and almond blossom and tiny twisted candles to burn, and the procession in the town, and brothers and sisters to feast on the hillside with. Those *festa* days—of which Sunday was the most often recurrent, always a holiday, always fun, always in one's oldest clothes so that one could get wet and climb about—how lovely they were. They make a kind of radiance in memory. And now nearly all that happy fraternal tribe are gone into the world of light, as Vaughan says. I do like the Requiem Mass in our Altar Missal; we had it this morning for someone. I have been trying to get hold of a second-hand copy of that book, it has so many good Propers, Introits, etc. It is out of print; but the S.P.C.K. has "sheets" of it, unbound, and *may*

---

[1] "O Day-spring, brightness of light everlasting (and sun of righteousness); come thou and enlighten (those who sit in darkness and in the shadow of death)." Fifth of the Greater Antiphones.

[2] "Send forth thy light."

[3] "And illumine the darkness of our minds."

[4] "(Thy word is) a lantern unto my feet." Ps. 119. 105.

sell me a set, I hope.[1] The S.S.J.E. here says it is to be reprinted. But a new copy would cost too much altogether. If I mayn't buy the sheets, I shall ask . . . if I may borrow the book in August when the Chapel is closed for 2 or 3 weeks and copy some of it. It is quite the best I know. Someone in the C[hurch] T[imes] complains of the bad translations in the English Missal[2], very justly. Worse is the withholding of the Chalice from the laity. I like your rendering of *digno*: "with feelings as little unsuitable as we can manage to put forth." "*Digno*" is discouragingly too much to aim at. Yes, I too like "*mysterium*"—that margin of mystery that is our circumambience, our doubt, and our faith; is, in fact God and ourselves. I keep going to memorial services; the last was my dear old friend Eddie Marsh; a charming and kind Maecenas to young writers and artists. I used to see a lot of him once, when he took up Rupert Brooke. He died at 81—a good age. Now I must back to my rocks. My love always; I do hope you are not too cold, and keep well. *Ora pro me.*

R. M.

20, *Hinde House, Hinde Street, W.*1
29th January, 1953†

My dear Hamilton,

Your a[ir] p[aper] of 24th to hand this morning, and thank you so much. I forget which day I posted my last to you, but since then I have had two of yours, 18th and 24th, both most welcome. Your Harvard undergraduate—did he mean, when "he wondered if such events as are described in *The M[an] on a D[onkey]* could bring into being a satisfactory, separated part

[1] *The Altar Missal*, edited by a Priest of the S.S.J.E. (Mowbray, 1936), is sometimes known as the "Cowley Missal." It is normally supplied in sheet form, to be bound according to individual needs.

[2] *The English Missal for the Laity* (W. Knott & Son, London, 1933); a translation of the Roman Missal which R. M. often used.

of the Catholic Church"—did he mean, could the events have been really as those described, or could our branch of the Church be satisfactory? Or perhaps merely that it was strange and wonderful that it should be so. But I agree with you that the Reformation had to be; and it was (wasn't it?) supported by a very large part of public feeling, which had sickened of Church corruptions, Papal interferences, clerical misbehaviour, Church services they didn't follow; all that Lollardry had been up against a century before. I think general feeling would have surged up, in the course of C.16, and *made* a reformation. So—and that is a very interesting thought—it *was* a good thing that Cranmer was there, a bulwark against the Puritans, or anyhow making a P[rayer] B[ook] that was this. What interesting lines of speculation you suggest! As to Belloc, he was, of course, an entirely unscrupulous lying historian, and thought only of making a case against Protestantism—how *dared* he write a book about Cranmer?[1] "Destruction of the hated Mass", indeed! I don't suppose B. had ever studied our P.B., or Cranmer's high sacramental communion prayers, both translated *and* composed by him. I was glad T. Maynard put him in his place.[2] The R.C.'s have a foolish bigotry about our not either having or wanting Sacraments—so *ignorant* of them. On Saturday last one of them defaced the Grosvenor Chapel noticeboard outside the door, which said " The Priest-in-Charge is in church on Fridays 5-6 to hear Confessions", and also announced the services. The objector had crossed out "priest" and put "parson", and crossed out " Holy Communion", writing " Heresy. See Article 31 " across it in block capitals. (I haven't looked up Article 31, and forget which it is, but probably the one about " the Romish doctrine of the Mass"; certainly not the one which speaks sacramentally about the Sacrament (which I think is 28).[3]) How rude and impudent

[1] H. Belloc, *Cranmer* (1931).
[2] Theodore Maynard (1890-1956), American Roman Catholic writer.
[3] Article 31, "Of the one Oblation of Christ," states: "Wherefore the

it was! . . . How incredible—that people can be so rude and
silly. . . .

I . . . lunched last Sunday after Mass with my friend Alan
Pryce-Jones, the editor of the *Times Literary Supplement*—a
most attractive youngish man—45, I think, who occasionally
comes to the Chapel. He made—perhaps I told you—a very
brief plunge into Rome last year, but didn't like what he found
and swam out quickly. And one thing he didn't like was that
arrogant conviction of having the whole and only truth.[1] My
old Aunt[2] died this morning (a good thing) and her Vicar is
having a Vespers for her at All Saints', Notting Hill, to which
any nephews and nieces who can are going. . . . I'm glad you
were interested in my father's Bible article. Yes, he did know
a good deal about Bible translations—and P[rayer] B[ook] ones
too. And had a great interest in the changes in English down
the centuries, from Anglo-Saxon on. Would this were more
wide-spread! As to the Bible, here is V. S. Pritchett, a very
able reviewer on the *New Statesman* saying that *Erasmus* first
translated the B. into English! What can he mean? I suppose
he got confused with E.'s trans: into *Latin*. But how ignorant.
Oh dear; here is *Finis*, before my mind has reached it. Much
love . . . Such a good Requiem Mass this morning[3] for my
poor old aunt—what a lovely mass it is. Did I tell you I have
now actually got the "Cowley Missal", unbound, in sheets,
from S.P.C.K. I need you here, to help me bind it.

R. M.

---

sacrifices of Masses, in the which it was commonly said, that the Priest did
offer Christ for the quick and the dead, to have remission of pain or guilt,
were blasphemous fables and dangerous deceits." Article 28 concerns "the
Lord's Supper."

[1] Alan Pryce-Jones comments that R. M. must be referring here to a
conversation in which he agreed with her doubts about the dogmatic
position of the [Roman Catholic] Church in regard to the Assumption. He
adds "I no longer share these doubts to-day" and points out that "the very
brief plunge" is now "a steady swim."

[2] Mary Macaulay.   [3] 30th January, the day this letter was posted.

My dear Hamilton,

Your Candlemas letter came yesterday; thank you so much, *and* for the one of 29 Jan. No, the floods did not come nigh me; only the east coast and the Thames estuary. Those *poor* people—and the Dutch. The stories are horrifying; families who sought safety in their attics, and the sea rose till it reached them, and tore away the roof and the attic floor on which they sat and washed them out to sea: a father, mother, and three children. They were at sea, in that bitter cold, all one day; when they were washed to shore the three little children were dead of exposure, and the mother died soon afterwards—only the father left. The Dutch death-roll is much worse, over 1300; ours only 300-odd, I think. But so many left homeless and without possessions. An appeal for clothes and money has been made, and I think is being well answered. I drove to the Eaton Square W.V.S. with some clothes, and found Church Army lorries taking hundreds of sacks away. Some are being sent to the Dutch. When I have time I will get Belloc's *Great Heresies*. What does he mean by "reason was given divine authority"? Does he mean the Logos? I am not sure I shall read his *Cranmer*; I feel it would be annoying and silly and untruthful (as you say it is). I have been reading (when I have a moment to read anything non-ruinous, which is seldom) a book called *Elizabethan Recusant Prose*, about the writings of the English refugee Catholics;[1] the author Alfred Southern (R.C.) makes a case for their having written much *better prose* than the Protestant English Elizabethans and Jacobeans. It is a strained case he makes; he seems to judge prose mainly by the religion of its writer. Actually the Recusant writings (mostly apologetics) can't compare with the non-Recusant contem-

---

[1] A. C. Southern, *Elizabethan Recusant Prose,* 1559-82 (1950).

porary prose; think of the Hakluyt voyagers' stories,[1] Purchas,[2] Hooker,[3] Ascham,[4] Raleigh,[5] Bacon,[6] etc., etc. *His* argument is that no-one in England wrote "good prose" between More and Dryden (another Catholic, of course). And he runs down Wycliffe's Bible (often excellent) and ignores Latimer and exalts the Douai Bible at the expense of all the English Prot-[estant] versions. Tiresome people they are when they argue a case. Belloc is one of the worst, of course. I wonder when he talks about "reason" as a prerogative of the Catholic Church, what he makes of Newman, who wrote " What is intellect itself, but a fruit of the Fall, not found in heaven more than in little children, and at the utmost but tolerated by the Church. Reason is God's gift, but so are the passions." " Faith and humility consist not in going about to prove, but in the outset confiding in the testimony of others". Mysticism too Newman runs down; he depends wholly on the authority of the Church. He had no use, apparently, for meditating on *rationabilia*.[7]

That is a nice story about Lady Knevet.[8] I suppose she was a Lollard born too late, if she always "kept from the popish church". One hopes it was the 1549 book she used in her latter days. She and Master Tollin were lucky to survive Mary's reign! Yes, when *did* she first feel so Protestant? I suppose she approved the Dissolutions. How one would like to meet and talk with her as she was in (say) 1500, as a young woman. There is a good subject—those belated Lollards. No doubt they read Wycliffe's Bible, what there was of it and when they

[1] Richard Hakluyt (1553-1616).
[2] Samuel Purchas (1575 ?-1626) author of the *Pilgrimes*.
[3] Richard Hooker (1554 ?-1600) author of *The Laws of Ecclesiastical Polity*.
[4] Roger Ascham (1515-1568) author of *The Schoolmaster*.
[5] Sir Walter Raleigh (1552 ?-1618).   [6] Francis Bacon (1561-1626).
[7] Some readers of Newman's works would disagree with R. M.'s conclusions.
[8] See John Foxe's *Acts and Monuments of Matters Happening in the Church* (1563), commonly known as Foxe's *Book of Martyrs*, Bk. xii, "The Lady Knevet, of Wymondham in Norfolk."

81

could get it. And delighted to see Cromwell's hacking down of papistical trash in the churches. I have never read Foxe. We didn't have it at home, and I think would never have been allowed to read such horrors. Nor have I wished to since; I always avoid tortures when possible. (History is frightful, because one can't really avoid them, they are everywhere.) I think you are right about the right timing of our Reformation. But how unpalatable a thing it was anyhow; if the timing was right, the *manner* was hideously wrong. I mean the Monasteries and Churches and Abbeys. I wish it hadn't happened. We could have reformed English Catholicism without it, and might now have a beautiful branch of that tree. But, of course, *we have.* Only *some* of its expressions are pretty poor, or seem so to us. I have had my *Altar Missal* bound in strong brown soft cardboard covers; it looks quite nice, and is firm. I do enjoy that book. Do you know *The People's Missal* (Mowbray, 1916) now out of print?[1] A v.g. little book, I wish I had it, but have only been lent it. By Rev. E. A. L. Clarke, A.K.C. (whatever that means).[2] There's a lot in it. No more now!!

Much love,

R. M.

20, *Hinde House, Hinde Street, W.*1.
Ash Wednesday
18*th February,* 1953†

My dear Hamilton,

I do hope that by now, in fact, many days ago, you had my letter answering your two of Jan. 30 and Feb. 4 (I forget the date of mine). And now I have yours of the 12th, which rather disquieted me, as it sounds as if you felt not too vigorous.

[1] A second and revised edition of *The People's Missal* (Mowbray, 1929) went out of print in 1950.
[2] Associate of King's College, London.

When you feel a shrinking from letter-writing (and how well I know that!) I'm *sure* you ought not to write, it is a real nervous strain and exhaustion, especially when you write several together. I find it tires me when I could write my own work for hours; it is a drain on one's time and energies that I resent. Still, they have to be written in the end; or some of them have. When you leave a long gap in your letters to me, I shall know why it is, and be very approving. Reading, collecting prayers, binding books, are *much* less tiring.

I have had to make a Lent resolution, not to be broken, to answer necessary letters and not let them lie by. I am trying to take Lent seriously this year, though I don't go without food, it wouldn't be healthy. The arrangement of time is more to the point. And keeping accounts, and sticking to hours of prayer—all that. Except for early Mass I didn't do any church to-day; had I more time, I would like to have gone to All Saints' [Margaret Street] for the Ashes Mass at 11; I have never been at this service. Being a one-priest chapel, we can't have such elaborate affairs at the Grosvenor. Though we do have blessing of the palms on Palm Sunday.

Yes, people *do* take sides about the Reformation people. (Though I am rather surprised at Westcott[1] not disapproving of, at least, Cromwell; a very base and cruel man.) Similarly, R.C. writers, such as Alfred Southern, whose *Recusant Prose* I was reading lately, can see no ill in More (and there really was some—he was very rude and unjust to Tyndale) . . . People are interesting largely because so mixed in character, bad and good together; though it isn't easy to see the good in Cromwell. But Cranmer had so much that was admirable; and one is for ever grateful to him for his liturgical style.

Yes, it is interesting to read of the religious feelings of those ordinary Marian Protestants. They were very strong and convinced. They felt they had at last really got hold of the

[1] B. F. Westcott (1825-1901), Bp of Durham.

Christian religion, so presented that they could understand and lay hold of it, and they didn't mean to let it go. The burnings had a tremendous effect on the popular mind, of course, and I suppose gave the English a Protestant bias for centuries to come. To many those cruelties were their only experience of Catholicism; the sailors who sailed the Spanish main brought home shocking tales of torture, etc., "the inquisition dogs and the devildoms of Spain",[1] and national and religious feeling were all mixed up. I think Margery Kempe[2] would probably have been a fervent Protestant in the 16th century, don't you, and have joined in that Norfolk supplication,[3] with much weeping.

I suppose most people have to be one-sided and fanatic about religion, if they are zealous at all. It shocks one when one reads history. So many didn't even try to see the good in the other point of view. Well, we have become more tolerant and less persecuting, if less zealous.

I, like you, have been collecting fresh collects, etc., from the Missal and Breviaries; I ought to learn more by heart, as one hasn't always got the words at hand. But I am still so hard-pressed, so jungle-drowned, in ruins that I haven't much time for learning anything.

It is late, and one of my resolves is earlier bed, so I must stop writing and go there.

There is a great new translation of the Bible on hand; a professor of King's College London is working on it. A friend of his showed him my father's *Quarterly* article,[4] which interested him. It will be a really fresh translation, from the original Hebrew and Greek, unburdened by echoes of the

[1] See Tennyson, "The Revenge."

[2] English mystic (c. 1373-after 1433), author of the *Book of Margery Kempe*.

[3] A Supplication signed by Protestants in Norfolk and Suffolk c. 1556; see Foxe's *Book of Martyrs*, Bk. XII.

[4] G. C. Macaulay, "The English Bible," in *The Quarterly Review* (October, 1911). See *Letters to a Friend*, p. 116.

existing ones. So is E. V. Rieu's Penguin N[ew] T[estament], but this seems too colloquial, I think.[1]

Much love. I hope you aren't really more tired than you say.

Yours always,

R. M.

20, *Hinde House, Hinde St., W.*1
28th February, 1953†

My dear Hamilton,

Your letter of 22nd came to-day, just as I was about to answer that of 16th. Thank you *so* much for *both*. You are right in saying I meant to have done with *Ruins* a year ago; indeed I did, but here I am, still struggling with them. But the end is in sight, if I keep at them. There is always a page of them half-typed in my typewriter, preventing me from using same to type a letter to you! I am interested in what you say about Foxe's Martyrs, poor heroic people. How lamentable the persecutors were, how glorious the persecuted—on all sides. How *could* people put themselves into that wickedly cruel position, in the name of the Church? It passes our modern understanding. Thank heaven for our greater humanity, at least. Yes, the Church *had* failed indeed. One can see that from all the writings before the Reformation—Chaucer, Langland, every writer except the mystical enclosed such as Rolle,[2] Hilton,[3] à Kempis,[4] Juliana of Norwich.[5] Did you ever come across the *Ancren Riwle*, that very interesting and rather charming set of rules for the guidance of some young ladies of

[1] E. V. Rieu, *The Four Gospels* (1952).
[2] Richard Rolle of Hampole (*c.* 1295-1349), English hermit and mystic.
[3] Walter Hilton (d. 1396), English monk; author of the *Scale of Perfection*.
[4] Thomas à Kempis (*c.* 1380-1471).
[5] Julian of Norwich (*c.* 1342-after 1413), English anchoress; author of *The Sixteen Revelations of Divine Love.*

good family in the 13th century—about 150 years before Chaucer, I think—who wanted to form a little religious community? It is in English (one of the earliest post-Conquest English writings) and one of the first and best examples of early Middle English. It is very engaging. My father was editing it when he died; his work has been of great use to other scholars, but was unfinished.[1] There, I suppose, was the Church at its best. It had to be in English, because, said its author, women know little of Latin. I suppose the teaching of Latin (and Greek) to English girls of the nobility only began much with the Renaissance. And, after about a century, unfortunately died out except in exceptional cases, until the mid-19th century and the Higher Education of women. As to Bible *v.* Church, I suppose both those two exclusive views made their ultimate synthesis (anyhow in the *Anglican* Church, for I think the dissenting churches incline too much to the one, and the R.C.'s to the other) and luckily "God fulfils himself in many ways, Lest one good custom should corrupt the world",[2] and one needs all the facets of truth. That book of David Mathew's is, I suppose, the one he wrote some time ago; I have it.[3] He has another Charles I book in hand,[4] and is dedicating it to *me*, which is nice of him. . . . He is so intelligent and scholarly— and I think must feel as Fr —— said to someone about the Assumption dogma, " This *isn't* going to help us". He makes kindly fun of Belloc's theories. . . .

That Collect (Lent 3, Friday); I like your "constant saving existence for us", but isn't it *better* than its original?[5] Well, I don't see why it shouldn't be. It is much stronger than "always prove wholesome to us", which I suppose would be more

[1] G. C. Macaulay, "The Ancren Riwle," in *The Modern Language Review* (January, April, July, October, 1914).

[2] See Tennyson's *Idylls of the King*, "The Passing of Arthur."

[3] *The Age of Charles I* (1951).

[4] *Scotland under Charles I* (1955).

[5] ". . . *nobis salutaria semper existant*"; see the *Secreta* for Friday of the 3rd week in Lent.

literal, but neither so euphonious nor so strong. I shall adopt yours.

My sister asks, what does the Bp of Bristol (Cockin)[1] mean when he says he *"repents"* of the disunited Church. Does he mean he feels personally that he is doing wrong about it? If so (she asks) why doesn't he amend, so far as he personally can? But I think what he feels is not quite repentance but a kind of collective guilt. He is *not*, probably, prepared to lead the way in abolishing barriers and proclaiming one united Christian Church because he thinks some of the barriers are right. He wants unity, but not to pay the price of surrender of Church principles. But he feels guilty, as I do about (say) war, and the preparation of terrible weapons; I can do nothing about it, having no power, but I feel guilty. Also about poverty. There is a very real sense in that one feels the guilt of one's human community, its dreadful cruelty and selfishness, while all one can *mend* is one's own individual share.

I am reading, when I have any reading time, Steven Runciman's *History of the Crusades*, the first of 3 volumes of it. It is fascinating reading. Those dreadful Crusaders—incredible barbarians. I have just been reading of their sack of Jerusalem, 1099; every inhabitant—men, women and children—was massacred, and they thought it right, those people being infidels. I suppose really they enjoyed it, as soldiers let loose in a conquered city always have until lately, and rationalized it by saying it was pleasing to God. On the other hand Saladin, retaking the city 80 years later, was very civilized and considerate. Very shaming for us! After the massacre the Crusaders held a thanksgiving service in the Holy Sepulchre Church; rather like Pius V[2] striking a medal in thanks for the Massacre of St Bartholomew. Can one translate *sanctificationibus* by one word? (See Post-Communion collect for to-day,

[1] Rt. Rev. F. A. Cockin.
[2] Pope Gregory XIII, not Pius V.

87

Saturday.)¹ Does "sanctities" do? "Holies" is obsolete (except in "holy of holies"). I must look at that P[rayer] B[ook] chapter in that French book. Oh yes, I *am* well placed in my unique chapel, indeed. In Cyprus, I hope to worship in Greek churches—they do accept us, don't they?² I should like to get acquainted with their Rite. Much love always. Lots more to say, but seems impracticable! Your loving

R. M.

20, Hinde House, Hinde St., W.1
13th March, 1953†

My dear Hamilton,

Thank you for two good letters, of March 2 and 7. I feel it is rather a shame, you always write the day *before* you get a letter from me, and then you feel you must write again to answer it. Since I wrote, on Feb 28, I have been having flue —a mild attack, from which I am practically recovered, but still in bed; up to-morrow, I hope. I shall write badly, therefore, and you will be able to read even less than usual of my weighty remarks—no great loss, as you know. I am very pleased to hear of the new R.C. fasting rules, and directly I can get there will go to Duckett and at least turn the pages of the number of *Worship*³ in which it is set out. I must ask... [a Roman Catholic friend] about it, too. But *she* has a notion that, as she is over 60, no fasting rules apply to her.⁴ I like the idea of those evening communions, that admirable Evangelical service that we little thought ever to see flourishing in Rome. I mentioned it to [an Anglican friend] ... the other day, and said I wondered how soon we should follow this

¹ Ember Saturday in Lent.   ² See below, p. 96*n.*

³ A periodical published by the Monks of St John's Abbey, Collegeville, Minn.

⁴ The Roman Catholic Church does dispense with the fasting rule for those over 60.

example. He said, " Oh no doubt when father says turn, we shall turn"; and I now expect that we shall. Really we *are* unnecessarily obsequious, don't you think, to that other branch of the Church. I'd like to know what *Worship* says about Lent and Easter, too.

Yes, those poor good fasting mass-priests—it [must] have been very straining for them. I wonder if your father did it, or was he a little before the time when they became so rigorous?[1]

I have been reading Rosalind Murray's *Further Journey*[2], her second book about Roman Catholicism (the first was *The Good Pagan*[3]). It interests me, and she is very fair about her religion and Protestantism and agnosticism (she insists still on calling this "paganism", which is quite silly; but she means her father's brand of high-minded humanist liberal agnosticism). She thinks these "pagans" have at least as high a standard of ethics and behaviour as R.C.s, if not higher; in fact, I gather she thinks it usually *is* higher, but she seems to mean only the best type of gentlemanly agnostic, and to be comparing him with the common run of often rather poor characters which make up the mass of R.C.s, and she quotes "an eminent prelate" as having said that cheating the customs was not sin at all, only ungentlemanly. Considering that it involves hard lying, you'd think that any Christian (as well as any decent non-Christian) *must* know it is sin; but she seems to think that many R.C.s think a shady deal like that is *less* sinful than not going to Mass on Sundays. I must say she is very candid about the defects of her Church. All the same, she believes that it is the channel of grace and that this grace is more important than ethical principles. Wouldn't you say that one purpose of the grace is to *create* right ethical principles? Grace to "perceive

[1] Presumably this refers to the strict fasting rules of the Tractarians, applied to priests celebrating at a late hour.

[2] *The Further Journey: In the End is my Beginning* (1953).

[3] *The Good Pagan's Failure* (1939).

and know what things we ought to do", and to perform the
same? If I didn't think that, I couldn't be a Christian at all;
it would seem a mockery of all Christ taught, and all that the
Holy Spirit teaches.

I must read *Spanish Tudor*.[1] I wonder what she makes of
Mary. Of course we can't judge them by modern standards;
our squeamishness about cruelty and pain is comparatively a
modern growth.

I haven't met Maurice Ashley, but have always heard a lot
about him; he does know his 17th century. I must get his
Penguin.[2] Though not yet, my hands being so full with
archaeological and other ruinous works. How lovely some
Mosques are! But all over Persia they are crumbling to decay,
their porcelain tiles fallen, their melon domes broken. Moslems
seem apathetic; and the Persian mosques are nearly all built of
clay. One feels that a Mosque is better perfect, and takes ruin
less well than Greek or Christian temples.

I suppose I am lucky, this flue of mine having been so mild.
Jeanie had it very badly, with bronchitis and then jaundice.
I hope your old Aunt Katie[3] has evaded it. I'm sure she loves
drama and catastrophes—I think all old ladies do! I remember
how my grandmother revelled in them. After all, their lives
are pretty dull and quiet. I don't feel, do you, that Stalin's
death is going to affect the world. I feel my temperature may
be rising a little, so will stop this. On Tuesday next John
Betjeman has planned a "corporate Communion" in Dr Joad's
sickroom. Several of his friends, and me too. . . .

Much love

R. M.

[1] H. F. M. Prescott, *Spanish Tudor* (1940).
[2] Maurice Ashley, *England in the Seventeenth Century* (Penguin Books,
1952).
[3] Mrs Catharine B. Johnson.

30th March, 1953†

My dear Hamilton,

Thank you so much for your letters of 16th and 25th. I last wrote to you on 14th, as you say, from bed. I . . . got about soon again, but rather weak in the head.

No, I won't write you "treatises", I didn't really mean my letters to be that, but I suppose I was interested in what I'd been reading, or perhaps in something you wrote, and meandered on and on. And perhaps when in bed I felt I had more time than usual. Now we are arrived in Holy Week. I got a blessed palm yesterday, for the first time in my life. Last Palm Sunday I was in bed; and in '51 I didn't, I remember, feel that I had got quite as far as palms yet. I have now, and liked getting it and keeping it. I believe they are burnt on Holy Saturday and the ashes used for the fire and candles service—or is it *next* year? Yes, I think we keep our palm crosses for a year, don't we?[1] I think of going on Easter Eve to the Blessing of the Candles at All Saints', Margaret St. . . . It is followed by midnight Mass (rather a new plan, I gather) but I think I shan't stay for that, but go on Easter morning to my own conventicle; I shouldn't really like to make my Easter communion anywhere else.

That is interesting about the psychological origins of the Reformation—I must get hold of it. It does sound a reasonable supposition that the Church services were felt to be un-intelligible and inaudible to the majority. By the way, *why* were they read so inaudibly? And sometimes are still? I suppose to emphasise the *mystery* of the Faith. But very bad for the intelligence of the congregation, who can never have learned to follow; I suppose they told their beads during the service, as Italians do now. Of course there was a very strong

---

[1] Traditionally the palm crosses are kept until Shrove Tuesday the following year, when they are handed in and burnt, and the ashes used in Ash Wednesday services.

subjective element in Catholicism, as one sees from the medieval books of devotion. Too much stress, I think, laid on devotional feelings and ecstasies. I was looking at a little French R.C. manual that had been left in Grosvenor Chapel; the tone of rather mawkish sweetness, its talk of "delicious visits to the Holy Sacrament", is rather repugnant. It reminds me of the way the nuns talked at our convent school, which we thought very foolish!

The public is much enjoying the obsequies of Queen Mary; they file all day past the coffin, and will do so all night. Women even shed tears, which seems affected for someone they never met and who was nearly 86. Royalty has a hypnotising effect on our nation, and considering what *real* tragedies go on all the time—the deaths of the young on the roads and in battle, the massacres in Kenya, the plight of the refugees, the cruel injustices inflicted on Africans in S. Africa (one has just been sentenced to 15 lashes and a year's gaol for some criticism of the government)—it is these things, and the preparations for war, that we should cry for, not the quite normal death of an old lady just because she has been a queen-consort. I can't understand it. Canon Collins of St Paul's has just sent me a letter to *The Times* for my signature, protesting against the treatment of Africans; he wants to get about 50 people, of different professions and opinions, to sign.[1] He is a vigorous kind of Canon.

No, don't bother to send me magazines. I imagine they don't always reach me. I haven't yet had time to go to Duckett and see *Worship* on the new fasting rules. My [Roman Catholic friend] . . . says they don't affect midnight masses, and that one could always eat up to midnight if the communion was just after midnight.[2]

I too like adding to my Prayer Notebooks. The last thing

[1] See *The Times*, 8th April, 1953, "Sentence on an African."
[2] Evidently a misunderstanding, as the 3-hour fasting rule applies to all Masses.

I copied was part of Isaiah, chap. 58, about the right kind of
fast, and the way to make the Light break on our dark minds.[1]
I have got some good Latin collects lately, too. Much love—
you can't think how much I value your prayers and good
wishes. But I do hope I haven't written another treatise!
I am still working much too hard. I fly to Cyprus May
16th.

Are you well? My love.

R. M.

20, *Hinde House, Hinde Street, W.*1
21st April, 1953 †

My dear Hamilton,

What ages since I wrote! I have had your two letters—
Good Friday and Easter Monday—lying on my writing-table,
and have tried for the last week and more to answer them, but
each day, and each hour, have been driven down and under by
the pressure of work, etc. I still am, having pledged myself to
deliver *Ruins* before I depart on May 16th. I really *ought* to get
rid of it by about the 10th, to have a week for journey preparations, visas, and what not. But I shan't, unless I work even
more strenuously than I have lately been doing. I have been
doing late night shifts, which is exhausting; but what can I do?
However, a month hence I shall be clambering about Cyprus
mountains, viewing crusaders' castles, monasteries, churches,
and antiquities in general. I plan to trip over to the Lebanon
coast, and possibly thence into Israel, but the Lebanon-Israel
frontier is an iron curtain, it seems. I have a 2nd passport,
endorsed only for Israel, which the Lebanese must not see, so
fiercely do they feel against their neighbour—and really who
shall blame them? It would be very thrilling to be in Palestine,
wouldn't it, [and] possibly to visit Galilee, and Nazareth? 1

[1] Isa. 58. 6-12.

shall write to you from Cyprus. You won't be able to write to me, as I shall have no fixed address, though " Poste Restante, Famagusta" would find me in the end. But I don't advise you to write. I am telling my sister the same, i.e. not to write unless there is anything urgent.

Thank you very much indeed for your two good letters. Did I tell you I went to an Easter Vigil Candle-Blessing on Easter Eve, at St Cyprian's [Clarence Gate]? It was at 6, not a late one, and I didn't go to Midnight Mass.

I liked the service, it was very charming, and the font-blessing, though got wet from the sprinkling. Of course it's all too *objective* for me; the idea that the water, when blessed, actually assumes qualities in itself. It's not my view; I expect too Protestant for it! Perhaps I feel the same about the Host. This is, I fear, quite un-Catholic of me. But it doesn't take anything away from the gift or the mystery, really; it remains the *remedium sempiternum*.[1]

I have just been reading in the newspaper about a priest who refused communion to a woman at the altar rail, closing her outstretched hands as he passed her, because he mistook her for a woman who had been divorced. Surely this is very shocking. I mean, to refuse any one who comes up, unless they are drunk and disorderly. If they want communion, even if they are doing wrong, surely they ought to be given it. The woman is making a fuss with the Bishop about it; he, apparently directed the priest to excommunicate the divorced persons in his parish. I wonder if he would take the same line with swindlers.

I am glad your brother[2] in S. Africa is in peace . . . But the loss of brothers and sisters must give a pang; one has shared so much with them, it goes down to the roots of life.

I saw Graham Greene's new play the other day;[3] it is most interesting, and leaves everyone discussing what he meant by

[1] "Everlasting cure."   [2] Kenneth Cowper Johnson.
[3] *The Living Room.*

it, and whether it is for the Church or against it, on the whole.
I shall like to see what *The Tablet* says of it. . . .

My love always,

R. M.

20, *Hinde House, Hinde St., W.*1

9th May, 1953†

My dear Hamilton,

I am shockingly late in answering your delightful letter
posted April 28th. I have been living pretty hectically, and this
next week will be worse, as I fly on Saturday 16th. If ever you
sent me an air letter (same as usual, same postage) to " Poste
Restante, Famagusta, Cyprus" (though, as I feel sure there are
cities of that name in the U.S., I don't know if you should make
it clear that you mean this Mediterranean isle—the P.O. will
know; but I expect "Cyprus" is enough) well, as I was saying,
I should be overjoyed, and shall, anyhow, write to *you*, if only
p.c.s, to keep you posted in my doings and seeings. How good
the second lesson for Evensong yesterday is, about St Paul &
Co.'s perilous voyaging round those parts—Alexandria,[1] Sidon,
Cyprus, then that gale and storm that threw them broken on
Crete—told in such a *sailorly* way (as my Macaulay grandfather,[2]
who was a sailor before he took orders, used, I believe, to say).
But I, flying serenely and with a rapidity S. Paul and my grandfather equally never dreamed of, through the heavens, shall
leave England at 8 a.m. and alight in Cyprus, dry and safe, at
8 that evening. *Mira fides:*[3] how lovely it will all be. I have
visas (and plans) for Lebanon, Israel, Jordan, Greece, Asia
Minor coast (opposite island of Rhodes); and kind friends have
loaded me with useful introductions, so that I shall have

---

[1] St Paul did not visit Alexandria, but part of this second voyage was
made in "a ship of Alexandria," see Acts 27. 6.

[2] Rev. S. H. Macaulay (1807-*c.* 1873).   [3] "Strange but true."

95

facilities for getting about, I hope. I look forward greatly to Palestine—Jerusalem, Nazareth, Lake of Galilee, Sea of Tiberias, etc. Will it make the Gospels more alive to me, I wonder? Not that they *aren't* alive; but it may add the vividness of visual imagination.

I shall miss the Chapel and Daily Mass very much. I shall go to Greek services, *and* Latin. Anglican? I'm not sure! Not if the Greeks admit us to communion—but I must find out.[1] Though nothing is usually *duller* than the churches of C. of E. colonies abroad. But there may be a good one on Cyprus that I shall like. I *must* try and keep up a little religious life; rather difficult, in the exciting circumstances which will take the whole of one's mind absorbing them. But they can be made part of the other.

I am interested in your 18th century readings. Have you included *Tom Jones*? And Richardson?[2] They are all so much *wordier* than we are now. I agree about Hardy: he is, on the whole, quite unreal. Where he is good is in atmosphere and landscape—oh yes, and some of the village scenes too. But his chief characters seem to me all sentimentalized.

Ascension Day on Thursday; and two days after it I fly. Whitsunday either in Cyprus or Lebanon or Israel, it depends how the Cyprus steamers go to those lands. I'm told it will be *very hot*. No thick clothes needed. Odd, in the N[ew] T[estament] so little *weather* comment. A storm on the lake—no sun, no rain, no cold. I must stop. All my love and thanks.

R. M.

I do hope you are, and will go on being, *well*.

---

[1] No intercommunion with the Anglican Church is recognised by the Orthodox Church.

[2] Samuel Richardson (1689-1761), author of *Clarissa Harlowe*, etc.

My dear Hamilton,

I got your letter of the 10th in good time to take it with me when I flew off at crack of dawn yesterday. I had a smooth and beautiful journey, and got to Cyprus at 8 p.m. One night in Nicosia, and now here for a week. After that, my movements are vague, but I am still having letters forwarded to Famagusta [as] I don't yet know my dates for Lebanon and Palestine and Rhodes. It is all very exciting and very beautiful. Famagusta is an old walled crusaders' city, but nothing left of it now but the walls, the citadel (Othello's supposed tower), and the great Gothic cathedral made a mosque by the Turks when they conquered Cyprus in the 16th century, and still a mosque —all whitewashed within, carpeted, all ornaments and altars and stained glass gone, and Moslems in corners saying their prayers aloud. Near the cathedral stand the ruins of a few medieval churches, and some domed Moslem buildings; all the multitude of churches and convents gone that were there 6 and 7 centuries ago, when Famagusta was a fine rich luxurious city. Now all is desolation, a littered waste, thistles and grass and palms and the sighing of the sea beyond the massive wall. I have hired a self-drive car, as there seems no other way of getting about Cyprus. No buses, no railways scarcely; one must either bicycle, walk, or drive. This morning I saw Nicosia, the little capital; it too has a great church turned mosque. The municipal elections are on, and the hotel manager warned me to be careful, I might get killed—I asked why. He said Cypriotes got excited and stampeded. How unlike municipal elections in London! However, the streets seemed to me very quiet.

I like your "steering past the monsters"—*much* better than the other. Yes, it does seem likely that the composer had sea monsters in mind. The metaphor of steering is excellent, and rather beautiful. What nice things you find. I always like the old use of *monstrous* in the sense of " full of monsters," like "the bottom of the monstrous deep", where Lycidas lay. I shall use *"vitiorum monstra devitare"*[1] myself. *How* prosaic most collect-translators are! (Not Cranmer, however.) About Wm Law: I agree with you that his notion of absolute renunciation goes too far, and is too ascetic. What I like so much about him is his ideas about God and Christ as our saviour—saving us not *in* our sins (like the Evangelical view) but *from* them; and the bringing of our wills into harmony with Christ, so that we may desire that which is good, and not be double-minded. He puts all that so very well. Quite a lot in him I ignore, of course.

Now I must take this down and get it posted. It brings my love—I wish I had time to finish the page, but haven't if it is to go out at 8.

They called for my Book at 4.30 the day before yesterday. I had just done it up. I then began to pack, and was up all night nearly. I still have one more chapter to write on my return. Yours with much love.

R. M.

Cyprus
2nd June, 1953†

My dear Hamilton,

This is a heavenly island! I think I wrote to you before from Famagusta; now I am at Kyrenia, but leaving this week for Beirut, Lebanon, Palestine. Then back here, then Rhodes, then home (by end of June). It is really gloriously beautiful here, and tremendously interesting. Famagusta is a remarkable

[1] "Eschew all forms of vice," from the Prayer for the Sovereign (used in England only) in the Roman Missal.

old place, and near it are the ruins of ancient Salamis, where St Barnabas is buried; he was a native of it. Then there is Paphos, where Aphrodite arrived in her shell, and where St Paul converted the Governor.[1] Wonderful Greek and Roman ruins all about. And now Kyrenia, by the sea (perfect bathing) and under the mountain range of Tröodos; St. Hilarion's medieval castle is up in the mountains above us, and Bellapais Abbey—both of extreme beauty, both ruined crusader buildings. In the harbour here there is another crusader castle. I like the Cypriotes so much, they are so gay and friendly. The Anglican churches seem deplorable, I can't go into them, they are built of grey porridge. On Whit Sunday I went to a Greek Mass at the Greek church at Paphos. The Bishop of Paphos preached, with eloquence, but I didn't follow all of it! *Sin* came in (*against* it, he was) and *church-going* (*for* it). But I liked the service. The island is full of old Byzantine medieval churches, some with charming wall-paintings of the medieval centuries. And some Latin churches of the crusaders, some have been turned into mosques, however.

I look forward to Syria and Palestine. Don't be surprised if you get no letters, as the air mail (not being British like Cyprus) will probably be no good. I will write if I can, though. I am very well and sunburnt and gay. I have made several acquaintances among the residents and visitors here—some are rather raffish young men, of the type who are apt to congregate in Mediterranean islands, and are not much approved of by the British residents.

The Coronation service came to us on the BBC fairly well, and was impressive. How glad I am to be away from the madding crowds! Cyprus is full of the gods of Olympus as well as of the Byzantine, Roman, and Turkish forms of worship: it gets to feel rather the same, a kind of merger—the Light that lighteth every man. But I belong to the best company, though it makes little show here. I am going to-

[1] See Acts 13. 12.

morrow up into the mountains (in a car) to see painted Byzantine churches. How lucky I am! Much love. *Ora pro me.*

R. M.

Jerusalem
18th June, 1953†

My dear Hamilton,

I last wrote to you from Cyprus; since then I have had a marvellous and interesting time. I spent a fortnight or so in Cyprus (superb bathing, crusader castles, ancient Greek things ...) then crossed to Beirut, on the Lebanon coast, and all about Lebanon and Syria, being very nobly entertained by people to whom I had letters, and others. I was driven out into desert places to see Baalbek and Palmyra, and down the coast to Tyre and Sidon (of both [of] which there is much more left above ground than Isaiah and Ezekiel would have wished), and to Tortosa and its crusader castle and cathedral, both now made squalid by Saracens.[1] Then I came south to Damascus, Amman (Rabbath-Ammon of the Old Testament, at the siege of which David did his dirty trick on Uriah).[2] It is in a rocky and mountainous land, and a few miles off on all sides ancient cities stand in ruin, and are being excavated; some of them I went out to with archaeologists in cars or jeeps. Round Amman and Jericho there are terrifying camps of the poor Palestinian refugees, driven out of their country by the Jews, and living in camps, supported by United Nations—no work, no life, nothing but existence. The children have evil, cunning, ferocious little faces, and stone foreigners like me. If ever I saw a criminal community in the making, it is that; there seems no solution and no hope. The Arab-Israel hate is

[1] See R. M.'s *Pleasure of Ruins*, p. 446.
[2] "Rabbah," see 2 Sam. 11. 1.

frightening. We ought never to have sanctioned the Israel invasion.

I am now in Jerusalem (yesterday I came) staying practically *in* the Anglican Cathedral, in a hostel frequented by rather mousey, nice people rather of the church-worker type. The Bishop[1] is in England, and his clergy carry on. They have 7 a.m. daily Mass, not quite what I am used to in Grosvenor Chapel (plain P[rayer] B[ook]) but it *is* Mass, and, after long Mass-less-ness, it is good to have it. I haven't seen much of Jerusalem yet, and don't know that I like it v. much (except for the Rock), it's so got up for the tourist. One of the clergy here advises doing the things in chronological order, going through Our Lord's last week; but space-order takes less time. The Garden of Gethsemane has several huge churches, all showy: R.C., Russian, and United Nations; and the tomb of the B.V.M. is at hand (when it was built, in the 4th c., they hadn't yet invented the Assumption) and the Mount of Olives is behind. I would rather see all this alone, but one is pestered by guides. Then there is the Via Dolorosa, along which Franciscans process every Friday; and I must go to Bethlehem and Nazareth and the Dead Sea. Then across the frontier into Israel (for which I have a second passport), to see Galilee, Lake of Tiberias, and some castles round Haifa. From Haifa I cross back to Cyprus, and my plane leaves Cyprus for London on July 1st. I am very well, and it's not *usually* too hot. I do hope you are well? It's much too long since I heard. Much love from your affectionate

R. M.

[1] Rt. Rev. W. H. Stewart.

My dear Hamilton,

I got home last week, to find your letter of June 27th awaiting me. Next morning my wireless got spontaneous combustion and set my sitting-room alight, and it burnt down a lot of pictures, furniture, curtains, carpet, etc., before the firemen could extinguish it, also a few books and papers, and the heat was so great that my big glass-fronted bookcase broke its glass front. The builders haven't yet got to work on re-decorating (that is my landlord's job, of course) and heaven knows how long they will be. Meanwhile I live in my bed-room, encumbered with books and papers and furniture, and the pictures have gone away to have their canvas repaired where possible, their glass mended (and frames), and the sofa is going away for re-covering and two tables for repairing and polishing, and the hair carpet for restoring if possible, if not I must have another. Luckily I am covered; I was afraid my insurance had run out, but it just hadn't. Of course the insurance won't pay for everything, as things cost so much more now than when I bought them; but I hope not to be utterly ruined. It is all very tiresome and uncomfortable, and my proofs are pouring in and I ought to be writing my last chapter, but it is very difficult in these circumstances. However, to soothe myself I think with joy of Cyprus and the Levant. Since I last wrote to you I have been over the frontier at Jerusalem, from Arab land to Israel, and then on into the whole State of Israel, the lake of Galilee, where I stayed in a Franciscan convent at Tiberias, high above the lake; it was very beautiful. Lovely bathing, and I drove round the lake to Capernaum, which is just a little group of ruins with a little church near, with a mosaic of loaves and fishes. Galilee was indescribably beautiful. Then I saw Nazareth, and so to the coast, where I saw Acre, Tortosa, Caesarea (now a few ruins above the sea), Askelon (also a heap of ruins) and the new capital Tel Aviv, a horrid modern city. On that side of the frontier I heard, of course, the Jewish point of view, after the furious diatribes I had heard about them from the evicted Arabs. I liked the Children of Israel, and I liked the Arabs, and there seems no solution of their quarrel. The Jews are making a good thing of their new State, if they can get hold of enough money. I returned from Tel Aviv to Cyprus on June 20, and had a few more days there before flying home in a rather limping plane that kept having to retrace its steps and held us up at Athens for a while. I certainly did have an eyeful and a mindful of beauty and interest, also of sunshine. Now I am back in the cold damp of an English july, and am just getting used again to never feeling quite warm enough. I am working uncomfortably hard, which would perhaps be more difficult if it was hot. . . .

I will read C. Dawson's *Oxford Movement*.[1] And the *Newman Letters*[2] again; I can't have read them for years. His reactions to the places he saw were, as I remember them, *all* part of religion to him; was he ever carried away by sheer sensuous beauty, with no religious afterthought? I imagine not. My reactions to the Palestine and Syrian country, apart from its clear, fine-drawn beauty of line and colour, were to deepen my sense of the essentially *Syrian* life they led there, and of the Eastern origins of the Christian church. I see what you mean about the Christ formed by Western Catholicism, the form in which He comes to us. But I always feel, don't you, that Western Catholicism made many mistakes and misinterpretations, and should go back without prejudice to the source, in as scholarly and honest a way as can be done. We do seem to have made so many muddles, and worse than

[1] Christopher Dawson, *The Spirit of the Oxford Movement* (1933).
[2] Anne Mozley, *Letters and Correspondence of J. H. Newman during his Life in the English Church* (2 vols., 1891).

muddles. They say it was the inspiration of the Holy Spirit: but I think they got this wrong extremely often. No more room to talk about this! Only my love.

R. M.

20, Hinde House, Hinde St., W.1
30th July, 1953†

My dear Hamilton,

This isn't going to be a real letter, as I can't write one till I have a free moment, and that means when I have got my proofs off. At present I am knee-deep in them, sitting on my bedroom floor, while the painters and carpenters occupy the sitting-room. I *have* to finish them by August 4, and after that shall write to you properly. This is only to send my love and to thank you for yours of July 14th and 15th and 21st, and for an old one you wrote to Famagusta; it followed me about the east, and arrived here 3 days ago! Thank you so much for it, and for the others. I will answer them all properly soon. At the moment my writing-table in my bedroom is piled with *unopened* envelopes and unanswered letters and they will just have to wait. I *shall* be glad when the long business is over; and when, too, I can get back to my sitting-room. My furniture (the burnt but not quite destroyed things) is being repaired; the pictures are being treated, those not too far gone. Curtains and covers and carpet are being replaced. I am here till August 8th, when I go for a fortnight to the Isle of Wight with my sister; then back here. The Chapel shuts for August, except for the Sunday services, which will be taken by Father Maycock,[1] Canon Hood's successor at Pusey House. I shall miss the daily Masses quite a lot.

When I have time to read at all, I shall read the various

---

[1] Rev. F. H. Maycock.

books you mention—Tyrrell I *always* find good. Now I must stop and labour. I am quite well, only rather exhausted with all this work and comfortless domestic conditions.

I am just in from the wedding of a friend[1] at St Margaret's, Westminster. A beautiful service and singing. But what an *odd* service the marriage service in some ways is! I can't help feeling that the Christ and the Church analogy, kept on all these centuries, is pretty blasphemous and silly. Who first conceived it? It always shocks me. But I like all the "for richer, for poorer, for better, for worse", etc.—it is very moving.

Much love. I shall write again soon.

Your loving

R. M.

Ryde, Isle of Wight
11th August, 1953 †

My dear Hamilton,

At last I have got my book OFF, delivered to the publishers, and no more worry with it till it comes back to me in page-proofs, and—horrid thought—*index*. And at last I can relax, lie about in the sun on this blessed island (not so blessed as Cyprus, but still blessed, when one is, as I am, away from the madding crowds on the beaches and sitting in a garden above the sea). And now I can write some kind of answer to your letters. One result of them was that I took some of the books you wrote of with me, and am reading them: Vol. 2 of M. D. Petre's (yes, surely *Peter*, not Petrie—I never heard it called that but I may be wrong) *Tyrrell*, which I have read, of course, long ago, but have forgotten.[2] It is the volume with the

---

[1] Nigel Nicolson.

[2] Maude D. Petre, *Autobiography and Life of George Tyrrell* (2 vols., 1912).

account of his middle years, his conflicts with the S[ociety of] J[esus], his friendship with von Hügel—all that. And I like *her* account of her R.C. mid-Victorian childhood. I also have her *My Way of Faith* but haven't got down to that yet. I couldn't get (at the L. L[ibrary]) Tyrrell's *Faith for the Millions*,[1] but have some Wm Temples. I couldn't get *Nova et Vetera*[2] either, which has some good essays in it. I possess several Tyrrell's, and do re-read them from time to time. It always makes me wonder how often it is possible for a convert bred in a more or less sceptical atmosphere to settle down intellectually *permanently* in Rome: I think nagging doubts, rebellions against all those dogmatic certainties, so authoritatively delivered as if from God not from fallible human beings, would always from time to time raise their heads and disturb. What an extraordinary position that Church has come to hold, in the minds of vague non-Catholics! In a novel I am now reading a dissolute young woman says, " I think I shall join the Church", and means the R.C. Church— no other crosses her mind. She adds that it seems the *only* escape from self. None of her friends say " How about the Anglican Church? " None of them has ever heard of it. But they beg her *not* to "join the Church", as they think she wouldn't be happy in it, or able to believe enough. It seems to me that rather ignorant people in novels always take this line —religion is the R.C. Church (which they call "the Catholic Church") and they know of no other. I was interested that the nice manager of this hotel,[3] who is an Anglo-Catholic, said to me, "Are you an Anglo-Catholic? " And when I said yes, said, " I somehow felt you were." Why, I wonder? He was telling me of "a nice church" near here with daily Mass. But so far I have been too sunk in dopey lassitude, after my exhausting labours, to get up early enough. I bathe, and lie about, and

[1] *The Faith of the Millions: A Selection of Past Essays* (2 vols., 1901).
[2] G. Tyrrell, *Nova et Vetera: Informal Meditations* (1897).
[3] Westfield Park Hotel, Ryde.

read, and talk to my sister, and answer piles of unanswered letters, and *sleep*. I must get that Latin and English Psalter you mention. And Dawson's *Oxford Movement*, which would interest me. What a good prayer, that "*contra adversa muniamur*",[1] I shall get it by heart, and transcribe among my *Preces Privatae*. I need it, for I am terribly *un*fortified against adversity, by nature. How wrong you are about me! I attach *far* too much importance to possessions, and loathe losing them. In '41, when my flat went, I was shattered (being then also without *coelestia alimenta*) and even now hate to think of it. Of course my conflagration the other day was a very minor affair; tho' it wrecked my sitting-room it didn't really *destroy* very much, except some pictures (which I mourn) and curtains and covers and a few books and lamp-shades, etc.

I don't feel quite happy about your Prodigal Son analogy. After all, the C. of E. *has* tried, however faultily, to be Christian (and not more faultily than the R.C. Church) and I don't feel that it was *eating husks* all through the Protestant centuries, do you? One thinks of George Herbert, of Bp Andrewes, of Hooker, Jeremy Taylor, the non-Jurors, the quiet Anglican rectors who did their duty (your ancestors and mine), who never felt they served a Church which was no good; and the millions of faithful people who belonged to it. But no more!

Much love,

R. M.

---

[1] See post-communion Collect for Quinquagesima: ". . . *Ut qui coelestia alimenta percepimus, per haec contra omnia adversa muniamur.*" (". . . That we who have received this heavenly food may by it be safe-guarded from all adversities.")

My dear Hamilton,

Thank you so much for yours of 14th, answering mine from I[sle of] W[ight]. This is in an envelope, as I want to enclose an interesting review from the *Sunday Times* of a book on the Clapham Sect[1] (an absurd name, as Raymond Mortimer rightly points out). It is, as he says, odd that it should have been, in the Church, only the Evangelicals who bothered about those social wrongs. I suppose the Tractarians were too much taken up with church reform to care about social reform. Or is there any other explanation? It is one of the shocking anomalies of Christianity—like the Inquisition. I do see what you mean about the C. of E. and the Prodigal Son. I suppose all branches of all churches have shown a terrible appetite for husks at various times; luckily sometimes they achieve the fatted calf in the end, but not always. The pity is that so many people really do prefer the husky diet, apparently, and don't see the beauty of the other—don't even know about it—and when, weary of husks, they hanker after a calf, they only know about the Roman calf, and make for it without a glance aside at the potentialities of the Church of their country. Somehow the larger Church has succeeded in imposing itself, and in stealing the limelight. Of course there are, all over the country, a great number of very dull and unsatisfying churches, which no doubt make a bad impression on those who look for a Church to attach themselves to. Two Irish girls in the I. of W. asked me why C. of E. churches smelt so musty. I said it was the smell of damp and ancient stones, also of hassocks. I added that of course we had the old churches, and they had had to build new ones. They retorted that *they* thought it was because our churches weren't much used. I rather like the smell, it

[1] E. M. House, *Saints in Politics: The "Clapham Sect" and the Growth of Freedom* (1953).

reminds one of all the country churches that ever were, and is very, very Anglican.

I have now got hold of the first volume of the *Faith of Millions*, and have read some of it with interest. *Nova et Vetera* is vol. 2, isn't it, which I shall get next time I go to the L[ondon] L[ibrary].[1] It is interesting to think that in 1897 he [Tyrrell] felt as he apparently did, in his admiration for the [Roman Catholic] Church (though even then with reservations) and by 1900 was writing "O Church of my baptism why did I ever leave you?". Now I am back here, I can get the other books too. I have now got to write a BBC programme on "Changing Morals", illustrated by quotations read aloud. I suppose I begin with the cave man gnawing his bone and snarling at those who try to take it away; a long step from him to the elaborate arrangements for people's welfare we make now. Yes, we are better. History is horribly cruel, people flogged to death, tortured, massacred, lunatics chained up and beaten, children worked to death in factories and pits, prisons what they were. I suppose even our partial advance in humanity is something to be glad of. But we have kept war. As to our moral teachers, I suppose "the Light that lighteth every man" has inspired in them much the same codes, from all ages, however shockingly misinterpreted. Buddha, Confucius, Socrates, the Jewish prophets—all speak of love, human kindness, forgiving trespasses. But all the time these horrors went on; and, of course, go on still, tho' less. And what of sex morality? It seems to undulate, have its ups and downs. I see the Kinsey Report about women is out;[2] one review suggests that some of the women questioned were probably pulling Dr Kinsey's leg. I am little by little getting my flat into shape again. . . . Actually the room gets to look rather smart . . . and hasn't been so clean for years! I won't write on the back of this, as it shows through. I had *such* a nice

[1] *Nova et Vetera* is not Vol. 2 of *The Faith of the Millions*.
[2] A. C. Kinsey, *Sexual Behaviour in the Human Female* (1953).

peaceful week on the Island, and feel very much rested by it The weather was nice. I hope you too feel well and fit. Much love to you. Your letters are *so* full of interest always.

Yours,

R. M.

20, *Hinde House, Hinde St.,* W.1

18th *September,* 1953 †

My dear Hamilton,

Your letter of 15th reproaches me (though not in words) for my dilatoriness in writing lately, for I have had three letters from you since I last wrote. But truly I have been impossibly busy since I got back from [the] I[sle] of W[ight], wrestling with proofs and other business, and have scarcely had time for reading or writing anything. . . . [I have been hearing] a terrible account of the state of things [in South Africa] . . . the tension between Africans and Europeans, and the frightfulness of the Malan government. The ill feeling grows all the time, and no wonder. The worst part of it is the way these injustices and cruelties are done in the name of religion, that horrible brand of Calvinistic Old Testament religion that Boers affect. One calls it O.T. because they keep referring to this, but it is really a libel on the O.T., with its magnificence and communing with God . . . No, I don't remember that line in Swinburne, and, as you say, it isn't like him; I will ask a Swinburne expert. Mrs Belloc Lowndes was R.C. like her brother.[1] So are her daughters, Elizabeth Iddesleigh and Susan Marques, who is married to a delightful Portuguese and lives in Lisbon. I will get hold, if I can, of *One Poor Scruple,* I've never read it.[2] Didn't I send you *Period Piece?* I know I thought of it. I certainly shall, for an early Xmas present! I know you'd love it. It is full of wit and observation and

[1] Hilaire Belloc.

[2] Mrs Wilfrid Ward, *One Poor Scruple* (1899).

Cambridge and the Darwins, etc. Thank you for all the books you put into my mind. I shall get from the L[ondon] L[ibrary] *The Wards and the Transition*.[1] For the next little while I must read books about "Changing Morals", for my BBC programme. They certainly have changed: and of course on the whole much for the better . . . I have been reading Lecky,[2] Aristotle, M. Aurelius, Plato, Leviticus, the Psalms; and, as you see, have not got yet very near our own times. But before I really tackle it I have to compile the index to my book; this I must do next week in Dorset, where I go on Tuesday for a week to stay with Raymond Mortimer, who is far from well and will be alone, so invited me to keep him company; I think he will be helpful about the index.

Your description of your over-replete cell that needs tidying is very like my flat! *All* my drawers and boxes are full to choking, and my tidyings are much too partial and inadequate. Should you not throw away a lot of letters, beginning with the 134 (now 135) that you mention? I really think you should. They must take a lot of space, and aren't worth preserving. My sitting-room has acquired a new neatness after its wrecking by fire . . . "homely and yet artistic", as the man who came to mend my clock remarked.

Yes, your reading *is* rather Popish just now. I am reading Christopher Sykes's *Two Studies in Virtue*, with his study of Richard Sibthorp, the Anglican priest early in the 19th century who was from time to time drawn over to Rome; it is interesting and amusing and attractive. I think if I had been born 50 years before I was, I might easily have made that journey, just to escape from the bareness of the C. of E. But now I feel we have as good as the Romans have, and with it far more integrity and intelligence in our worship. What should you say is the central point in the Christian faith? I suppose the belief that Christ is God and became incarnate and

[1] Maisie Ward, *The Wilfrid Wards and the Transition* (2 vols., 1934-38).
[2] William E. H. Lecky (1838-1903), Irish historian and essayist.

lives to help us now and is the indwelling light in every man.
I can never get much further than this—and that He is Love.
But all the Churches have got much further, of course, and
the Rom: Church furthest of all. No more space to expound
on this! Don't worry when I don't write. You are so steadily
there to me that I can talk to you sometimes in my thoughts,
without writing.

And I send my love always, even when I don't write.

R. M.

20, *Hinde House, Hinde St., W.*1
8th October, 1953 †

My dear Hamilton,

I seem always to be answering two letters from you, the
2nd having arrived before I had had time to answer the 1st,
but it is quite unintentional, as I always think I shall have time
to write, and then each day submerges me again. Since my
return from Dorset and getting your letter of Sept. 22nd, I
have been feverishly rushing round to libraries etc. trying to
check up on the captions for my illustrations; where the
original pictures are, who by, etc. etc., my publishers having
lost some records. It has been a great hunt, interrupted by five
days of pleurisy on my part, but that is now cured by assiduous
doping with M. & B. and penicillin, and I am now entirely
recovered. And the book chores are over, I think, so I can now
get down to all the other arrears of chores, including "Morals",
and two reviews over-due. What a life! To-day I got *W. G.
Ward,* by his son, from the library (I mean *W. G. Ward and
the Oxford Movement*).[1] *The Transition*[2] is still out, but is being
sent for, as it is due back. I shall read that with interest; also
One Poor Scruple. The Ward I have is interesting. His pre-

[1] W. Ward, *W. G. Ward and the Oxford Movement* (1889).
[2] *The Wilfrid Wards and the Transition,* see above p. 111*n.*

conversion attitude towards Rome reminds me of you. "He recited its liturgy constantly, he studied its devotional literature unceasingly. The existing Catholic Church had to him all the romance which days of chivalry have to the youthful readers of Scott." But you don't hate Anglicanism, and he did. It "caused him torture," he told people. He thought it was oppressive and had no liberty. This view may seem a trifle biassed, but he was too wholly enchanted by Rome to admit any such defects in it. Just as Belloc was. And any defects which he (Belloc) saw, he loudly denied, and hit out at the heretic enemy. Not an admirable character; but an admirable writer. He had the great faults of scorn and arrogance.

I believe myself that our Reformation had positive virtues; don't you grant it any? In spite of the destruction and the crudeness and the bareness of church and worship, it had an element of truth and moral integrity, and did end many corruptions, surely, that had to be ended. Had it been led by Erasmus and Colet . . . [sic] but, as you and Horace rightly point out, one can't change the past. Or have we, to some extent? Anyhow, we have now something in which I, at least, can live and find nourishment—well in the treacle.[1] I certainly don't want anything else; only the power to use better and more profitably what is accessible. In short, I am a happy Anglican, even though a pretty unprofitable one. And of course I couldn't be a happy Papist, or an honest one. Though I dip into their devotions and their liturgy at my pleasure and suck no small advantage from it, especially from the bits you pass on to me from time to time. But I read it myself too, quite a lot, and it is all part of the treacle. From treacle to cantaloups. Pronounce (says the O[xford] D[ictionary]) cántaloup. No, not cantellopies. It is from the Italian place near Rome, Cantalupo, where it first grew, brought there by Armenians.

[1] In earlier letters to Father Johnson, R. M. had written metaphorically of "treacle wells"; see *Letters to a Friend*, p. 39, and Lewis Carroll's *Alice in Wonderland*, chapter VII.

" Highly esteemed by the curious" (1763), and thought a great delicacy. Talking of delicacies, did you know that old St James's Day, August 5th, used to be Oyster Day, because the oyster season then began.[1] Hence the grottoes made by children of oyster shells. Did they in Norfolk "go grottoing", begging "a penny for the grotto "? And is it still anywhere done? A friend of mine says he remembers it in Battersea Park some thirty years ago. And the Shropshire children always did it when my father was a child there. I wonder if the custom ever got to America. It is supposed to be derived from the days of pilgrimages (with scallop shells) to St James of Compostella, when they built grottoes to his honour. The origin of all these customs interests me to track out. I dare say the New Englanders thought it popish, like the maypole, and didn't allow it.

I am now recovered from my conflagration, and sit sur-rounded by its fruits: new curtains, with a pleasant design as of large blue sunflowers in squares—very nice, I think; and a new deep blue weave sofa cover, and new haircord carpet, and polished up writing-table and cabinet (inlaid), and a new cabinet with drawers, for the new wireless to stand on; and on the new wireless stands my new and beautiful Parthenon of cork, under a glass dome like a bubble, which Raymond Mortimer gave me in Dorset; and newly painted walls of deep cream, and the pictures now nearly all back, except the totally destroyed; some remain rather scorched, but I have hung what I could. The room looks very clean and re-furbished, and is an incentive to tidiness, for me an unattainable virtue except by fits and starts. I really must try to keep my litter under; I am glad that you too find this difficult.

You have given me no news for a long time of your friends the Paines. Is Mrs P. well, and the girl and her baby? Do

[1] By "old St James's Day, August 5th" R. M. presumably means St James's Day according to the Julian Calendar, which was in use in England until 1752.

you see them much? And how is Father— oh dear, can I have forgotten his name?[1] I forget everything just now, and he so kind to me when over here. It will come back to me when I am less sleepy; it is after 11, and I have had a busy day. And my *ostium coeli*[2] awaits me at 8.15 to-morrow. Mark Bonham Carter, a friend of mine and the son of Lady Violet B.C., a most intelligent young man in his early 30s, wants to come to the Grosvenor with me one morning;[3] he . . . thinks he will try what it is like at the Chapel. I hope he'll like it. . . . [I] saw the new T. S. Eliot play . . . *The Confidential Clerk*; not v.g., I thought. I always feel he could do better, somehow. But some people see deep meanings in it. Well, who knows? Good-night. Thank you for everything in your two letters, and much love.

R. M.

20, *Hinde House, Hinde St., W.*1
25*th October,* 1953 †

My dear Hamilton,
    Thank you v. much indeed for your letter of Oct. 12th. I am interested in what you say about the validity of Catholic sacraments and orders outside the Rom: Church. I always feel it is largely from *vanity* that the Papal claims to be the unique Catholic Church of Christ rise; they can't bear to have any non-Papal rivals. Apropos of this, I will send you *Infallible Fallacies*,[4] the pamphlet by some anonymous Anglican priest which has lately been published. . . . It is called "An Anglican reply to R.C. arguments", and opens with a protest against the

[1] R. M. means Fr Pedersen, s.s.j.e.
[2] "Doorway to heaven."
[3] The idea originated with R. M.
[4] *Infallible Fallacies: An Anglican Reply to Roman Catholic Arguments, by some Priests of the Anglican Communion* (S.P.C.K., 1953).

R.C. anti-Anglican propaganda, which is to be found in all those booklets which lie about R.C. churches, and elsewhere. I think a reply was wanted, but perhaps they go too far in criticism down too near the ill-mannered R.C. level, which is a pity. But I gather they meant to answer the questions of many Anglicans who are upset and shaken by Roman propaganda. I shall like to know what you think of it, when you receive it. How nice it would be if each Church were to publish a pamphlet full of *compliments* to the other! Why should there be all this ill-feeling?

Mark Bonham Carter came to Mass with me, and liked it v. much. . . . I hope he will go on coming sometimes. That Bonham Carter you knew may have been Sir Maurice, Mark's father and Lady Violet's husband—a pleasant, able barrister of about 70-odd. Are you a reader of George Santayana, and did you ever come across him? I've just been reviewing his last autobiographical volume[1] (he died last year[2], I think). A curiously egotistical philosopher-poet, who never fitted in anywhere; Spanish birth, American and Harvard upbringing, long stays in England (Oxford and Cambridge). But, tho' a sceptic, [he] could like no religion but the R.C. Church, which he never practised, but felt a patriotic devotion to, and loathed Protestantism (oh dear, my new pen is *not* a success, it comes through the paper—I shall type instead). Fr Waggett[3] asked him to lunch at Cowley, and (except Fr W. himself) he utterly despised the Fathers, and described them most rudely. That was about 1896, I think: before your time, of course. But dear Fr Cary must have been there,[4] and many other delightful people. I think Santayana was angry with them for being non-"Catholic" monks at all; he found it hypocritical

[1] *My Host the World* (1953).
[2] 26th September, 1952.
[3] Rev. P. N. Waggett, s.s.j.e. (1862-1939), whom R. M. knew at Cambridge before World War I.
[4] Rev. H. L. M. (Lucius) Cary, s.s.j.e. (d. 1950), formerly R. M.'s confessor.

and absurd. He didn't like King's either,[1] except the architecture of the Chapel etc., which he describes very beautifully, but implies that it was unvisited by God. As Bertrand Russell says of him, he was full of "facile contempt", therefore difficult to love. I am going to a lecture on the Gospels by E. V. Rieu, who has lately translated them, hasn't he?[2] And I want to read C. H. Dodd on the Fourth Gospel, which was reviewed the other day; it sounds interesting.[3] You will see that I am trying to improve my N[ew] T[estament] knowledge, which wants doing. Meanwhile my sister is engaged in trying to introduce an unbeliever to Christianity; she plies her with books, which the unbeliever reads with interest, but so far can't envisage a God. Jeanie has never unbelieved; I have, so am useful in suggesting means of cure. Perhaps, in the end, it must be a movement not of intellect but of will. Perhaps sin, perhaps unhappiness, help sometimes to open the doors; perhaps sometimes mere loneliness, often of course personal influence. But reading? I don't know if that often opens the *ostium coeli*. Corresponding with a Cowley Father in Cambridge, Mass. is not a bad plan, followed by attending a Chapel in Mayfair. I have got the *Transition Wards* from the Library now, and read a good deal of it with interest.[4] It must have been a stimulating time and set of people. Quite different from the circle of Arnolds, Stephens, Huxleys, etc. that my grandparents moved among, and who seldom (except Tom Arnold) had R.C. leanings. Tho' several of my mother's cousins were converts actually. Yes, Sam: Daniel[5] yearned after old times, yet remained Protestant; like Bishop Corbet[6] and many others. All Hallows next Sunday: that at least the Church has always celebrated. And All Souls has returned to us; I wish we put

[1] King's College, Cambridge.
[2] See above p. 88.
[3] C. H. Dodd, *The Interpretation of the Fourth Gospel* (1953).
[4] See above p. 111*n*.
[5] Samuel Daniel (1562-1619).
[6] Richard Corbet (1582-1635), Bp. of Oxford and Norwich.

fairy lamps on graves here, as we did in Italy. Much love for All Hallows.

R. M.

20, Hinde House, Hinde St., W.1
3rd November, 1953 †

My dear Hamilton,

Your letter (Oct. 26th) came soon after I had posted mine of 25th; and now you have answered that one on 28th, so I have *two* of yours before me. I wonder when you'll get *Infallible Fallacies.* You will probably dislike it v. much; indeed, we mostly think it a mistake. It may hinder some wavering would-be converts and set them thinking more critically about Roman claims and Anglican ditto, and may tell the ignorant things they hadn't known before about both: but this doesn't compensate for the aggressive tone of much of it, which can only do harm. Perhaps I shouldn't have sent it you, because I know you'll hate much of it.

Did I ever tell you of my little god-daughter, Mary Anne, now 12?[1] I sponsored her at a time when (I now see) I was in no fit state to be sponsoring anyone—but there it is, I *am* her godmother, and I did promise to see that she was brought up a Christian. She now goes to St Paul's school, and her sister of 10 to a smaller day school in Kensington. There they get some church and scripture teaching, I suppose . . . . Now I feel it is time I took up my responsibilities more, and tried to introduce them to some attractive church that has good children's services—masses or afternoon services, or both . . . As smaller children they sometimes went in and out of a Roman church close to them, off Kensington High Street, and probably that is about all they know of Catholicism. They know nothing, certainly, of Anglican Cath: and I should like to

<hr>

[1] Mary Anne O'Donovan.

118

introduce them to this, in an attractive setting. . . . St John's, Addison Rd[1] [has, they say] . . . services for children of a Catholic type. So I shall go there to inspect it, and then take the two young ladies there on Sunday, and try and tell them something about the Church. . . . I wish you would bear these children in mind from time to time, and my efforts for them. They are intelligent, charming, lively, and we are mutually fond of each other; I am, of course, their "Aunty Rose". Mary Anne reads some of my books. I fear she won't get far with *Ruins*, which comes out at the end of this month.

All Saints and All Souls were v.g. . . . A really first-class sermon on Sunday, mostly about All *Souls*, and yesterday we had 2 early Requiem Masses.

Unusually, I have been writing a letter to a paper (*The Listener*) in reply to a broadcaster on Newman and Manning who charged the C. of E. with having "slept a deep sleep" for nearly two centuries when Newman came to Oxford in 1817.[2] What a thing to say of the Church of the Caroline divines, the tremendous religious conflicts between Churchmen and Puritans, the rich stream of Cathol[ic] piety and tradition that ran thro' both 17th and 18th centuries, tho' rather thinly in the latter. But remember the Non-Jurors, Wm Law, the groups of pious churchmen and women, in the Little Gidding tradition, the theological pamphlet wars that excited London so much, the innumerable books of devotion that ran into so many editions and were so widely used, the sacramental teaching in them, so much in advance of the B[ook of] C[ommon] P[rayer]. Then the speaker referred to the bibulous, toadying parsons of the early 19th century. Searching the records of my clerical forbears of that time—Conybeares, Macaulays, Roses, Fer-

---

[1] A slip for St Barnabas', Addison Road.
[2] R. Furneaux Jordan, "Rome and Oxford: A Study in Environment," *The Listener*, 29th October, 1953. R. M.'s letter was published in the issue of 5th November.

gusons—I find sobriety, scholarship, integrity of life, piety. And in so many others as well. These stale second-hand clichés are so silly. Oh dear, I have scarcely begun on the many topics raised by your letters. *Musophilus*,[1] Carthusians,[2] etc., and several admirable prayers that you quote. I will write about these next time. Your in some ways unwise hemisphere is sending us an evangelist called Billy Graham to convert and rouse us. I fear he may have some success, those hysterical missions always do, specially in "the Protestant underworld". I have lately met several people brought up dissenters, now nothing at all (can one blame them?) who, I foresee, will end in Rome. Our chapels are breeding grounds for that church, and it should be grateful to them. They know how horrible is the religion they grew up in—how unlovely, dull, unshining, stark, often vulgarly expressed—and they know of no other, but assume that Rome is the alternative, and fly to it with relief. Now I go to the L[ondon] L[ibrary] and shall get out that Mathew book, which I did read once, and that edition of *Musophilus*, which I have read, but elsewhere; and [I] should like to read it more carefully.[3] Thank you for those v.g. prayers, and all the interesting comments in your letters. I have finished the Wards (Wilfrid[4] was hard on Tyrrell, so is Maisie [Ward]: I prefer M. D. Petre's picture of him[5]).

Love always.

R. M.

---

[1] Samuel Daniel, *Musophilus, or a General Defence of Learning* (1599).

[2] This refers to David and Gervase Mathew's *The Reformation and the Contemplative Life* (1934).

[3] R. M. nowhere makes it clear which edition of *Musophilus* Father Johnson had recommended.

[4] Wilfrid Ward, son and biographer of W. G. Ward.

[5] In her Life of Tyrrell, see above p. 105.

20, *Hinde House, Hinde St.*, *W*.1
16th *November*, 1953†

My dear Hamilton,

Yours of Nov. 9th (posted then) came quickly, and was most welcome. Thank you for reminding me of *Musophilus*, which I got, in that edition, from the Library, and read with great interest. How sane it is! Every merit except poetry and clarity, don't you think, for poetical or clear it isn't. But eloquent and moving, and oh what good sense! Exactly what we feel now: " For with the worst we will not spare the best, Because it growes with that which doth displease". I like "th'opened and invulgar'd mysteries". But I don't quite get "the *Norman* subtleties".[1] The whole poem is very interesting. As to the Mathews' Carthusian book, I haven't yet got hold of that.[2] I am meeting the brothers at lunch next week, and will mention it. The Bishop will soon be leaving Mombasa for good,[3] and will probably take work in England.

Did I never mention before my 12-years-old god-child, Mary Anne? By the way, the Conybeare infant, to whose Eton baptism I went, was *not* a god-child, only a cousin.[4] At that time I shouldn't have had the cheek to take on a god-child, things being as they were. Twelve years ago I was much less aware of such matters, and had therefore more cheek. It really was quite wrong, in my then circumstances. Still, I did it, and now her faith is my concern. I took her and her 11-year-old sister Jane on Sunday afternoon to a very nice children's service at St Mary Abbots, taken by an admirable curate[5], who really seemed to be interested in the children and eliciting answers

---

[1] R. M. has added a marginal note here: " See overleaf for more about it"; i.e. see below p. 122.

[2] *The Reformation and the Contemplative Life.*

[3] Mombasa had been Abp Mathew's headquarters while Apostolic Delegate in Africa.

[4] John Bruce Conybeare, see *Letters to a Friend*, p. 32.

[5] Rev. Charles Wright.

from them; he talked about Christ at twelve in the temple, and about St Hugh of Lincoln, and interested my two very much. After the service they went up to get stamps to stick in books each week, and are keen to go again. Then I took them out to tea, and gave them little copies of the catechism, telling them they might learn the answers to the first two or three, and I would ask them next time. Perhaps I made a mistake in telling them that the proper answer to " What did your godfathers and godmothers then for you?" was " Silver mug, spoon and fork"; this joke stuck, and I fear I shall get this answer only. I remember we used to think it funny! Afterwards I rang up the curate, and told him their names, and asked him to take an interest in them, as . . . it would be good if they took root at St Mary's. So I hope for the best. I would like them to strike roots in some Anglican church. Mary Anne told me at tea that they "didn't believe anything yet", but that later on she thought of becoming a Roman Catholic. I said, " You'll have to believe plenty if you do that, you know", to which she replied, " No, I shan't believe it. But I like the churches, and they have prayers in Latin "—which you would have liked. The point is that they, when smaller, used to run in and out of the R.C. church close to them in Duke's Lane [off] Church Street, Kensington, and the priest was nice to them and fed them chocolates. I told Mary Anne that they were now think-ing of having the prayers in English; she has begun Latin at school, and likes it. If ever she really does "vert", I fear she may just take it as a nice thing to belong to, and believe none of it really. Still, she may grow to. Meanwhile, I must do what I can about giving them an idea of the thing; no, I won't impart any doubts or negations, only what I do believe and value. . . .

Really S[amuel] D[aniel] does write awkwardly sometimes. [For instance in *Musophilus*,] line 698: "Norman subtleties".[1]

[1] See *Complete Works in Verse and Prose of Samuel Daniel* (ed. Alexander B. Grosart, 1885), where "the Norman subtleties" occurs in line 668.

The O[xford] D[ictionary] sheds no light on these. I think it means "arguments", but why Norman? The next two lines seem to personify them.[1] Then (l. 704) what is *"it"*??[2] I can only suppose that it refers back to "the estimate" in l. 695; but how awkward this is. So is l. 722, in its relation to 721.[3] One sees what this means, but it has no syntax. All page 90 is good and clear. Mostly I think his sentences are too long, which leads him into grammatical confusion, forgetting what was his predicate and subject. One feels that what he had to say exceeded his powers of saying it, like a river brimming over its banks and rushing unbridled and unchannelled. But what good things he was trying to say, and how one sympathises! I must look up in the *Worthies* all that Fuller says about him. S.D.'s was a different view of the Reformation from Fuller's; but obviously F. had great esteem for him. I suppose S.D.'s view is very much ours; certainly mine and yours.

Now I have to sally out to a party given by Graham Greene and Wyndham's Theatre on the 250th performance of *The Living Room*. I seldom meet actors, they are to me bright strange fishes swimming in an element alien to me; I feel that to meet them is to See Life. Not that I want to see much of them. But I shall like to meet this cast, particularly the girl Rose Tutin,[4] and the man who acts the old priest who can do nothing to help her in her sad plight. It is a moving, odd play; I wonder how it will fare in New York, if it should go there. A party beginning at 10.30 is rather late for me, and will bring me rather too near the hour of getting up for Mass. I used to

[1] Who (being mounted up into their state)
   Doe best with wrangling rudeness sympathise.
[2] Yet would this giddy innovation faine
   Downe with it lower, to abase it quite:
[3] To alter course may bring men more astray,
   And leaving what was knowne to light on none.
[4] R. M. means Dorothy Tutin, who took the part of "Rose" in *The Living Room*.

123

go to more late parties once; but there were then more of them, I was younger, and got up later!

My book comes out on Dec. 4th[1]; I hope to see some copies in a day or two. Shall I send it you? I think you must have it, tho' you needn't read much of it. Much love. Thank you for 2 good little p[ost] c[ard] prayers.

R. M.

20, Hinde House, Hinde St., W.1
2nd December, 1953†

My dear Hamilton,

I think the posts have already begun to go hay-wire for the festal season, don't you. Your last letter, posted Nov. 24th, took 6 days instead of the usual 3 or 4, and no doubt they will get worse soon. But thank you so much for it; I shall probably have to write this letter in instalments, as you sometimes do, my time at the moment being rather cut up.

I am interested in all you say of *Musophilus*. As regards his [Samuel Daniel's] poetic gifts I rather agree with Ben Jonson, who said he was "an honest man, but no poet" and with Michael Drayton, who thought that his manner better fitted prose. Ben Jonson, of course, disliked his anti-Latinism, and was probably prejudiced. But as to Tudor English, surely he had many splendid models, both in poetry and prose. Writing *Musophilus* in 1599, he had all the Elizabethans behind him in their stately glory—and what a glory they were! The great and smaller poets, the great musical translators, such as North,[2] Philemon Holland,[3] Florio,[4] the travel writers collected by Hakluyt, Sidney, Tyndale and Coverdale, Cranmer, Hooker,

---

[1] *Pleasure of Ruins* was published on 7th December, 1953.

[2] Sir Thomas North (1535?-1601?), translator of Plutarch, etc.

[3] Philemon Holland (1552-1637), translator of Livy, Pliny's *Nat. Hist.*, etc.

[4] John Florio (1553?-1625), lexicographer and translator of Montaigne's *Essays*.

the racy Latimer,[1] Nashe[2] and the romance-writers, Bacon—
what models to choose among! The awkwardness of the 15th
century English outgrown, and all the renaissance of imagination and language and freedom of expression surging up like a
great river set free after long running soberly between narrow
banks. This at least the Reformation did help to bring about,
with all it cost in other ways. And, after all, it was an age of
great scholarship and learning. Of course I agree with you
about the "beastly business," but it had other sides, that made
for nobility and genius. If only the Puritans could have been
kept out of it, what a thing it might have been. I suppose it is
true to say that *all* movements have good and evil sides:
Protestantism, Catholicism, agnosticism, monasticism, roman-
ticism, democracy, etc., etc. I think Daniel exaggerated the
sickness of learning in his time; there was plenty of learning,
and of a very fine kind, though scholastic theology had waned,
or sickened from its own excess. I think you must be right that
" Norman " as S[amuel] D[aniel] uses it must mean medieval.
You have elucidated the meaning of several of the lines for me.
I haven't still got the book at hand, but remember it pretty
clearly. As to Simony, and such venal goings-on, from the pre-
Reformation accusations there must have been as much of these
in the medieval centuries as in the 16th, so here too the poet
was prejudiced, probably. I suppose people are apt to be; about
their own times. But he had an interesting and attractive mind
and angle. What interesting things you bring to my notice
always. . . .

My *Ruins* emerge on Monday, and the publishers are giving
a party for them and for a book of Cyril Connolly[3] to-morrow.
There is a BBC review of *Ruins* on Sunday afternoon, by John
Raymond, the literary editor of the *New Statesman*, which I
shall listen to with interest. And I gather Raymond Mortimer

[1] Hugh Latimer (*c.* 1485-1555), Bp of Worcester.
[2] Thomas Nashe (1567-1601), romance-writer and dramatist.
[3] *Ideas and Places* (1953).

has done it for the *Sunday Times*. So it will get a good start. Of course a book like that doesn't expect large sales. It will cost 25/-, which, as it is large, illustrated, and nicely produced, isn't expensive at current prices. Then I won't send it you;[1] but at Xmas I shall send you *Period Piece*, I hadn't forgotten that. I think you'll like that. I hope your cold is gone now. I saw the death of your cousin T. F. Powys, I suppose the most famous of the family. Did you know him well, or not so well as John?[2] *Mr Weston's Good Wine* was interesting and able, tho' not wholly likeable.[3] His too was, I suppose, a godless world.

Did I tell you that I met Bp Mathew and brother Gervase at lunch, and they were much indignant at *Infallible Fallacies*. We agreed it was very ill-judged and discourteous. They admitted that the anti-Anglican leaflets published by the Cath : Truth Society were also discourteous, but . . . these acrimonious criticisms . . . are a frightful mistake, and must surely envenom relations.

Dec. 3rd. This morning came your good letter posted Nov. 30 —quite good going. It has come in time for me to comment on it in this. Yes, isn't that a vivid Vesuvius story of Pliny's.[4] No trace identifiable, I think, of Uncle P.'s house. All the old town of Misenum is perished, but there are a few ruins of villas on the Cape, and some moles of the harbour. I don't know what was the site of that villa. Of nephew P.'s Laurentum villa near Antium there is no trace either, but the approximate site is known. Uncle P. must have been a very great man, so full always of noble and courageous curiosity. Thank you for your encouraging words about my little misses and the Church. I

[1] Father Johnson had evidently replied in the negative to R. M.'s question, "Shall I send it you?" see above p. 124.

[2] Theodore F. Powys, younger brother of John Cowper Powys, was Father Johnson's first cousin.

[3] T. F. Powys, *Mr Weston's Good Wine* (1928).

[4] Pliny the Younger, in a letter (VI. 16) to Tacitus described the death of his uncle, Pliny the Elder, during the eruption of Mt Vesuvius in A.D. 79.

do hope they will get on. No. I shan't minify the mystery. Odd; *my* complaint of R.C. teaching is that it tries to do this, by its detailed, clear-cut, rigidly dogmatic instruction, that leaves no place for the mysterious and unknown. I remember this at the Convent school we attended for a time in Italy.[1] The nuns and priests knew just how everything happened, and *all* about heaven, purgatory and hell, and what happens in the Sacraments. I feel we leave much more on the margins of certainty.

P.S. I meant to tell you about the gorgeous Greek Orthodox (Pan-slav)[2] [service] that I went to last Sunday. A radiant golden affair, and such singing!

20, *Hinde House, Hinde St., W.*1

5th December, 1953

My dear Hamilton,

As I want you to have my Christmas card, I am putting it into an ordinary letter, surface mail (too heavy for the air) and posting it now, to reach you, I *hope*, in time for Xmas Day. The card I took from the same engraving (1760) I have for the jacket of my book: happy Turks enjoying themselves in Greek ruins. I have composed a Christmas verse for it.[3] My other

---

[1] R. M. and her sisters Margaret and Jean attended a convent school when the Macaulay family was living at Varazze (1887-94).

[2] R. M. probably means *Pravoslavni*, which is the word for "Orthodox" in various Slavonic languages.

[3] It's said that Turks, when we keep Christmas Day,
    Smoke pipes in Asia Minor by the sea,
    Lolling among Greek capitals, so gay
    You'd never guess the Ottomans they be.
    They know not why they smile, but on their ear
    Beats from the west a carillon of bells,
    Rocking and tumbling; in a dream they hear
    And suck their hookahs, the grave infidels

enclosures are two reviews; one by me, about a new anthology of children's poems[1]—do you agree with my views on children's poetic tastes? But I forgot, you said you never cared for poetry. I can't imagine my early life without it—I was steeped in it. The other review I thought might interest you; it is about the attitude of the English Recusants.[2] The passage I have marked reminds one again what our Reformation might have been had it been left to More and Erasmus and their kind. Even you might then, perhaps, have approved it.

What you say sometimes about our Church saddens me a little; it sounds almost as if you disliked and despised what to me is a beautiful treasury of riches and mystery, and a source of spiritual life and strength. In your last letter, e.g., you speak of "all mystery" being "eliminated" by the child being called "a member of Christ, the child of God, and inheritor of the kingdom of heaven". You say this makes it sound "quite ordinary and dull", whereas to me it sounds mysterious, beautiful and exciting; far more so than the dogmatic and clear-cut teachings of Rome, against which so many intelligences have revolted. I suppose one difference between me and you is that I have lately (and largely thanks to you) refound the Church, and to me it is still a wonderful and lovely heritage, and its Masses a glorious mystery, interpenetrating our life with God. There is too much in R[oman] Cath[olicis]m to repel me so that I could never quite get *that* from it. I feel the Anglican Church more Christian and more what I want in religion. I know you don't, and sometimes I feel a little sad for fear *you* are sad about being in the wrong Church. No,

---

"Mahound," they grunt, and puff and bubble away,
Not knowing that they smoke for Christmas Day.
I wish you all as merry a feast as they.

[1] *The Faber Book of Children's Verse*, compiled by Janet Adam Smith (1953).

[2] Probably a review of Geoffrey Anstruther's *Vaux of Harrowden: a Recusant Family* (1953).

I should never try to "explain the rightness of our Church" to Mary Anne; only try and make her see it as a channel for God's beauty to enter our lives, and make her, above all, *want* this beauty. She is a child who will be able to reason, and I know, if she got instead into the R.C. Church, would eventually want to get out, seeing much of it as "mumbo-jumbo" and untrue; she is that kind of child, clear-headed, and not very romantic. The 10-year-old Jane is a more likely R.C., I think. Anyhow, I must do my best with them. Meanwhile, we have quite entertaining Sunday afternoons together. Perhaps one day I'll take them to a R.C. service; but they couldn't follow it much yet. I don't mind what they are, so long as they have some form of Christianity to hold on to.

But please, dear Hamilton, to whom I owe so much, don't run down my Church too much to me, because I love it, and don't like it called "dull and ordinary". For that matter, lots of R.C.s find their services this, too, when used to them. Perhaps one day I shall find the C. of E. dull, but I don't so far. Of course I do see the best of it, in my Chapel. Perhaps if I had to attend a Sunday-matins church, I should be bored and repelled.

I sent you *Period Piece* to-day. I shall be writing later, by air paper, for Christmas; this one is only for the enclosures. "*O Oriens*" (that you quote) is one of my favourite prayers and I often use it.[1] Much love. Forgive my C. of E. bias!

R. M.

20, *Hinde House, Hinde St., W.*1

12*th December*, 1953†

My dear Hamilton,

I sent you on Dec. 5th my Christmas card with a sea letter, *hoping* it would reach you by Christmas Day, but it may not.

See above p. 76.

Anyhow, it won't for some time, so I am filling the epistolary gap with this very handsome Coronation air paper, so that you may not think I haven't answered your last letters, which were so full of interest. I expect transatlantic posts are already haywire. I sent you also *Period Piece. Not Pleasure of Ruins*, which saw the light on the 7th, and has had, so far, a very nice kind press; charming reviews in *The Times, Sunday Times, Observer, [Daily] Telegraph, New Statesman*—that, so far, is all. I am surprised and relieved, having got myself rather tired of the book, to find that people do, apparently, like it. No American publisher has yet taken it: perhaps they won't. Though, considering what tourists they are, a book about the great ruins of the world might have a sale. It has a lot of nice illustrations, and looks handsome.

I have had such a good Christmas present . . . a *History of Christian-Latin Poetry* up to the close of the Middle Ages; a very exciting work, which you would like.[1] . . .

I hope you are well, not tired, not overdoing, and not too submerged by Christmas jobs. Do you ever attend Mass in any neighbouring R.C. church? Perhaps the Society's rules don't encourage this; I don't know. I have sometimes done it, but I like ours better, it has less gush, more restraint. On the 8th we kept the Conception of the B.V.M. Our (the Cowley) Missal doesn't call it "immaculate", of course, but I believe they probably do at the very extreme churches. . . . To-morrow I take my two little misses—*parvulae indoctae*[2]—to their weekly service, which they rather enjoy. Mary Anne is v.g. at answering questions. Yes, I know you will say I ought to be taking them to St James's, Spanish Place. But there they would hear all kinds of things about the B.V.M. and the Saints, and all that can come later if they want it. The first thing I feel is Christianity and God, if only they can get a hold on this. This

[1] F. J. E. Raby, *A History of Christian-Latin Poetry from the Beginnings to the Close of the Middle Ages* (2nd ed., 1953).
[2] "Unlearned little girls."

letter brings so much love for Christmas, but I may write again before that.

Your loving R. M.

My dear Hamilton,

A word written amid the rush and bustle of Christmas, to thank you so *very* much for your letter posted 21st, which came this morning, marvellous at this season! My sea letter didn't do so badly either, it seems. That sea letter: I feel remorse that it made you remorseful; but thank you for your wonderful letter, which completely reassures me, and shows me that I was stupid to be even a little disturbed or saddened by the things you have from time to time let drop about these two branches of the Church, both of which you love. You know, I do owe you more than I can say for introducing me to so many lovely things—prayers, graduals, etc. etc.—in the Roman liturgy and breviary. These prayers have much enriched my *Preces Privatae*; and I am always rather pleased when I find that I have discovered and appropriated for myself the same prayers that you have later pointed out to me, as well as getting hold of the new ones. All this you put me in the way of. All this, and, of course, the being inside *Ecclesia Anglicana*, which is the best thing I have. So forgive me if I seemed to grumble and to be apprehensive of your criticisms of it; of course I make many myself, even now that I so much love it. Who can criticize it rightly, except those who are in it and love it? Of course I sometimes feel that I love too exclusively one side of it, and should feel pretty forlorn and chilled and unsatisfied if I ever had to make do for long with the middle kind of church, the kind that abounds all about the country and suits, apparently, so many devout people, and which one does feel affection for so long as one doesn't have to attend its services. But I suppose

131

even that one would make a *modus vivendi* of if one had to. And, after all, one could still enrich one's public worship with the little Mass prayers. So, you see, I am prepared for anything! And why should I be entitled to a better kind of thing than my pious forbears had and were nourished by in their good and spiritual living? Still, I am thankful that I have it.

I am in the middle of the Christmas rush; I am going to my sister's to-morrow morning, after midnight Mass here. . . .

My *parvulae* are coming on pretty well, I think. On Sunday my godchild is to be one of those who join in reading the lesson for the day; part of St Luke, I think. I was so pleased when the nice curate asked her at the service if she would, and she said yes. She is now apprehensive but eager, so is her 10-year-old sister. I hope it will go well! She is a child with brains and a strong personality, for good or ill, bless her. They are both good companions, and we always have fun together. But they are too much concerned with the lusts of the flesh, in the shape of chocolates, which I tell her I have promised that she shall renounce. Illogically, I usually produce some for them.

Now I must get ready to go out and lunch with Archbishop Mathew, now back from Mombasa for good, and still uncertain what he will next do, besides literary-historical work, such as going on with the life of Acton. Did I mention to you in my last letter the life of Gasquet by Shane Leslie that I have been reading,[1] which revealed such shockingly dishonest and un-scholarly juggling with his texts on the part of the good Cardinal when he was given Acton's letters to edit? "Lacordaire sees through the hollowness of the Roman system", wrote Acton; which Gasquet renders " Lacordaire is rather unsettled just now". The sanctity of quotation marks is a sanctity continually violated by him in the interests of the impression he wants to give; an unforgiveable sin in a historian, and one about which the scholarly Dr Coulton always attacked him, but he never replied or altered anything. It seems so much

[1] Shane Leslie, *Cardinal Gasquet: A Memoir* (1953).

honester just to leave out what you don't want to publish than to alter it. "*O Sapientia*" is a great antiphon which he should have taken to heart: but perhaps he thought he was following the higher wisdom in perverting truth for the greater glory of the Church.

I may go to mid[night] Mass at All Saints', [Margaret Street,] not the Chapel to-night; I believe the music and singing are extremely good there.

Sometime I'll send you a few reviews of *Ruins*. All have been kind; except the *Daily Express*, who said it "may be worthy scholarship, but it makes jolly dull reading!" They rang up my publishers to ask for the book, as they hadn't thought it worth while to send the *Express* a copy, so it seemed ungrateful! But every other reviewer has seemed to enjoy the book, which relieves my mind, and I hear it is selling quite reasonably well. This brings all my love for 1954, and so much gratitude for everything. Forgive me if I say stupid things sometimes, and *ora pro me* always.

Your loving R. M.

I hope you are *well*?

1954

20, *Hinde House, Hinde St., W*.1
New Year's Day, 1954†

My dear Hamilton,
Thank you so much for your letter of Christmas Day, which
came to-day (posted 28th). You hadn't, of course, yet got my
a[ir] p[aper] of the other day, answering yours of the 19th, but
will have got it by now. I'm glad *Period Piece* also has reached
you. Let me know sometime what you think of it. It seems to
have had good reviews in America. . . .
I'm glad you found that article about the Recusants
interesting. I did too, and thought you would. Yes, I expect
it is for ever sunk and lost among that Father's Christmas
correspondence. What a time we have made of Christmas!
And what a litter its tide leaves deposited when it recedes. I
must clear up mine soon; my room is at present a shocking
mess. I had a nice peaceful day and night at Romford, after
midnight Mass here. We lit the candles and set out our
Provençal Crib and heard a carol service from King's College
Chapel in the evening—very peaceful. I got back on Boxing
Day evening, in time to dine in Hampstead; and on Sunday
I heard my godchild reading (very well) part of a lesson in St
Mary Abbots; I was quite proud of her, so was her little sister.
The curate who presides at the Children's Service was pleased
with her, I think.
It *is* difficult to know exactly how to get things across to
children. Looking back, I remember that we got religion
through the prayer-book teaching of my mother; she used to
give us most stimulating lessons on the collects on Sundays,
and it was really exciting and inspiring. We did also go to
parts of the services in one or other of the churches near us
[in Varazze], but I don't remember getting there anything like
that stimulus or feeling of the excitement and fineness of the
Christian battle. There was too much of the B.V.M., too much

137

of what seemed to me to be rather "soppy" devotions; you know what R.C. devotions can be. I think it came to us through my mother rather like a Marathon or a Thermopylae, and we thought of striving for the incorruptible crown, though I fear our strivings were fitful. But we did glimpse the glory and the courage and the beauty of it all, and it was never made tedious for us, or drab. I think my mother was a very wonderful person, with an extraordinary magnetising gift, and she kindled a kind of fire when she spoke of religion and being good. I have never since met anyone with so much gift for it. The Churches speak in more muffled tones; their approach is "here it is, if you can take it", and one has to learn to find God in it. At Mass one can; and I find our Anglican Mass wholly satisfactory; much more so than the Roman, which contains a great deal that I just don't want and which doesn't answer to any ideas I could have about it all. This in spite of the many first-class prayers set about in it, many so beautiful, which I use often. But, after one of these admirable prayers, follows some piece of what to *me* is gush and sentimentality, though this is probably my fault, but it is a thing I have felt from childhood about R.C. prayers (I mean, some of them); they embarrassed me then, and do still. From such a tone our B[ook of] C[ommon] P[rayer] is blessedly free. The mystery is there just the same, and I don't feel it is explained away or "eliminated". It is difficult about mystery. Too little, and it is commonplace: too much, and one gives it up as improbable and out of reach; one has to try for a balance. I'm sure one doesn't want all that about "not three incomprehensibles" etc. etc.; I suppose one wants the shadow and the wavering mirror and the poetry, and the being able to make what one needs out of it somehow, out of all the imagery and the dark and the light, and not to be too much bound with words and statements, all man-made, all falling short. The Romans *say* too much, try to net it all into words and doctrines, instead of letting it interpret itself into each life and soul as the communion is made. I could do without all that, without all those Angels, O[ld] T[estament] analogies, prophecies, irrelevant holy people. I seem to be talking rather nonsense perhaps. . . . I went to St Paul's on New Year's Eve to enter on 1954, with a friend; but it was rather dead. . . . We sat and pined for Dr Donne, who thundered about "this minute makes your eternity, because it may be your *last* minute; God is speaking to each soul here, and may bless or curse you according to your acceptance or refusal of Him"; and the people began to swoon, and lay inert as if their Eternity had already arrived. . . . More spirit and fire would be good, but one seldom gets it. Have you heard of a book (new) about the C. of E. from 1800-1900, by a C. K. Francis Brown?[1] It sounds not brilliant but sound. Oh I do see just what you meant and felt and mean and feel about the two branches of the Church, and I partly feel the same. Certainly four centuries ago I should have. No room to expand on this. So much love for 1954. Don't get overdone with answering letters and shriving penitents. I only do the former, but find it a tough job!

Yours with my love,
R. M.

(The 4th new year since I took up with the Church again, thanking you.)

20, Hinde House, Hinde St., W.1
15th January, 1954†

My dear Hamilton,

Your letter posted Jan. 11th came yesterday, thank you so much. The one posted 2nd I have too; I opened it wrong way up, cut the wrong end, and the result is most peculiar, and I read it with difficulty, but I *have* read it all. If you try this way of cutting an a[ir] p[aper] open, you'll see what I mean!

[1] *A History of the English Clergy, 1800-1900* (1953).

I am much interested in what you say about *Period Piece*. Those Darwins were, of course, quite un-religious. But Frances, Gwen [Raverat]'s first cousin,[1] succumbed to religion in the end; as Gwen writes "it got Frances in the end", and she is now High Anglican. Don't you like the pictures of those two little cousins together? And of the family out tricycling. And of Gwen under the nursery table, praying that her dancing mistress might die! She *is* a clever and charming artist. I didn't know her, as when we went to live in Cambridge she was already in London with her uncle. But my Conybeare cousins did. I have met Gwen and Frances since, of course.

Yes, we did owe a lot in religion to our mother. Though, you know, I discarded it at 14 or 15, and during my later teens was what the 17th century called "nullifidian". I regret it now. If I had been church-minded at Oxford, I should have gone to Cowley, I dare say. I got it again later, as you know. Of course we were never, as you were, brought up in a Church and Vicarage atmosphere; but we did have those collect lessons, and I remember them still, and the excitement and inspiration they caused. I imagine Gwen Darwin's mother was quite worldly; the *Darwins* were very unworldly and good, but without religion. For the R.C. services of our childhood, I had affection, but not exactly *attraction*. We were bored by the convent school nuns, and not inspired by the very repetitive prayers in church. Perhaps we knew it too well, for it never held any *glamour*. Not the glamour and beauty that Anglican Catholicism had for me later. . . . Of course in the 1890's there was a lot of Anglo-Cath[olicism], but not, I suppose, very much in the country parishes.

Such a silly outcry by Protestant Truth etc. against the televising of the Roman Mass by the BBC last Sunday. "The Mass is against the Law", they wrote. What *can* their minds be like? They seem 400 years out of date. The R.C.s were pleased by this protest, and by the assumption that

[1] Frances Cornford (1886-1960).

Mass in the Anglican church had never been heard of. The BBC *has* sometimes broadcast an Anglican Mass but not televised it. The R.C.s said, " Now the public has seen the Mass in which the Coronation *used once* to be enshrined". They implied that our Coronation last year had omitted Mass altogether; well, from their point of view, of course, it had.

I'm sorry I forgot to answer what you said about Joyce Cary. I like him very much as a person, and his novels are very able, though I have never found them absorbing. The last one I haven't read.[1] . . . I think next Sunday I shall, at 11, go to St Stephen's, Gloucester Place.[2] . . . That is where T. S. Eliot is a sidesman; I wonder if he takes the bag round!

You know, Virginia Woolf *wasn't* really "an unhappy person", though she had that side. But she had so much fun, and humour, and a kind of genial friendliness, though also much malicious comment (discreetly *not* published).[3] Did you ever read *To the Lighthouse*? It is a very amusing and brilliant picture of her father, Leslie Stephen, and her mother. Yes, you are right about Novels. And I must begin another soon. You are a great encouragement to me to do so! *Ruins* is still having a kind press; quite beyond my expectations. A nice stranger writes to me that he likes its "sustained note of ecstasy"! Lots more to say, but no room to say it, only my love always.

R. M.

[1] Joyce Cary, *Except the Lord* (1953).
[2] R. M. means St Stephen's, Gloucester Road.
[3] See *A Writer's Diary: Being Extracts from the Diary of Virginia Woolf*, edited by Leonard Woolf (1953).

My dear Hamilton,

I write from among snows; not deep in London, but quite deep in some parts of the country, and to-day, Sunday, flaking steadily down, so that the slopes of Hampstead, where I drove after church, are slippery and white. However, it doesn't last long in this temperate land; you, no doubt, are deep under for many weeks to come. I hope you don't go out in it, and are *well*. Thank you for yours posted 20th: yes, the *Punch* review was very nice. . . . I think *all* my reviews have been kind, except the *Express* . . . and the *Manchester Guardian*, whose reviewer, a Mrs Sprigge, abused it on the grounds that I obviously didn't *like* ruins, and why, therefore, had I written of them? . . . I should have thought my ruins-passion only too evident on every page. She thought I was "ribald", which seems most odd. However, every one else has taken the book as I meant it, and has praised it much more than I dared to hope. No American publisher has yet taken it, but my publishers have hopes.

That is interesting, von Hügel's view of Darwin as an unconscious deepener of Christianity. I'm not sure I agree with him, do you? To me, Christianity, or even belief in God, have nothing to do with the natural sciences, or the order of the universe; they are, to me, in a separate world, and I should never draw any conclusions about them from Nature. But I know many Christians do. Odd, how differently people's minds work, in this matter of religion.

I think that, however Virginia W[oolf] and E. M. F[orster] had been brought up, they wouldn't have retained Christianity when adult, or ever really *believed* in it. All E. M. F.'s principles, and I suspect most of his actions, are what I should call deeply Christian in the *moral* sense; but intellectually he would never accept it. Virginia was naturally less loving and humanly unselfish and kind than he is; but her intellect equally remote from religion. As were the Darwins, and so many other intellectuals. One is lucky to be able to come to it, not only from upbringing, which taught one the lie of the ground, so to speak, but from later developments and sense of need—in my case always there. Always one felt in one's soul what someone has called "the God-shaped hole", where God has once been, or will be, or (anyhow) ought to be. Even non-believers have that hole; but they fill it with different sub-stitutes. I have done the same myself, for long years.

Joyce Cary, being Irish, was certainly brought up Church of Ireland—I don't know what he is now. I doubt his knowing much about Dissent. But he should have remembered about the Psalm versions Dissenters would know.[1] At least, I *suppose* they would. Or do you think their prayer books (after all, they *have* prayer books) would take the Psalms from the B[ook of] C[ommon] P[rayer]? I suppose they might.

I'd forgotten that More[2] came into *John Inglesant*—I must read it again sometime. I was slightly repelled by hearing that he [J. H. Shorthouse] had taken so much of it (without acknowledgment) from John Evelyn. But it is a good book. Yesterday we celebrated the Feast of Blessed Charles the Martyr at Mass, and gave thanks for his life; but I don't know that I do. He was a shifty and tiresome monarch, and his tiresomeness opened the doors to that abominable civil war and puritan revolution, whereas a wiser king would have averted both and we should have ridden the puritan storm and not, perhaps, have been affected by it ever since. . . .

Much love always.

R. M.

[1] See *Except the Lord*, chapter 28, where a Dissenter quotes from the Psalms.

[2] Henry More (1614-87), Cambridge Platonist.

My dear Hamilton,

As usual, your letter of Feb. 4 crossed mine of Jan. 31st; my letters always seem to reach you just in time to be acknowledged at the end. I expect this will do the same. However, never mind. I must get hold of Fr Gardiner's *Norms for the Novel.*[1] It is an interesting theme, and one I have no definite principles about, I think; I form an *ad hoc* judgment of each novel as I read it. Have you come across *The Go-Between,* by L. P. Hartley? I think it very good; I wonder if you would. It has had a great success here, so no doubt is published in America too. If not, I will send it you. Do you see the *Church Times,* by the way? It had an excellent review of *Ruins;* one of the best I have had. I don't know who wrote it. If you *don't* see the *C.T.,* I'll send you this review sometime, if you like seeing reviews of books you haven't read. H. F. M. Prescott has now written another book, about Pilgrimages to Jerusalem in old days;[2] it sounds interesting, and she is scholar enough to get it right and not fanciful.

I have been busy correcting *Ruins* for its 2nd edition. Kind friends have sent me a lot of Errata, and some I found for myself. My publishers now want to send me, at their expense, somewhere, to write about it. But Collins (Mark Bonham Carter, that is to say, who is a great friend of mine) says I have promised to write a novel for Collins next, and that Weidenfeld & Nicolson (who want me to write for them) are tempting me like Satan, showing me all the kingdoms of the world in order to seduce me. . . .

[The sermons at Grosvenor Chapel] on the Sundays till Easter [are to be] on "the Christian mythology" which will interest me. Perhaps it will make me change my heretical mind

[1] H. C. Gardiner, *Norms for the Novel* (New York, 1953).
[2] H. F. M. Prescott, *Jerusalem Journey* (1954).

about the order of the universe, who knows? But I have long since renounced any hope of understanding the universe. I have never read or heard any account of it which gives any clue. As to God's relation to it, I feel that He may regard it as *irrelevant* to His purposes for humanity's salvation. Perhaps I talk nonsense.

Feb. 20. I have Dr Joad's last little book,[1] just out (some months after his death) to review for the *Times Lit. Sup*. It is a kind of Peacockian set of imaginary discussions between a group of people, the central character being obviously himself, called " Mr Longpast". It has a preface by Canon Hood and John Betjeman, about his religious development, during his last illness (including how I used to drive up G. Irvine . . . to bring him Communion). I'm not sure that all that is not a little too intimate, but perhaps he wouldn't have minded. The conversations themselves give a last run to all his prejudices and ideas; which may be, I think, a pity, in a way. He could be, and often was, unfair to the point of unkindness, in his comments on contemporary writers, musicians and artists, and [he] loathed Americans, and despised women (but got over this before the end, when he became kinder).

Your brother seems unjust about your air papers. They are *always* legible and clear, in spite of being closely packed. I never misread a word. (Alas, I fear you couldn't say the same about mine.) Did you answer me when I asked if you would like me to send the *Listener* article about J. C. Powys? I don't remember. Perhaps you hadn't space to in the small piece of what you so nicely call "surface" that remained in your letter after mine had arrived. But I will, if I can find it. . . .

My love always.

R. M.

[1] C. E. M. Joad, *Folly Farm* (1954).

20, *Hinde House, Hinde St.*, W.1
1st *March*, 1954† (*St David*)

My dear Hamilton,

Thank you so much for your letters of Feb. 18 and 23, the second one answering mine of 20th. I suppose I can't have asked you about the *Listener* talk on J. C. Powys before. But I will look for it when I get a moment, and send it you by surface mail, which is slow but sure. It is a cutting, that will go in an envelope. It is considerate of you to think of the trouble of doing up parcels. All the same, I expect I *shall* one day send you *Ruins* (perhaps for a birthday present?). Then you could turn the pages and look at the pictures, and read a bit here and a bit there, when in the mood. It's not a book to read through, I think, but in small doses.

It seems difficult to be certain what that collect really means;[1] I suppose it might be one of several meanings: profit by, progress or advance in (or by), thrive upon. The trouble with so many Latin words is that they have so many possible meanings. This was a bother in one's youthful Latin-learning days, I remember. Cassell's Dictionary I always thought very needlessly difficult in its arrangements. . . .

I'm glad you reminded me of John Marquand. I've read very little of him, but shall now read *Point of No Return*, and *B. F.'s Daughter*. I think he is good. Of course you would know the people he writes about better than I can, but I like to meet a rather unfamiliar world. Did you read Lionel Trilling's novel—I forget its name—about the Communist who left the Party?[2] Very interesting; and sheds a sinister light on American politics and Communist vengeance.

Yes, it *is* interesting exploring alien worlds. I always feel I ought to understand more kinds of society than I do; it is

[1] Collect for Friday of 4th week in Lent; see below p. 149.
[2] Lionel Trilling, *The Middle of the Journey* (1947).

stupid not to. G. K. Chesterton said somewhere that he was fascinated by *clergymen*, finding them strange and unfamiliar as cats! I know too many to feel quite that.

On Shrove Tuesday I am bidden to a cocktail party given by the Editor of *The Month*, Fr Caraman, and Longmans. It may be a rather interesting set of guests, I dare say. I don't often see *The Month*, but it always interests me when I do.

You ask about "the Christian Mythology" . . . [the Grosvenor Chapel] sermon topic at present. . . . [It] means the Biblical story, as containing the truths it enshrines. . . . very interesting . . . The world myths, Virgin and child, the risen God; all culminating in the Christian story. I put it badly, I know.

I am reviewing too many books; they take my time. I must really refuse them, and get down to my own work—the novel, anyhow. My publishers offer to send me somewhere, that I may write about it (Weidenfeld & Nicolson, I mean). I thought of Russia, and wrote to their Consulate about visas. But they hold out no present hope, *what* odd people they are! In my letter I said I wanted to look at the landscapes and rivers and architecture, which sounds very innocent and unspy-like. But I don't suppose they believe me, though it's true. I want to roam about steppes, see the Caucasus, the Volga, the Black Sea, white horses cantering with Cossacks on back and long tails floating. I could *not* care less about their political regime or the way they live. But no, I see I shan't get to those steppes and those great rivers. I came in two days ago to my flat and interrupted two men. " What are you doing here? " I asked. " Who let you in? " Upon which they knocked me down and rushed away downstairs and I couldn't catch them. And *every* drawer was emptied on to my floors higgledy piggledy. Luckily I had interrupted them in time to stop them taking much. They had put out my father's silver cups and other silver, and some more things, ready to take, but only did take

a little clock and other small objects. I was furious. I wasn't
hurt, to speak of. They had no cosh, luckily. My love for
Lent.

R. M.

20, Hinde House, Hinde St., W.1
14th March, 1954†

My dear Hamilton,

Thank you so much for yours of 5th. I didn't mean to
alarm you with my burglars; they got away with little, owing
to the short time they had, and scarcely hurt me at all, I only
bruised my arm a little when I fell, so it wasn't really "grievous".
I was *very lucky* to lose so little and not to have been coshed
or tied up and gagged! These men are very ruthless and wicked
just now. Are they especially bad also with you? But they
won't come back to *me* for a long time by any laws of chance.
(I have changed my lock, but they can pick "Yales".) I am
afraid the police will never get them, as there is no clue. But
they may very well get them for some other "job"; I hope so.

Russia has receded a little. The more I hear of the prospect,
the more I feel it might be something of a bore. I mean, I
should be with a party, and *they* might be bores.[1] And, as the
Soviet government would have paid our return fares to Prague,
one would feel bound in civility to look at the tiresome things
they might want to show us, such as schools, hospitals,
maternity homes, etc. Whereas all I want to see is landscape
and old buildings. I feel sure guides would take one round,
telling us how splendid it all is, and that, though funny for a
time, would get tiresome. Stephen Spender told me that even
a literary visit to Russia might make it difficult if ever I wanted
to visit America again so I went to the U.S. Consulate and

---

[1] R. M. had been considering going to Russia in a party in honour of
Tchekhov.

asked. The Consul said it might make a visa slow and difficult to get. I asked him " How long is this nonsense of yours going to last ? " He smiled sardonically, and said merely, " It's getting worse". Consuls don't like such goings-on, it hampers their job. Meanwhile George Weidenfeld (one of my publishing-firms) is bribing me with a publisher-paid trip to the East: the old trade route Venetian merchants used to take. I suggested going through Greece and the Islands to Turkey and the Black Sea. Steven Runciman says they have built lidos on the shore out of the old Byzantine walls and that the Turks don't bathe much, so the Black Sea is nicely under-populated with swimmers. Then, *if* I could somehow coax a permit out of the Soviet government, I could cross the B.S. in a steamer to the Russian side. Anyhow, there would be Turkey, which is full of Roman ruins, and it would be very exciting and lovely. This would be in late July and August, if it comes off.

Yes, I *think* it is the Church that is going to avail us for the eternal ordinances, and not profit by them itself.[1] It obviously could mean either, and we could take it, I suppose, now in one sense now in another. But the former seems the more practical prayer for us to make. Possibly it is deliberately ambiguous, so that it can mean both! I confess that in this Ember week just over I have been using it in both senses; [in] the ablative that the ordinands and the Church may profit by the eternal institutions, which they so sorely need.

I must read some Tyrrell this Lent; I think I have *Christianity at the Cross-roads*[2] somewhere. . . . [Those] sermons are being really admirable; this morning partly on the pre-Incarnation Light of Christ in man's soul, the eternal *Sapientia*. . . .

We have your Billy Graham here, converting thousands

---

[1] See Collect for Friday of 4th week in Lent: ". . . *praesta quaesumus, ut Ecclesia tua . . . aeternis proficiat institutis*" (". . . grant, we beseech thee, that thy Church may avail us for the eternal ordinances").

[2] George Tyrrell, *Christianity at the Cross-Roads* (1909).

by his meetings! I will send you the *Spectator* with a fair-minded article on him by John Betjeman! I wonder what are really his permanent effects. John quotes Canon Hood as predicting good from them. But *how repugnant*!

My love and thanks always.

R. M.

20, *Hinde House, Hinde St., W.*1
24*th March,* 1954†

My dear Hamilton,

Your letter of 18th pleased me much, with its glimpse of you in the Confessional, telling young ladies not to say "grievous", and that it wasn't a sin, but a thing they should know. Why didn't you tell her also not to "propose" to amend? But perhaps she is not one of those who say that. I rather like it, and may adopt it myself. . . . I have got an invitation to go to Canon Hood's installation at St Mary Aldermanbury, Bow Lane,[1] on April 9th. He is very pleased to have a City church; it was one of the City churches very little bomb-damaged, I think, and is anyhow now restored.

What you call my "oriental projects" are still very much in the air. I am *not* going in a party to Russia in honour of Tchekhov, that is certain. I *may* go to the Turkish side of the Black Sea, but this isn't at all certain. But wherever I go will be *safer* than London, and "moving rapidly over the face of the earth" is safe and wholesome, and I think should be done while it is possible, while one has good health, and can get someone else (such as publishers) to pay one's expenses. It would be so interesting to see the Black Sea, and Turkey, and the Crimea from a ship, even if I couldn't land there. I find the surface of the earth, its cities and landscapes, very exciting and beautiful.

[1] R. M. means St Mary Aldermary.

But I quite likely shan't explore it this year, I think. I shall send you *Folly Farm* and my review of it, when I find it. And John Betjeman on Billy Graham, too. How I agree with you about B.G.! Fundamentalism is such a *barbarity*. I doubt if he is having any permanent effect here. My sister has got her catechumen on some way now, but she can't believe in the " Divinity of Christ", so won't be baptized. It seems you have to say the creed when baptized. I am reading an interesting book on Lamennais.[1] No more space! But lots more love.

R. M.

20, *Hinde House, Hinde St., W.*1
6th April, 1954†

My dear Hamilton,
    Thank you so much for your letter of March 30th. . . . *Ruins* isn't yet published in America, by the way, so couldn't be noticed in reviews. If and when it is published there, it will be interesting to see how it goes, and whether the Press and public like it. My *novels* have always gone well there, except *They Were Defeated*, which was *not* their cup of tea (except for a few scholarly people, who included Herbert Agar), but I left a long gap between *The World my Wilderness* and the novel before that, and probably passed out of memory rather. My next novel may restore me a little, but not *Ruins*, I fear. Did you like what you saw of it? Six dollars is a lot; over £2, isn't it. Here its price is only 25/-. One of my publishers, George Weidenfeld, is over there just now, and is seeing about getting a publisher to take it if he can. But all your bookseller can have meant by not expecting it to be noticed was that it's not yet published, so couldn't be. Of course it *may* never be

[1] Probably A. R. Vidler's *Study of Lamennais; The Church and the Revolution* (1954).

published there. Thank you for telling the bookseller it had done well here. I believe George Weidenfeld took the reviews over, to encourage the publishers.

I have been reading a book on the "Cambridge Platonists",[1] translated from German by an American. The style is dreadful, therefore; but the matter is interesting. I love those Cambridge 17th century men, with their Alexandrian and Platonic philosophy, and their stress on the light that lighteth every man and the Deiform seed in the soul. I have been reviewing this little book on them.

So here we are in the middle of Passion Week—not my favourite season. I don't mean because of its events and their meaning for us, but because of the way the Church (Roman, Anglican, and Nonconformist) has always taken it. It's probably my fault that I am alienated by so much of the language used in the prayers about it, both Latin and English. I believe, when left to myself, I can get into it much more easily. But the Church seems always to have clung to its ancient sacrificial Hebrew notions, which haunt its interpretation of Good Friday. You will think this impertinence on my part, perhaps; but I don't think it really is, only an admission of inaptitude for a standpoint and teaching alien to me. Those great early Latin hymns about it are magnificent, but no use to me as religion, only as poetry.[2] If the ocean did not roll between us, we could discuss all this. Still, we make a pretty good shot at it on air papers. Yes: *Exeunt omnia in mysterium*,[3] indeed. As to "the obsequies", I see the O[xford] D[ictionary] gives "rites" as one meaning, and quotes from 1550 "the ceremonial obsequies in the house of God". "Obsequy" (in the singular) meant obedience or homage, but in the collect it is plural, so

[1] E. Cassirer, *The Platonic Renaissance in England* (trans. J. P. Pettegrove, 1953).

[2] Hymns such as *Vexilla Regis prodeunt* and *Pange, Lingua, gloriosi proelium certaminis* of Venantius Fortunatus (*c.* 540–*c.* 600).

[3] "All things end in mystery."

must mean "rites". Anyhow, as you say, the handles by which we lay hold on heaven. . . .

Much love for Easter.

R. M.

Mottisfont Abbey,
near Romsey, Hants
May Day, 1954†

My dear Hamilton,

It is too long since I wrote; I have been grossly busy. I have had your letter of April 11 lying by me, waiting to be answered, but have had no moment till now, on this week-end, when we have breakfast in bed and a little leisure after it; a nice plan. It is an interesting old house, built out of a dissolved abbey, with fragments of abbey and church in corners about it—not much, as at Rothley Temple,[1] but hints, as it were—an arch here, a piscina there, a re-modelled door, great monastic walls under the Georgian stucco. And spacious lawns, where we play croquet. Nice fellow-guests: Raymond Mortimer, Clive Bell, Peter Quennell, and others; and animated conversation all day. Quite fun, really.

Thank you much for your good letter . . . [and] for those prayers you quote; I have noted them for use.

I did an unwonted thing lately. John Betjeman gave me a Press ticket to go and hear Billy Graham, the U.S. Evangelist, at Harringay; so I went there with Joe Ackerley, a friend of mine who is the literary editor of The *Listener,* and we sat under him, in a packed stadium full of thousands of people, while he addressed us on the 7th Commandment, to which he gave the exclusive name of "immorality" (the breaking of it, that is). He was very fervent, preaching with great gesture and power,

[1] The Leicestershire seat of Thomas Babington, R. M.'s great-great-grandfather (1758-1838), which had formerly been an abbey.

very crude and simple, even illiterate (in phrasing and thought, not in accent). Of course it was *not* what Joe Ackerley or I could stomach. But the packed thousands did, and *hundreds* afterwards walked up to be "saved"—a very impressive crowd. Vulgar, yes: God saying to us, " You thought no one saw you on that day. But *I* saw you, *I* took a picture of you"; suggesting those photographers who stand about at the seaside snapping people. The audience seemed to us half dopey, somehow. Ever and anon we sang a vulgar hymn, with great enthusiasm. All very strange. God certainly does move in a mysterious way, His wonders to perform. I think he really *is* converting many people to a Christian life; he is a Baptist. One day I must ask some Baptist about this "being saved". What happens when they sin again, and go on sinning? Can one be saved again? Well, *quot homines, tot sententiae,*[1] and good luck to them all. Joe Ackerley came out murmuring " Dreadful creature! " I tried not to feel this, because I think he is sincere, though melodramatic.

Easter over, and here we are in May. And about Whitsun I probably go to Turkey for about 4 weeks. Black Sea, Constantinople, Ionian coast; all very interesting and beautiful. I shan't drive this time.

How good and how welcome your letters are. It is good of you to write just what I need and want.

I hope you had not too strenuous a Holy Week and Easter. . . .

My love always,
M.

---

[1] "As many opinions as there are men."

20, *Hinde House, Hinde St., W.*1
16th *May*, 1954† (or *Deus qui fidelium*)[1]

Oh dear, Hamilton, I seem to have mislaid your two lovely letters; I was carrying them about in my hand to answer them, and must have put them down somewhere in the flat, but where? Anyhow, for the moment, *non sunt.* They will turn up; but meanwhile I am answering them without the book. However I remember lots of nice things out of them, in particular *"Deus qui Errantibus"*[2] which pleases me very much. That letter isn't in my selection of Paston letters; I must look at it in the full edition at the L[ondon] Library. I don't think particularly well of our P[rayer] B[ook] way of adding "almighty" to "God" in so many collects; it is unnecessary, and not v.g., it seems to me. We do it on this Sunday too. I see that "to those that go astray" is another rendering of *"errantibus"*, which I rather prefer to "those that be in error", I think. *Qui errantibus* rather comes home to me just now, owing to this and that; so does *"veritatis tuae lumen ostendis"*. How fortunate one is to be able *in viam redire.*[3] . . .

On being reminded by you of poor Ovid, I got out *Tristia* and *Ex Ponto* and read his sad accounts again.[4] *"Orbis in extremi jaceo desertus harenis . . . aequora semper ventorum rabie solibus orba tument."*[5] It doesn't promise good bathing! All the same,

[1] "O God, who (makest) the faithful (to be of one mind and will . . .)"; see Collect for 3rd Sunday after Easter.

[2] "O Almighty God, who (showest) to them that be in error (the light of thy truth)"; see Collect for 3rd Sunday after Easter.

[3] "(To the intent that they may) return into the way (of righteousness)"; see Collect for 3rd Sunday after Easter.

[4] *Tristia* and *Epistulae ex Ponto* were written when Ovid (Publius Ovidius Naso, 43 B.C.—*c.* A.D. 17) was in exile from Rome at Tomis, on the Black Sea.

[5] " I lie abandoned upon the sands at the confines of the world. . . . the seas deprived of sunshine for ever swell beneath the wrath of the winds." Ovid, *Ex Ponto*, 1.3.49.

"*obligor, ut tangam laevi fera litora Ponti*",[1] and no doubt poor
Naso made the worst of it. Anyhow, he was at Tomis [*sic*], at
the bleak Thracian end of the Black Sea. I am sure that on the
southern shore, where I shall roam (as well as to other places)
it won't be like that, with icicles perpetually hanging on the
hair and the beards of the fierce locals; no, it will be bland
and sunlit, *aprica litora*,[2] and the Euxine Sea will be smooth and
blue. I shall also be on the Ionian coast and the southern coast
(I mean of the Mediterranean, not the Pontus) and in the
interior; Ankara and the other inland places. And especially
Istanbul—Constantinople or Byzantium as I prefer to call it—
where there is so much to see. I always think S[anta] Sophia
must be one of the very most beautiful things anywhere, inside
and out. And the Byzantine palaces, and the Theodosian wall
crumbling to ruin. I will send you picture p[ost] c[ard]s, which
Naso never did to his friends. I suppose Poste Restante,
Istanbul, Turkey, would find me, on and off; I can't be sure
of any other fixed point. I shall be back at the end of June.
The posts may be odd between Turkey and Cambridge, Mass.,
so don't worry, if you don't hear; you will eventually. I fly
on June 4th, just before Whitsunday. I always seem to spend
Whitsunday, that ghostly feast, in some heathen land. Not that
Moslems are heathens, of course. Talking to a young Jewish
friend to-day, I said without thinking, " Let me see, do you
have the 10 Commandments, or are they only in our P[rayer]
B[ook] " ? He replied, "After all, WE made them, didn't we?"
and I had to hand it to him that they had. And the Moslems
made the Koran, which I believe is a very good code of morals
on the whole. " Very superstitious people," a Christian Arab
said to me in Syria, " they pray in their mosques all day." Your
letters have turned up—good. I now have again before me
your explanation of the kind of salvation that such as Billy

[1] " Here am I making vows, and all that I may reach the savage shores
of the ill-omened Euxine." Ovid, *Tristia* I.2.83.

[2] "Sunlit shores."

156

Graham sets going in people, and of the metaphors that help in this. I do see that it may be very valuable and saving. But tends too much to depend on emotion; and, as you say, that passes. Thank you for saying that about *Salutis fundamentum*;[1] I like that. I sometimes wish you nearer at hand, so that I could discuss things with you. It would be good for me.

I have noted Lacey's "*A. C. Faith*"[2] and shall get it from the L[ondon] L[ibrary]. Also the *Historic Christ*.[3] That chapter on Worship sounds interesting. I have to review a history of the Church in England 597-1688, by Dr S. C. Carpenter, late Dean of Exeter.[4]

> Much love always,
> *R. M.*

*20, Hinde House, Hinde St., W.*1
29th May, 1954†

My dear Hamilton,

This letter is *aimed* at June 2nd, that auspicious feast, but I dare say it will reach you too early. (I thought better too early than too late.) Anyhow, it brings much love to you for your birthday, and for the coming year. I see you are patroned by the Martyrs of Lyons and Vienne, Pothinus the Bishop and Blandina the Virgin, and their companions in holy martyrdom. I have ordered to be sent to you a book you won't read, but I feel you ought to have it from me, and you may like the illustrations, and bits here and there. Anyhow, it brings my love and good wishes, and gratitude for all you've done for me since August 1950. I don't think this book (*Ruins*) is likely to be published in your adopted continent.

[1] "The essentials of salvation."
[2] T. A. Lacey, *The Anglo-Catholic Faith* (1926).
[3] Probably James MacKinnon's *The Historic Jesus* (1931), see below p. 220.
[4] S. C. Carpenter, *The Church in England, 597-1688* (1954).

I should have begun by thanking you for your letter "begun May 19", of which I absorbed every word. I might take a Marquand novel to Turkey, perhaps. Yes, in ccmmon with most novelists to-day, his world has few supra-mundane communications. Compare George Eliot: she was a rationalist, yet her Maggie Tulliver is guided through her life by the communications of conscience and God; G. E.'s world was open to that always. On the other hand, I have just been reading two new novels, both by friends; the people get into dire straits, and never a cry for help to God, never a prayer, never even a dim faith. Their desperate human problems have to be resolved in human terms. I am just now in touch . . . with a desperate human problem: this business of husband throwing over wife . . . and taking a mistress. . . . No religious faith in either . . . or in the mistress . . . It is all so squalidly unrelated to any principles; or rather, the principles are unrelated to goodness as I see it. And it is on my conscience that we—my generation, who had codes, often deserted the codes and disrupted them, damaging them for the next generation so that now they scarcely seem to exist, in many people. I have a very personal remorse about this, though I was only one of many. But what is to come of it all? . . .

No, don't try and write to Turkey. I'll send you news of my travellings when I can. But no air letters from there, alas.

I admire your enterprise in making the Colonial rebels pray for the descendant of Geo: III. Do you add the President of the revolted colonies? In *this* country, royalty-worship has become a lunatic hysteria, guyed, I am glad to see, in *Punch* ("Our Palace Page") and elsewhere. Now I must get on with my review of S. C. Carpenter's book. This is, I suppose, my last word to you from England for the present. *Fera litora Ponti*[1] call me.

My love always. I shall think of you on 2nd June at Mass.

---

[1] "The savage shores of the Euxine."

20, *Hinde House, Hinde St., W.*1
8*th July*, 1954†

My dear Hamilton,

I arrived home at 4 a.m. the day before yesterday, plunging from extreme heat to icy cold and wet. Turkey *was* hot; particularly in the south (Antioch, etc.) but [also] all over. I found waiting for me, among a great pile, your letter of 27th June. I am very sorry for its sad news of the loss of the two Fathers. It will cast a sad melancholy over your Retreat, I am afraid. Sudden accidents like that are so much more of a shock than death from illness.[1]

Turkey was most interesting and exciting. *Too* hot: I was slightly ill from it while I was there; [with the] exhaustion of getting a lot done under that fierce sun, scrambling about, frustrated by not knowing Turkish; though kind English friends sometimes turned up opportunely. But it *was* interesting. I went from Constantinople down the Black Sea to Trebizond, the last little Byzantine empire, not conquered by the Turks till 1461, eight years after Constantinople fell. It was a very famous place in the Middle Ages: "the emperor of Trebizond" has many references in poetry. Now it is completely Turkish, the last Greeks turned out 30 years ago, and all the Greek churches now mosques. But there is a Byzantine ruined palace and castle on a high crag above the town, and I climbed up there and felt forlorn Byzantine ghosts pattering about it. Apart from that, it is a very Turkish town; women still muffled up to the eyes and mouths (a dress discarded in the large towns, but still common in remote places). Women are being ill-treated, having been looked on as slaves for centuries; they walk while the man rides the donkey; they stay at home while the men eat out in cafés and restaurants;

[1] Two Cowley Fathers (Rev. Richard Morley, s.s.j.e., and Rev. Francis Hanlon, s.s.j.e.) were drowned when their boat capsized in the Lake of Bays, Ontario, Canada, on 29th May, 1954.

they are pushed aside in the scramble for tram seats (as I found —I never once got a seat) and almost pushed into the sea in the stampede for getting on to a boat. A shipwreck among Turks would be a poor time for women; none of them would ever get on to one of the boats. Nor have they (quite) souls. Nor may they eat with men: not even the Consul's wife in her own house when her husband has Turks to lunch. While as for bathing (in remote places such as Trebizond) one would probably be stoned. It will take at least 50 years before they catch up with the West in this matter. Constantinople is a very noble and exciting city—the Bosphorus is glorious. S[anta] Sophia is now a museum. I got South to Antioch, and saw the earliest Christian church (a cave, supported by columns), and to Smyrna and Ephesus, the latter extremely moving. The great Temple of Artemis was destroyed in C.3, and its ruins lie in a swamp. But the ruined city—the Roman one, that St Paul saw—is very extensive: forum, Marble Way, theatre (where the Ephesians shouted for 2 hours about Diana), etc. Then, on my last day, I got to Troy—imagine the thrill. The sea is now 4 or 5 kilometres back, so the Greeks couldn't now watch the walls from their ships.

I didn't mean to bore you with my *Ruins*; don't do more than look at the pictures. But when I write a book, I feel you should have it.

By the way, I have been looking in vain in the Missal for a collect you once quoted, *"Domine, in manus tuas sunt exiti"* [*sic*], or anyhow something like that, I may have got the words wrong.[1] I wonder just where it is? If you happen to remember, tell me sometime. You'll by now be out of Retreat, I suppose. . . .

Much love.
R. M.

---

[1] A misquotation from a Psalm not a Collect; see below p. 162.

My dear Hamilton,

Thank you so much for yours of 14th. How interesting to meet a Roumanian[1] who knows Tomi (more correctly Tomis?)[2] and has seen Ovid's grave! Is it kept in nice order? It is the present-day Constantius, of course;[3] no chance of my having got there, as it is behind that annoying Curtain. As I heard an ingenuous American youth in an Istanbul hotel say to his friend, "I promised my father I wouldn't go anywhere near the Iron Curtain." I suppose his dad feared that if he did, hands from the Other Side might reach out and drag him over. So I couldn't visit the scene of Ovid's woes, or see those terrible Getans with icicles in their beards. (Though actually no doubt in June and July they would have thawed out.) It always makes me rather sad to think that the barbarians of Tomis were hurt by the accounts of them and their country in *Tristia* and *Ex Ponto*; though one wouldn't really have thought they would have got hold of those works. I am sure that is the least agreeable part of the Euxine. The other end, the Colchis end where I travelled, was, do you remember, the home of the Golden Fleece and its ferocious custodians, and the more ferocious Medea and her father. I like to think of the *Argo* voyaging along that sea, and visiting the ports which I saw. The ship *Argo* was a familiar craft in my family; we called our canoe after it and struck out into the waters of the Mediterranean to some rock where the fleece hung. I think it is a good thing to be brought up on the classical tales; they register deeply and for life.

Of course I soon found that phrase I was looking for, in

[1] Then an employee at Phillips Book Store in Cambridge, Mass.
[2] Of these alternative spellings "Tomis" is the more usual.
[3] Usually known as Constanza.

Psalm 68: *"Domini, Domini, exitus mortis."*[1] It is expanded in our Visitation of Sick Children into "to whom the issues of life and death belong."[2]

I am sorry about the disturbing changes in the disposal of your Fathers. You will miss those who are going far away, like Fr Pedersen. . . . Well, as you say, the thing goes on, irrespective of personalities. Yesterday in chapel we sang "Disposer supreme". . . . "To frail earthen vessels, and things of no worth, entrusting thy riches, which aye shall endure. Those vessels soon fail, though full of thy light, and at thy decree are broken and gone; thence brightly appeareth thy truth in its might, as through the clouds riven the lightnings have shone".[3] Let us hope so. I wonder if the Roumanian ever sent you *Ruins*. My sister is still reading it, a small piece each evening. She says she likes to go to bed with a nice picture in words in her mind; she has now got to the end of the section called "The Haunting Gods", which deals with ruined temples, churches, abbeys, etc. I am now embarking on my novel, but haven't properly got down to it yet, as I have been busy with recovering from Turkey, odds and ends, and writing some poetry, besides seeing a lot of people. Also writing a longish article for the *Times Lit. Sup.* about *A History of the Crusades.*[4] Are you interested in John Addington Symonds?[5] He left an interesting MS diary, now in the hands of the London Library (on whose Committee I am), and the question is, is it fit to publish or not? It is full of rather surprising things about

[1] "God is the Lord, by whom we escape death." Ps. 68.20.

[2] See "A Prayer for a Sick Child"; one of the occasional Collects appended to the Order for the Visitation of the Sick in the Book of Common Prayer.

[3] See *The English Hymnal*, Hymn 178:
 Then brightly appeareth the arm of thy might,
 As through the clouds breaking the lightnings have shone.

[4] See "The Tragedy of the Crusades," *Times Literary Supplement*, 29th October, 1954. See above p. 87.

[5] Historian and translator (1840-1893).

people, such as Dr C. J. Vaughan, Headmaster of Harrow (*brother* of my great-uncle by marriage)[1] under whom he was in the 1840's. No more space, as you observe! But much love.

R. M.

20, *Hinde House, Hinde St., W.*1

4th August, 1954†

My dear Hamilton,

Our last letters crossed, yours of 27th July, mine of a few days earlier. I was much interested in yours, and very sorry that your friend Mrs Paine has "poped", as we call it here. Why do they do it, these sane, intelligent, reasoning Anglicans, who have had the faith and the sacraments all their lives, been nourished by them and known God through them? I do find it hard to understand. I really, I suppose, agree with someone who said lately that the Roman Church is not a Church for adults. Perhaps the Anglican Church is the only Church which is this, do you think? But worse than the rather trashy nonsense they have to swallow is, of course, the barrier they set up, the iron curtain between themselves and other Christians. Surely a Christianity which won't worship with other Christians, outside their own exclusive body, is self-condemned? I hate to read their interpretations of what they believe Our Lord meant and said about it; how *can* they be so astray as to a character and purpose so clearly shown us in the Gospels? If you ever talk about it to Mrs Paine, I wonder if you will get much light on that question. A Portuguese friend of mine once said the Church *had* to show by its exclusiveness

[1] In an earlier letter to Father Johnson R. M. had said that C. J. Vaughan was an *uncle* of her great-uncle Canon E. T. Vaughan, though she later corrected this to *brother*. See *Letters to a Friend*, p. 286.

163

that it had the truth in a unique way and mustn't seem to condone the worship of those who hadn't. But I am very sorry it has come between you and your valued friendship. Though perhaps it won't. My cousin Jean[1] and I never discuss it, and are very good friends, with so much common ground. She was really delighted when I came back to the Church, and did feel it was a supremely important thing. . . . Well, it seems that some people must see things in that way; I think argument with them achieves nothing. I am interested in what you say about English and American Anglicanism. Yes, *how* different are their roots and background and growth. I don't know nearly enough about Amer: Anglicanism, or Anglo-Catholicism. When did it start? Did they get the repercussions of the Tractarians? I doubt if there was anything of our 17th century A.Cism among the Episcopalians of Virginia and Maryland in that century. A pity, in a way, that more of our High Church refugees from Cromwell didn't go across the Atlantic, to counteract the Mayflower. Or the Non-Jurors of the end of the century. But when did it begin? When the S.S.J.E. first set up a branch there, what kind of reception did they have? And when was that?[2] I vaguely remember in an American novel or two early this century noticing that some of the Episcopalians went to "high" New York churches; I mean, somewhere round 1914, I suppose. If there is a history of the Ang: Church in America, I would like to read it. There should be something like Dr Carpenter's *The Church in England*, which is an excellent account of the shaping and development of the Church. I will send you my review of it, if I can lay hands on it, and you could probably get hold of the book itself from your Roumanian bookseller or another. I think it v.g.

[1] Jean Smith.
[2] Between 1870 and 1880, when the Cowley Fathers first started working in the U.S., they met a good deal of opposition from Low Churchmen on account of their "ritualism."

I am just off for a week to the I[sle] of W[ight] with my sister, and am choosing books to take with me. I shall be writing, too (my novel). And (since it is not Turkey) bathing, if the weather allows. And driving about with my sister and her friend[1], picnicking and exploring the corners of that nice island, which I love. I might take T. A. Lacey's book that you mention, perhaps, and Dr Kirk's on the Church, not *The Vision of God* but another.[2] I must go to the L[ondon] L[ibrary] to-morrow and look about on the theology shelves.

I only learned the other day a thing that interests me about Alice Meynell, and that you probably know. I always thought that it was Coventry Patmore whom she loved, and to whom she wrote that poem "Renunciation" ("I must not think of thee . . .")[3] but it seems it was a priest of her own persuasion, whom she loved so much that his superiors had to move him elsewhere. What a lot of this priest-devotion there must always have been! I expect you know it from personal experience. It may be quite innocent, and quite unreciprocated; but what an embarrassment to the priest, and how difficult to know how to meet it! Without, I mean, being either unkind or dangerously encouraging. . . .

My love always,
R. M.

20, *Hinde House, Hinde St., W.*1
19*th August*, 1954†

My dear Hamilton,
Again our letters have crossed. Yours (begun Aug. 2) reached me on the I[sle] of W[ight]; mine was posted Aug. 5.

[1] Nancy Willetts.
[2] Probably K. E. Kirk's *The Apostolic Ministry* (1946).
[3] See "Renouncement" by Alice Meynell (1847-1922).

I am now returned, after a nice but not very warm or dry ten days. Such was the weather that I bathed only twice. But my sister and I enjoyed driving about the island, its downs and little lanes, which are much more attractive than the over-built-up coasts. The best thing is the ruins of Quarr Abbey, lying in a field above the sea, huge fragments of a great Cistercian Abbey. But I rather like it all, except the vulgar sea resorts. I understand your difficulty about talking to Mrs Paine.[1] Though wouldn't it be interesting and enlightening if you were able to? I always want to know what are the real reasons behind these conversions from Anglicanism. One understands those from agnosticism or from the unlovely Protestant churches. But I am interested in what urges High Anglicans, who have something so good already, and have believed in it so firmly. Did someone persuade Mrs Paine, or did she think it out alone? . . .

20th Aug. Your letter of 16th came this morning, so we just avoided crossing again. I don't much like crossing; for one thing, you tend to answer again my letter before the last (in case I might not have got your first answer to it) and not comment or reply to the one you got later, so I don't know what I told you, and may repeat myself. I do quite forget what I said in my letter of the 5th; did I ask you if you had ever suffered from excessive devotion from those who come to you? . . . You are right about *pars tibi*. It is one of the errors I discovered too late, and listed at the end of my copy for future correction.[2] There are only too many such, alas. I'm glad you too like "*Supreme, quales, Arbiter*."[3] In stanza 3, are "they", who are borne like clouds to do thy will, the vessels (broken

[1] R. M. has added a note here: "This was written before your last letter, of course."

[2] In *Pleasure of Ruins* (p. 12) a quotation from the elegy on pagan Rome by Hildebert of Lavardin (1056-1133), "*Par tibi, Roma, nihil*" ("there is nothing thy equal, Rome"), is misprinted as "*Pars tibi . . .*"

[3] "Disposer supreme . . .".

and gone) or the lightnings?[1] It's not in Phillimore's *Latin Hymns* that you sent me.[2]

I expect those Latin rhymes may be by the Dean.[3] In 1888 he would be about 30, after all; he was a contemporary at Eton with my uncle Regi. Or of course it may have been his father. They are a classical family. I have just been giving Noel Annan, a young King's don, data about my own family connections for an essay he is writing for George Trevelyan's 80th birthday, about families and their inter-relationships and hereditary qualities.[4]

Do many Americans confuse *purpose* and *propose*? It does seem illiterate. I remember your telling of a penitent who did it in confession. On the Isle of Wight we heard the *most* illiterate sermons. I think preachers should have a special licence before they mount the pulpit. It must put off so many people. I believe St Paul's, Knightsbridge is v.g. I might try it sometimes.

Much love.

R. M.

---

[1] See *The English Hymnal*, Hymn 178:
> Those vessels soon fail, though full of thy light
> And at thy decree are broken and gone;
> Then brightly appeareth the arm of thy might,
> As through the clouds breaking the lightnings have shone.
>
> Like clouds they are borne to do thy great will,
> And swift as the winds about the world go; . . .

[2] *The Hundred Best Latin Hymns; selected by J. S. Phillimore* (1926).

[3] R. M. probably means W. R. Inge (1860-1954).

[4] See N. G. Annan's essay " The Intellectual Aristocracy" in *Studies in Social History, edited by J. H. Plumb* (1955).

20, *Hinde House, Hinde St., W.*1
29th *August,* 1954†

My dear Hamilton,

Thank you so much for your entertaining letter written on the Feast of St Bart's. " Bartlemy the Bright " it was *not*, in this land; but to-day and yesterday really are, miraculously and for the first time in this dreadful summer, *warm*, with the sun appearing. I am driving up the Thames Putney-ward, with a companion who always seeks to bathe;[1] we think we can find a spot somewhere in the reaches of the river where we can go in. He works in Madrid and Salamanca, but spends August here, and always when we lunch together has his swim-suit in his pocket in case.... I am feeling rather happy to-day, after a long and fruitful talk yesterday with ——... It is encouraging when someone one trusts, and someone with understanding, thinks one has "grown". How I hope I have, a little. After all, it would be strange if one didn't grow *at all*, going to daily Mass; though how pitifully little effect these great things have on one's life is a matter not only for distress but for wonder. How can it be, coming away day after day from that mystery, that one lives on this low level? "Confession, absolution, communion, then at it again," as H. G. Wells gibes. Well, that is life....

Now my space is gone, and I wanted to ask you if you know where is that prayer I once copied out beginning, "*Ut qui me, non meis meritis, intra viatorum numerum dignatus est aggregare, luminis sui claritatem infundens. ...*" I have put no reference to it, and don't know where I found it.[2] You, who know all, may know this. With this nice bit of flattery I send my love and end my letter, which seems a trifle crowded.

---

[1] David Ley; see *Letters to a Friend*, p. 295.
[2] It is adapted from the *Exultet*, see above p. 30.

My dear Hamilton,

Your letter posted 31st Aug. was rather especially good.
Thank you for it. How endlessly kind you are to me, and how
you manage to say just the things that I need, and that give me
fresh stimulus. Also, thank you for reminding me where that
fragment of prayer came from. Of course I remembered at
once when you told me, and looked it up. I had stupidly
forgotten even that I got it from you, and that you had supplied
the "*viatorum*" in it. I read the whole thing through again;
how beautiful it is. Canon Hood might well have used the bit
about the candle this morning at his solemn Mass on the name-
feast of St Mary's Aldermary, before which he blessed his new
candles, candlesticks, and crucifix, which someone had presented to the re-built church. I went to this on his invitation;
a beautiful service, though for my more austere taste rather too
much motion and gesture and fuss and intricate weaving about
among the clergy. All part of "the structure", no doubt; and
amazes the poore devat[*sic*], of course, but my bit of the
structure is quieter and more to my taste. . . . Is [it] . . . right
that there is very little Anglo-Catholicism in America? Are
there scarcely any churches which gorgeously sit deckt, are
nearly all plaine and quite threadbare? What a great pity, and
how lucky we are in London, with so many to our mind. No
wonder people like Mrs Paine feel they must go where there
is more beauty. I like the look of St Paul's Knightsbridge very
much; it is beautiful, rather dark, very ungarish. . . .

Interesting about "*felix culpa*."[1] I had always supposed it
St Augustine's; if so, end of C.4, I suppose. How old would
that Mass be, I wonder? It could be before that; but also

___

[1] "O happy fault (which was counted worthy to have such and so great
a redeemer!)," see the *Exultet*.

might be after. Pope Zosimus in 417 ordered candles to be blessed; many church writers spoke against it as heathen, both before and after this. The origin of the Paschal candle, says the *Encyc. Brit.*, is lost in the mists of antiquity. Probably the Jews had it. Fr Martindale might well have done a 3rd book, *"Dates* of the Missals." But there are more specialised studies of Missals; some I have read, and will look up again. . . .

Much love,

R. M.

20, *Hinde House, Hinde St., W*.1
24*th September,* 1954†

My dear Hamilton,

I am horrified by your account of your four termagants who have been sweeping over your parts.[1] I read a little about them in papers here, but not very much or very graphic. What an intimidating thing it must have been. I am thankful they have now swept by, and that "Carol"[2] didn't destroy your Monastery, as she well might have. I have been thinking about you with much concern. . . .

I am learning to meditate a little, or trying to. I am doing the Book of Wisdom, chapter by chapter, it is such good and delightful stuff, isn't it?—so full of the Spirit of God and of *Hagia Sophia.* And how I like the gay career of the ungodly, vanishing away like the soft air, but meanwhile missing no flower of spring and crowning himself with rosebuds, how lovely.[3] . . .

Yes, I remember Dr Addison's book on the Episcopal Ch[urch] in U.S.[4]; it interested me. People say now that

[1] During September 1954 hurricanes caused much damage and many casualties on the east coast of the U.S.
[2] One of the hurricanes.   [3] Wisdom 2. 3-8.
[4] Daniel D. Addison, *The Episcopalians* (New York, 1904).

a great deal of religion is spreading about, both in the Universities and elsewhere, but not predominatingly A[nglo-] C[atholic], in fact much more the middle and the slightly Evangelical type of churchmanship. What *I* mainly hear about is A.C.ism; at Cambridge the Franciscans at St Bene't's are attracting undergraduates, men and girls, and there are several good Deans and Chaplains, and Little St Mary's is a great centre; at Oxford St Mary Magdalen's, and I suppose still Cowley? And perhaps St Barnabas still? I don't know. I am interested that you think it a stronger movement in America. Yes, I must ask Canon Hood about it; not that I ever see him. . . . Perhaps I might ask him sometime to come and drink sherry with me. . . .

Much love,

R. M.

Long Crichel House,

nr. Wimborne,

Dorset

1st October, 1954†

My dear Hamilton,

   I have a notion that I haven't got your latest letter with me here (where I am week-ending), but only the one posted 16th Sept., describing the four dreadful harpies who swept round you, and saying a lot more, which I have answered in my last letter before this. But I'm not quite certain whether I have had another letter since that or not: it is stupid of me, but when I get back I shall know; if I did have one, my having forgotten doesn't mean that I wasn't interested in it. . . .

   I think I shall often go to weekday Mass at St Paul's, Knightsbridge (8.30, and only 5 minutes longer in the car [than to Grosvenor Chapel], and good both in Mass-execution and the church itself, which is very attractive). I think they have there rather a large organization and staff and ecclesiastical Bustle; but this won't affect me. . . .

I am week-ending with my friends here—Raymond Mortimer [and] Eddy Sackville-West. . . . Also here for week-end are Jacobine Hichens that was (who wrote that novel about a girl who didn't go R.C. . . .)[1] now married to Lionel Sackville-West. . . . They and I form a little Anglican enclave in this delightful company of agnostics and one convert; we have just been a walk and enjoyed a Church gossip—most unusual in this house! Now I must get ready to drive out to luncheon a few miles away. Much love. I shall write again soon.

R. M.

20, *Hinde House, Hinde St., W.*1
11*th October,* 1954†

My dear Hamilton,

Your letter of 28th Sept. arrived some days back; thank you so much for it. I find in your letters a lot of food for thought; that Ember Wed. collect you quote turned my mind towards "sedulous service"[2], and that, at least, should be one's aim. . . . Canon Hood is . . . coming [to sherry and I might ask [him] . . . about the Church in America. . . . I have also Gerard Irvine and his brother James and wife (both [Grosvenor] Chapel members), Jacobine Hichens . . . and my cousin Jean Smith the Papist. So I must be careful that Jacobine doesn't talk about the Bp of Rome and his detestable enormities. . . . She is now married to a nice quiet Anglican (quiet, but wildly High), and about to bring forth a nice little Anglican infant. . . .

---

[1] *Noughts and Crosses.*
[2] See post-communion Collect for Ember Wednesday in September ("... *ut quae sedula servitute* ...").

I wish I could get Fr Talbot's *Addresses*;[1] they are still re-binding, but I've ordered them from Mowbrays. I must tell you about my sherry party when I next write; I hope the guests will all get on together! Under the mellowing influence of alcoholic liquor, people usually do. How I wish you could drop down among us and join us. Only then I suppose I shouldn't want to converse with anyone else, which wouldn't do.

Love,

R. M.

20, Hinde House, Hinde St., W.1

21st October, 1954†

My dear Hamilton,

Thank you for two admirable (and very helpful) letters, of 12th and 17th, the latter received to-day. I was going to write to you to-day, so am glad your letter came before I did so. I think my last letter to you was written on the 11th, the day before the sherry party. . . .

By the way, Canon Hood, when I mentioned you as a distant cousin, radiated pleasure. He referred to "a delightful sight of you in 1919," when he stayed there [Cambridge, Mass.] a few days, and said what a delightful person you were. I don't think he has seen you since? . . . Another priest who praised you was Fr [Cecil] Wood, who came to the Chapel to assist in the noon celebration last Sunday; he spoke to me outside afterwards, and said he had tremendously enjoyed an evening with you in September, during his American tour. I don't think he had known that I knew you, before I asked him if he had seen you. Your name seems to light people up!

Thank you for your advice about Mass. I am glad you think I needn't feel tied to . . . [Grosvenor] Chapel; though it

[1] Edward Keble Talbot, *Retreat Addresses*, edited *by Lucy Menzies* (1954).

does pull at me with the bonds of gratitude and deep affection, and remembrance of all I learned there and the habits I formed, which can never be abandoned while I have health and strength for morning outings, and these show no signs of flagging, indeed, long practice has made me much tougher about them. But I now plan to divide my days between the Chapel and St Paul's [Knightsbridge,] and am glad you approve. On Mondays ... and Wednesdays and Fridays, I go to St Paul's ... which I like extremely. . . . They have it in a small chapel in the south aisle, always several people there, nothing could be better. The confessional seems to me to be rather publicly placed (and unusually), in the very middle among the seats! But I presume that during confessions the chapel is otherwise empty, or it would be all quite audible. . . . On the other mornings—Tuesday, Thursday, Saturday and Sunday—I go to Mass at the Chapel, only communicating on Sundays. . . . I think this compromise is satisfactory, don't you? I don't want to desert the Chapel more than this . . . I was very anxious while that horrid " Hazel "[1] ploughed her destructive way overland, lest she should take Mass. in her stride, and much relieved when the news came that she hadn't. Re intercommunion, *of course* we must keep and pass on our sacramental heritage; but is there harm in praying with those who have it in another form, such, e.g., as Wesleyans, most devout communicants who use, I think, our P[rayer] B[ook], but have no bishops? It seems to me to be Christian oneness to do this. . . .

Much love.

R. M.

[1] A hurricane.

7th *November*, 1954†

My dear Hamilton,

Remembrance Sunday. A poppy on my coat, another on my car. I attended divine worship in Knightsbridge, a very beautiful service with excellent discourse from the incumbent,[1] whom I like more and more (so far only from afar). I went there also for All Saints' Mass; All Souls to the Chapel. . . .

Thank you for your interesting letter of 26th Oct. I like the picture of the devout and luckless people of Worcester all at church while the cads of Droitwich bought up their markets! Of course you are right about the rather proletarian clergy; they are needed, and it is right that we should have them. I must try and not feel, as the Preacher puts it in Ecclesiasticus 38, that to some it is given to follow the plough and turn the potter's wheel and uphold the fabric of the world, but *not* to sit in the places of counsel and where parables are spoken. Of course it isn't so; but a trifle of polish does oil the wheels, so to speak. It is much to be hoped that the other type will soon present themselves in greater numbers. . . .

I have just cut out from the *Sunday Times* an article by J. B. Priestley about your cousin J. C. Powys, whom he much admires. I can't send you this herewith, but will put it in an envelope and despatch it overseas, and you will doubtless receive it in some weeks. There are some interesting books in to-day's reviews: the autobiography of Edwin Muir,[2] [and] two books by men who entered monasteries, one Redemptionist, where he stayed 6 years and was then turned out, he knew not why,[3] the other by Fr Bede Griffiths, O.S.B., who stayed in and was happy.[4] He was a convert, the other an Irish

---

[1] Rev. E. B. Henderson.
[2] Edwin Muir, *The Story and the Fable* (1940; revised ed., 1954).
[3] Gary MacEoin, *Nothing is Quite Enough* (1954).
[4] Bede Griffiths, *The Golden String* (1954).

born R.C., quite poor by origin. Both are reviewed by Philip Toynbee (Arnold T.'s son, and Gilbert Murray's grandson), himself a young man of no creed, who marvels at this entering into rigorous religious rule and shutting out the delightful and valuable world around, which he himself so greatly enjoys; but he is much impressed by this sacrifice for something they believe in, and which he sees must, therefore, have some truth in it.[1]

I am reading Arnold Toynbee's new vols. of his history, which I find extremely interesting.[2] His ex-father-in-law, Gilbert Murray, complains that he has "gone all mystical", which is wrong for a historian. But I like it, though I do see that he isn't always on sound ground in his deductions. . . . 10 p.m. I went into St Paul's Vicarage at 7.30, with about 20 others [for the Sunday evening "Open House"]; Fr Henderson I liked very much; he read aloud a speech of a Bishop at Minneapolis,[3] and there followed a kind of fireside chat or discussion about all manner of things, very nice, though rather low-brow. They talked, *inter alia*, about the Roman Church, which is rather aggressively attacking Anglicanism just now, and how far it was wise to make criticisms in return. . . . I didn't raise my voice, feeling too new—except once, to tell them the meaning of "eirenic",[4] which no one knew and they were sending for a dictionary; but I imagine Fr H. must have known, and was kindly coming down to the level of his company, so as not to seem a know-all. But I enjoyed the talk; he is very entertaining, nice and friendly. . . .

We are having floods here; perhaps a few just men will be spared. I should like a voyage in an ark. I wish when in Turkey I had climbed Ararat and found splinters of the ancient

[1] See *The Observer*, 7th November, 1954.
[2] A. J. Toynbee, *A Study of History* (Vols. VII-X, 1954).
[3] At the Anglican Congress at Minneapolis in August 1954.
[4] "Tending to peace."

ark, as travellers were used to do; they made good relics, and wrought miracles. . . .

Much love always.

R. M.

20, *Hinde House, Hinde St., W.*1

10*th November,* 1954

My dear Hamilton,

Here is the J. C. Powys article I wrote of; I don't know when you will get this, I've quite forgotten how long the ocean mail takes. I remember we used once always to use it, but that was 4 years ago.

I wonder if *The Cornerstone,* by Mme [Zoë] Oldenbourg (translated) will come your way. It is a historical novel about the Albigensian period—very vivid and full of graphic pictures. I have only just begun it; but it is being hailed as a masterpiece in its *genre.*

How *very* ignorant even clever and educated people often are about history sometimes! I have just read *The Golden Thread*[1], an autobiography by Bede Griffiths, O.S.B., who some years ago became R.C. and entered Prinknash. When at Oxford he read for Honour Mods, read privately Aristotle, Aquinas, Dante, St Augustine (in Latin), much in the way of Greek and Latin literature, and instead of Greats took the English Lit. School, and was obviously able (as well as a natural religious mystic). But, can you believe it, he knew so little of the elementary history that is in every child's history book, that it never occurred to him that the churches he saw about him and attended (he was a devout Anglican, for a time) had ever in the course of their history used anything but the English B[ook of] C[ommon] P[rayer], which he must have supposed to have been produced about 1000 years before it was! That

[1] *The Golden String.*

177

they had said Mass in Latin never struck him. Nor did he know that England was Christianized from Rome in C.6. When these facts burst upon him, he turned towards Rome and decided it was the True Church, and joined it. Such gaps in the knowledge of an intelligent and educated young man are very odd. I suppose most children of literate families learn about St Augustine and the English conversion in their first history lessons.

I know R.C.s who are getting rather worried about the Pope's recent pronouncements; he is said to be failing and getting senile. Can Popes be retired on grounds of health? This new Day of Mary certainly seems redundant.[1] People wonder what he will pronounce next. . . .

My love as always,

R. M.

20, *Hinde House, Hinde St., W.*1

3rd December, 1954†

My dear Hamilton,

You must try and forgive my over-long pause between letters: it's not that I forgot, but that life lately has been, with one thing and another, rather harassing, and I waited till things cleared a little before writing, since you aren't one of the people I can write to about other things while my mind is full of things I don't refer to. . . .

This . . . letter is a poor return to your two very good ones, of Nov. 9 and 28. I am glad you liked to have that Priestley article on J. C. P[owys]. I thought it good and interesting. He is a critic of good sense. About Arnold Toynbee's new vols. of his history: I am finding them very interesting, because, besides his tremendous learning, he has ideas. I know these

[1] Presumably R. M. means the Feast of the Assumption of the B.V.M.; but this doctrine was defined by Pope Pius XII four years previously, in 1950.

new vols. have had a lot of criticism, and especially of course from R.C.s, who are annoyed with him because he gives good reasons why he shied away from going over to Rome some years ago. . . . In his earlier vols. he took a much more R. Catholic standpoint, and I believe thought seriously of going over, but thought better of it. In vol. 10 of this new part of his history, he has changed his standpoint, explains that he was put off by the unchanging faults of the Church, and now has a much vaguer and more universal religion, towards which he believes that history, led by God, is working. Of course this doesn't please his R.C. critics, who seem to me unfair to him. Canon Roger Lloyd takes a much fairer view. Of course some criticism is justified. His father-in-law, Prof. Gilbert Murray, a lifelong agnostic, complains that Arnold has "gone all mystical"; and some historians have said that he twists facts to suit his theories. All the same, it is interesting. He is so amazingly learned that one learns an immense amount from every page; he seems to have been that kind of infant prodigy who read Xenophon in Greek at the age of 4, and remembers all he has learnt, so that his mind is a wonderful storehouse. One must allow such a man a few quiddities. But it is unfair to say that his historical trends are impersonal; on the other hand, they are, in his view, guided by God, towards some far-off divine event to which we are working. I must read *The Everlasting Man* again.[1] But G. K. C[hesterton] wasn't a man of A.T.'s intellectual stature, of course.

Yes, our liturgical funerals are very beautiful. I am glad you got to that one, and were able to see the daughters. Our short requiem Masses are also v.g. We had one in G. Chapel yesterday morning. . . .

"Marjorie Bowen" is now dead; her name was Mrs Campbell, I think.[2] I didn't know her, and not her books much

---

[1] G. K. Chesterton, *The Everlasting Man* (1925).
[2] Gabrielle M. V. Long, *née* Campbell (1886-1952) used the name "Marjorie Bowen" as one of her pseudonyms.

either. No, she wasn't a Christian, I believe. But she ought to have admired the Wesleys. I haven't read that book[1], though I have read one or two of hers. She began at about 17, with *The Viper of Milan*, and wrote historical novels for many many years. Not first class, but competent. . . . I like Advent to be here. I have been reading those Advent Benediction things, *"Rorate Coeli,"* for Advent I ". . . *et iniquitates nostrae, quasi ventus, abstulerunt nos . . ."*[2] beautiful, but desolate. The Roman "Stir-up Sunday" collect seems better than ours, with its *"remedia majora"*[3] instead of "plenteously be rewarded". I must send you my Xmas card, in a sea-letter. My love.

R. M.

20, *Hinde House, Hinde St., W.*1
16*th December* (O *Sapientia*), 1954†

My dear Hamilton,

Thank you for your letter begun on the 8th. I'm sorry mine came unstuck; I can't think why it should, except that they don't make the edges sticky all round, only one bit. Still, it is meant to hold and if it doesn't the P.O. should sticky more of it. I don't know what they do to these letters in the planes. I wonder if this will reach you for Christmas; I hope it will. I sent you my card by surface mail, and that may or mayn't reach you before the day; you never know. . . .

It is odd how differently people react to faith; some receive it so much more easily than others. . . . You know, Hamilton, there are and always have been a lot of things I can't and don't try to accept; I just can't feel they matter, and don't strain after them. I have God, Christ, the Holy Spirit, and the Mass;

---

[1] "Marjorie Bowen," *Wrestling Jacob: A Study of the Life of John Wesley and Some Members of the Family* (1937).

[2] "Drop down dew, ye heavens . . . and our iniquities, like the wind, have carried us away."

[3] "Greater blessings"; see Collect for 25th Sunday after Trinity.

the rest I don't concern myself with, except as the ancient idiom which enshrines these central things for me. Does this shock you? I don't think it will; you understand so well. Anyhow, as I said, minds are so different, and must work on things in their own way, and God will make allowance for our limitations. . . . O *Sapientia*: we must pray that she will lead us all along the road.

I hope you will have a good Christmas. I shall go to be shriven at St Paul's, Knightsbridge, and, I think, go to the Midnight Mass there too though perhaps I may feel drawn by old affection to go to the Chapel. Then to Romford on Xmas morning early, to stay with my sister till 27th. I expect you will [be] under snow. Not so (I trust) we. My love for Christmas. . . .

R. M.

20, *Hinde House, Hinde St., W.*1

28th December, 1954†

My dear Hamilton,

How good to get your letter begun Dec. 20, posted 22nd, arrived 28th (not bad for this season). You say a lot of things in it that sustain my mind in its present somewhat drooping state. . . . Yes, I did indeed need the Church, and still do; however unfit I sometimes feel for it, I hope to find more and more in it to appropriate till I die—CRESCAT *nostrae salutis effectus*.[1] Thank you, I like too that Advent ember prayer, very much. What a rich storehouse the Missal is!

I had a quiet Christmas at Romford; my sister rather over-tired; she can still see to work, but expects the cataract to stop her before long. I'm sorry about your snow; I hope it didn't block you altogether. None here yet; in fact, it is wonderful mild weather so far. This morning I had, as it were, two

[1] " May the fruits of our salvation be *increased.*"

Masses; one at the Grosvenor at 8.15, then came home and heard a broadcast of one at 9 at my other place of worship; it came over very well. I suppose not to perplex prayer-book listeners, the prayer of oblation was put after the communion. Fr Henderson has a very pleasant quiet voice, which came over well. . . .

I am sending you by surface mail a page of the *Sunday Times* containing " Books of the Year", a symposium to which a lot of writers contributed. I wrote about Arnold Toynbee's new vols. of his *History*; difficult to compress what I wanted to say into 300 words, but I had a shot at it. Have you come across *Dialogues of Alfred Whitehead*, by an American Boswell called Price?[1] They interest me a good deal; I was given it for Christmas. This Boswell took down Whitehead's conversations over a number of years, when the Whiteheads were living in Memorial Drive, Cambridge, close to you, I suppose. Mrs W. joins in, and it is good talk. All manner of discussable questions turn up. One doesn't always agree with the great man, but he is always interesting. I think he gets St Paul rather wrong; he regards him as very dour and stern, and regrets his giving Christianity the shape it took. He forgets the splendid lyrical passages, about Charity,[2] putting on the whole armour etc.,[3] a hundred more, which make his letters so full of the *poetry* of Christianity. But he (Prof W.) doesn't much like the Jews, on the whole. I have been reading also another American book, by Wallace Notestein of Harvard, a history professor, on the state of the English people 1603-30, just before the colonization of New England.[4] That too interests me, though badly written, like so many American books. On the whole, so many American writers, even those of plenty of scholarship, seem to have little feeling for style. But they are

[1] *Dialogues of Alfred North Whitehead, as recorded by Lucien Price* (1954).
[2] I Cor. 13. 1-13.   [3] Eph. 6. 1-20.
[4] W. Notestein, *The English People on the Eve of Colonization, 1603-30* (1954).

very good scholars. This Notestein writes for Americans, to explain to them what their first colonizers were like in England. He obviously has great sympathy with puritanism—more than I have, or you, for we think it nearly wrecked our Church. On this, and the religious conflict in C.17 that led to the Civil War, C. V. Wedgwood writes excellently, in a new book that I am also reading, the first volume of the long book she is writing on the Civil Wars.[1] She is v.g. Dear Hamilton, I do hope you will have a happy year, beginning your second half century of celebrating Mass. You are very kind to me, as always—where should I be without you?

Love,
R. M.

---

[1] C. V. Wedgwood, *The King's Peace* (1955), the first volume of her History of the Civil Wars, *The Great Rebellion.*

1955

20, *Hinde House, Hinde St., W*.1

13th January, 1955†

My dear Hamilton,

Yours of 4th Jan. came on the 10th, thank you so much for it. I have been thinking about several things in it; mostly concerned with the various different approaches to religious faith. I do agree that the specifically Protestant approach is much more difficult than the Catholic one, which is a daily entry into—or anyhow to the gates of—the visible symbols of the kingdom, with its rites and acts and words and mysteries; all we have to do is to look and listen and feel we are in it. Whereas the Protestant is, I suppose, much more thrown on to looking back at what he believes happened long ago, and accepting some interpretation of it, with difficulty often. Yet it is extraordinary with what conviction and ardour evangelical Christians have done this; making their redemption hang on the death of Christ, to which they seem to give far more importance than to his life. Whereas the Catholic enters the visible courts, enters into his "myth" ("myth" is defined by someone as "a popular concept encircling a nucleus of truth") and gets at the truth, or some of it, that way. It is much easier; I could have done no other, with any success or benefit, I think, though so many thousands have and do. Without frequent Mass, I don't think I could pray, except in a very barren and sceptical way. Mass sheds the light by which we perceive and know what things we ought to do; though I suppose the power to fulfil the same could come by prayer, only with more difficulty. Don't you prefer—I do—the Latin form of that collect?[1] I always use it now. I like the greater terseness of *"ut et quae agenda sunt, videant; et ad implenda quae viderint, convalescant"* (good word).[2] This is the form I have copied into

[1] Collect for 1st Sunday after Epiphany.
[2] ". . . that they may both perceive what they ought to do, and may have strength to fulfil the same."

187

my *Preces Privatae*. By the way, why does Knox say he is translating from the Vulgate? He so often gets right away from it, and obviously is referring to the Greek.[1] As in Romans 12. 3, where the Vulgate (and the Missal) has "*Non plus sapere quam oportet sapere, sed sapere ad sobrietatem*," which is rather nice, but Knox has (like the Authorized Version more or less) "not to think highly of himself beyond his just estimation, but to have a sober esteem of himself," which is I suppose probably what the Greek means, tho' it could mean either, couldn't it? I don't know how the Revised Version renders it. But the two are quite different.

I haven't seen the Reinhold Niebuhr article you quote from. But I can't ever feel in touch with him, somehow; he lays emphasis on *history*, rather than on the present working of the Logos, which I find a more possible approach. One must have both: but perhaps people are divided as to which is the more significant, and the more saving, for them personally.

I agree with you that the Notestein account of the early C.17 Englishman's attitude towards his nation and his religion is very unpleasing, tho' I fear it was to a great extent so, and that this was the attitude those puritans took with them to New England. I have been reading (and reviewing) C. V. Wedgwood's *The King's Peace*, which I think you would enjoy; it deals with the years 1637-41, very graphically. The picture it gives of the militant puritans, as of the Laudian tyranny, is rather dreadful, though not worse than we knew already, if we have studied the period at all. Such shocking bigotry and cruelty on all sides, except for a few reasonable and peaceable men, such as Chillingworth,[2] Falkland,[3] and those like-minded. Laud actually wanted to burn alive a poor illiterate stonemason

[1] R. A. Knox's translation of the New Testament is, according to the sub-title, "newly translated from the Latin Vulgate". But in the footnotes frequent references are made to Greek and Hebrew sources.

[2] William Chillingworth (1602-1644), Anglican divine, author of *The Religion of Protestants*.

[3] Lucius Cary, second Viscount Falkland (1610?-1643).

188

who had spoken disapprovingly of the Anglican hierarchy in public. Certainly we are more humane now. If we have "morals without religion" often, we don't have so much religion without morals as once—or rather with perverted and cruel morals. Though that is just what the South African government has, and all those Calvinist Dutch adherents. . . .

It is nice to have the Christmas turmoil over, and be able to settle down to work. I haven't got far with my novel, but shall get on with it, I hope, now. I had a sudden invitation from my cousins in Ipswich, Mass.,[1] to join them in a Jamaican bungalow in February; it sounded delicious, bathing in a warm sea, coconut palms, boating about among the islands—my idea of heaven. But of course I can't. Much too costly to get there, and I am tied here at present, by a number of things. Strange to think of those warm seas now when the snow lies in the London streets so thick that it is hard to drive through, where it hasn't been cleared. I hope you keep reasonably warm. I drive to Mass through the untrodden snows of Hyde Park, which looks very beautiful. No: surely the difference between prose and poetry is a matter of *sound*, not of subject? No space to pursue this, or for anything but my love.

R. M.

20, Hinde House, Hinde St., W.1
5th February, 1955†

My dear Hamilton,

This can't be much of a letter, because I am deeply snowed under by jobs, including my piece that I have to write for the BBC "Critics", a programme of criticism of current shows (theatre, films, books, art, radio) which I have just gone on to again, after about a year. We meet on Thursdays for lunch and record our discussions, which are broadcast on the following

---

[1] William and Isadore Smith.

Sunday afternoon. I write a short script on radio, but we all discuss all the subjects, so have to see all the things. I am just in from a matinée of *Richard II* at the Old Vic and still have ahead before Thursday a film about escapes from German prison camps, some modern Italian pictures, and the reading of a book I don't particularly want to read. So my time gets pretty well filled up, and I get little for my novel. *Thank you so much* for yours dated 19th Jan. That was a fatal evening for me, for my car was stolen while I dined at the Athenaeum Club, and turned up next morning in a ditch outside Peterborough, after having been used in the night for "several serious crimes," the police say. Unfortunately the criminals had vanished. So my poor car is still in Peterboro' being repaired, while I ride perilously (and coldly) about London on the old bicycle I used during the war. Traffic seems thicker now. However, I am acquiring skill and expertise in the art. It is nice between 8 [and] 9 a.m. when I ride to Mass either at Gros. Chap. or St Paul's, and get back before the traffic is really thick. And I can ride nicely to the London Lib[rary], which is a route with two one-way streets. All right too at week-ends, and in the evenings. My main trouble is the wind! But I am quite enjoying it, tho' it will be nice to be lazy in my car again soon.

I am interested in your comparison of Evang[elical] and Cath[olic] religion, one basing itself on subjective experience, the other on sacramental life, which seems utterly true. How lucky I am to be in the second, "well in." I am sending you a *Tablet* review of *The Great Prayer*, by Hugh Ross Williamson (still just an Anglican . .). Surely he goes too far in his claims for what Anglicans all believe! You won't get this for some time, of course. All this R.C. harping on "authority" seems so narrow; they seem to look at religion in blinkers. And it is characteristically unfair to say that 400 years of protestantism have given us an "irrational prejudice against the teachings of Christ and his Church." It is this tendency to rule out Protestants (including Anglicans) from the Church of Christ that is so tiresome and silly. And imagine saying that *Quakers* are prejudiced against "the teachings of Christ"! I should say they know much [more] about these than most R.C.s do.[1] But I do think that in many quarters there is a growing tolerance and willingness to admit the Christianity of non-Romans, and willingness to co-operate with them in humane works. There is the very broadminded type represented by my friends the Brothers Mathew, for instance, of whom Lady Violet Bonham Carter says that the Bishop is "the only free-minded R.C." she knows. I know several more myself, actually—though "free" isn't perhaps quite the right word. . . .

No more room! But my love.

R. M.

20, *Hinde House, Hinde St., W.*1
20*th February*, 1955†

My dear Hamilton,

Thank you so much for yours of the 10th. It is good of you to write, and to answer my letters so splendidly, even when perhaps you don't feel like writing but more like book-binding, a state of mind I can so well understand. Last night I felt so little like doing any writing work that I decided I must instead change the linoleum cover of my large kitchen table; so I moved everything off it, stripped off the blue lino I had had there for some years, replaced it with a fine scarlet one that I had ready for it (after scrubbing the table), washed and put back on it all the crockery, tins of rice and sugar, etc., polished the lino with lavender polish, and now it looks so smart and smells so nice. This was really because on Shrove Tuesday I am having a little cocktail party, the last gaiety I shall have of

[1] R. M.'s comments on Roman Catholic attitudes relate to opinions expressed by the reviewer of *The Great Prayer*, see *The Tablet*, 5th February, 1955.

that kind till after Easter. So I must tidy up the living-room and bedroom too, get out and wash my glasses, provide enough to drink, and generally abandon books and devote myself to worldly and social joys. This party will be *after* I go for shriving to St Paul's, so it will be a mixed day. I went to St Paul's this morning for Mass; Fr Henderson preached the best Lent sermon I have ever heard. He really is an inspiring person. ... I go to Mass through snow and ice (shocking weather has returned!) on my admirable bicycle, car being still under repair. I find a bicycle slips less on iced roads than one's feet do, and feels quite safe, so don't worry about that. And one gets quite used to the traffic. Still, I shall be glad to get the car back! Your remark about being sacrificed by Druids made me laugh. Actually, one's bicycle used to be stolen sometimes over half a century ago; and one was thrown off it, and from ponies, and fell from trees, and was all but drowned, and people were robbed and assaulted ... no, we weren't secure, even in the 1890s. The fact is, this is a dangerous planet; perhaps all planets are? But a rather nice one, all the same; I shall miss it when I have to leave it. Yes, you are right; I *am* wasting my time over these "Critics" plays and films. It is nearly over now; in Lent I shall settle to my book firmly and renounce the world, which will be a good thing.

I must look at Overton & Relton.[1] That Bish. John Conybeare was my great-great-great-great-(or was it 5 greats?) grandfather.[2] I have his *Defence of Revealed Religion*. He was one of an unbroken line of Conybeare clergy down to my mother's brother[3] (who later turned R.C. however) and *his* son, my cousin James,[4] who was Provost of Southwell and is now retired, but actively helping in the parishes round Oxon.

[1] J. Overton and F. Relton, *The English Church from the Accession of George I to the End of the Eighteenth Century (1714-1800)* (1906).

[2] John Conybeare (1692-1755), Bp of Bristol, was R. M.'s great-great-great-grandfather; see genealogy of R. M. in *Letters to a Friend*.

[3] Rev. J. W. Edward Conybeare (1843-1931).

[4] Very Rev. W. James Conybeare (1871-1955).

(He wrote a little book I once sent you, *Here's a Church*.)[1]
Several of these Conybeare priests were more or less distinguished; one was professor of Anglo-Saxon at Oxford in the 18th century and very learned.[2] The Bishop of Bristol was a great controversialist, and was always at odds with Thomas Hearne the antiquary. I am glad Overton & R[elton] approve of him. The line of priests of that *name* is broken now, but not the line of succession in blood, as two of my uncle's grandsons are in Orders, but their name is McCormick, their mother having married the one-time Dean of Manchester of that name.[3] ...

You kindly ask questions about the car situation. (How I value your never failing sympathy, by the way!) I hope to get it back in a week or two. I pay nothing, all being covered by insurance; except [for] a little work I am having done on it which needed doing before it was stolen. It will be made quite safe and sound again. I shall feel happy in it when I have used bell, book and candle in it to exorcise the spirits of those bad men. ... I do look forward to having it back. It will be driven from Peterbro' by someone from the garage there. So all will end well. ... I do hope you keep well?

My love,
R. M.

20, *Hinde House, Hinde St., W.*1
8th March, 1955†

My dear Hamilton,
Thank you for yours posted 28th Feb. I'm sorry you have no Max Beerbohm in your library. He is one of my very

[1] W. J. Conybeare, *Here's a Church—Let's Go In* (1946).
[2] Rev. John J. Conybeare (1779-1829).
[3] R. M.'s first cousin Alison Conybeare m. Very Rev. J. G. McCormick (1874-1924); their two sons being Canon J. C. McCormick (1906-1960) and Rev. M. E. McCormick (b. 1909).

favourite writers. His urbane irony and humour, his exquisite mannered style, his particular slant on his environment, are so endearingly charming. I have always loved him. I used, some 20 and 30 years ago, to see him in London sometimes; but now he never comes, he lives wholly at Rapallo. He is, of course, in his 80s now. But from time to time he gives a delightful talk on the wireless. There is no one quite like him; after reading him, almost every one else seems coarse. . . . Lately I have been reading Elizabeth Bowen's new novel *A World of Love*. It is rather fascinating, though not to every one. I reviewed it in two columns of *The Times* (not the *Literary Sup.*, that was by someone else, who liked the book much less than I did). By the way, I wonder why you say the critics "don't like me?" I should have said I got quite my fair share of praise from them, and in the *Lit. Sup.* I am fairly often mentioned in general literary articles, besides getting nice long reviews when I publish a new book. Sometimes, of course, I write an article there myself, and in that I naturally am not mentioned! I don't think any of my literary colleagues would agree with you that I am unfairly treated; I sometimes think I get *more* than my fair share of appreciation. Though naturally not every one likes my books, nor any one else's for that matter. Ivy Compton-Burnett is a writer I don't think you would care for. I find her entertaining and sometimes brilliant; but her novels are certainly odd, and often awkwardly written. Is she praised in American papers? I wonder if the fact that I haven't for some time myself published a book in America, and therefore haven't been in the public eye there, has made you think this is also so in England. But it really isn't.

Yes, G. M. Young's *Victorian England* is excellent.[1] Though I can't remember if it is EARLY *Victorian England* that I am thinking of. But possibly he has added on to it and made it

[1] G. M. Young, *Victorian England: Portrait of an Age* (1936; 2nd ed., 1953).

all one book now?[1] Anyhow, he is v.g. A very intelligent, civilized mind. Is it a Penguin?

Yes, my Shrove Tuesday party was quite fun. About 14 people, all of whom are my near friends. Goodness, how I shall miss my dear, amusing, intelligent, friendly, affectionate circle of friends when I have to leave them. Whatever "social joys are there", these won't be—or most of them won't, for some little time, I suppose. The day before my party, I got shriven . . . [and] Fr Henderson is . . . giving some good Lent addresses . . . So my religion is being kept together, more or less . . . and mostly by daily Mass. . . . I am very much interested just now in "character", and how each moment and each thought builds it up. I have been reading a little book by Bishop Austin Pardue, Bp of Pittsburgh, which is partly on this subject. He says a lot of sensible things. His little book (1952) is called *A new and contrite heart*.[2] I wonder what you would think of it. Some of it is rather too American for me. But he has the right angle. Oh yes, the C. of E. is a far better business now than a century ago. I don't think that, if I had left it in those days, I should ever have returned; perhaps one would have, if urgently minded for some Church, have gone Roman: but I couldn't have been happy or honest in that for long. . . . So I should no doubt have remained an unsatisfied agnostic. And now, here we are, with all this at hand. Tough going at times; but always a visible path, if at times obscured. I wish someone would write a long, really long, religious poem, that one could read bits of when one felt like it. There is David Jones's *Anathemata*, but it is rather confused and scrappy and too obscure.[3] And Eliot's *Ash Wednesday*, and his *Four Quartets*; but again they are rather twisted and obscure for easy reading, say in bed at night. This is my last week of the "Critics," I am

[1] *Early Victorian England*, edited by G. M. Young (2 vols., 1934), contained an editorial essay which formed the basis for *Victorian England*.

[2] Austin Pardue, *New and Contrite Hearts* (New York, 1952; London, 1953).

[3] David Jones, *The Anathemata; Fragments of an Attempted Writing* (1952).

rather glad to say. My car is still in Peterbro', and I am home-sick for it. Snow still falls. What a winter! But my love always.

R. M.

20, Hinde House, Hinde St., W.1
5th April, 1955†

My dear Hamilton,

I have been a long time answering your interesting letter of 13th and 14th March, partly because I have been more than usual busy. . . .

We are now arrived in mid-Holy Week, which I am keeping at St Paul's; we are having some good addresses there from the Provost of Southwark,[1] also Fr Henderson at mid-day. I feel a little mean about the dear Chapel, but there it is. Meanwhile, in the intervals of devotions, I am busy with my novel; now that I am off the "Critics" I have much more time and attention to give it, and am quite enjoying myself.

I don't recognise "where error is irreparable repentance is useless"[2] but hazard a guess that it is Gibbon, it has his anti-thetical rhythm, don't you think? G. M. Young would be looking at him as a master of history when he wrote that about "the greatest of our masters." But I may be quite wrong about this; if I come on it, or on any one who knows it, I'll let you know. Not a good slogan for this week, I feel, which should be spent partly in repenting one's irreparable, as well as reparable, errors.

It has been an odd week otherwise; Churchill resigning in the hush created by the cessation of newspapers;[3] but every

[1] Very Rev. H. E. Ashdown.
[2] See G. M. Young's Introduction to *Victorian England.*
[3] Winston Churchill resigned the Premiership on 5th April, 1955; this was during a newspaper strike.

one knew of it, and crowded Whitehall last night to cheer him, and besieged 10 Downing Street when he appeared at the door to welcome the Queen to dinner. I heard all about that dinner afterwards from Randolph Churchill, who turned up at eleven p.m. at the house where I was dining, and gave a very lively account. . . . The wireless gives more news than usual, there is also the *Manchester Guardian* (which I can't get), and the weeklies for comment.

I also met Evelyn Waugh last night at dinner . . . I don't think his writing will ever be what it was in his brilliant and unregenerate youth; his conversion did him no literary good, however spiritually improving. I hadn't seen him for some years, and he accused me of agnosticism; I was able to retort that I was now a practising Anglican and went daily to Mass, which is, I suspect, more than he does. . . . Of course you are right in your diagnosis of the wholesale attitude R.C.s have towards their religion; though there will always be some few who, like Von Hügel and Acton and Tyrrell, can't believe certain doctrines.

I have been reading Phillips Brooks's sermons and addresses; do you know them, I wonder?[1] I like them; though they seem to belong to a different and perhaps outdated religious world, on the whole.

Well, here we are nearly at Easter: Good Friday to-morrow (time having moved on since I began this letter) so it is too late to send Easter greetings, which, however, I belatedly do. It seems likely to be as chilly and occasionally rainy as usual here. I'm not going away anywhere. . . . Evelyn Waugh says the next Pope may be a Chinese! That would be very impressive; they look so wise, one could almost accept their infallibility when they said " Me speakee *ex cathedra*". . . .

A new curate (middle-aged or elderly and an ex-missionary from New Guinea) has just arrived at St Paul's to help for a

[1] Phillips Brooks (1835-1893), Bp of Massachusetts, published several volumes of sermons.

time—one Canon Benson. When someone introduced us, he at once broke out into pleasure about *Told by an Idiot* and other of my novels which it seems are read by New Guinea missionaries, which surprised and pleased me. To-morrow I shall attend the Three Hours at Holy Trinity, Clapham Common, where my evangelical Macaulay relatives used to worship 150 years ago (Zachary, I mean). It seems to have gone Higher now than he would have cared for! Fr Henderson is taking it.

My love for Easter.

R. M.

20, *Hinde House, Hinde St., W.*1

30th April, 1955† *(Feast of Sta Caterina da Siena)*

My dear Hamilton,

I was very sorry to hear in your Easter Sunday and Monday letter than you hadn't been well, and still weren't. I have been bothering about that a good deal, and hoping you were better, and weren't trying to do too much. Perhaps it is better now that Holy Week and Easter are over.

I didn't tell you the glad news that my car is back, greatly furbished up and refreshed by the repairers in Peterborough who had it in hand for so long; they not only repaired the damage done by the thieves who finally flung it into a ditch, but the small dents and scrapes on the paint made in the course of ordinary wear and tear; so it looks better and goes better than for a long time past. So, except for making me bicycle about in the arctic winter for two months, the criminals did me a service. I must say it is nice to have it again, and get about in it so snugly—if "get about" can be used for the incredibly jammed-up driving we do in central London. Now, with this railway strike beginning to-morrow (Sunday) night, even more people will bring their cars up to London, and the confusion will be worse. I don't use mine much in central London except in the quiet hours of morning and evening (comparatively quiet, that is) and during week-ends. Of course I do use it sometimes, I have to. But in many cases walking is quicker. . . .

Meanwhile I am writing at my novel, which I think is rather foolish and frivolous, but I like doing it; it is very restful after the toil of *Ruins*. I am not going far afield this summer, so shall have the more time. Only short visits; of which one is a week at a Butlin's Camp at Skegness with my two little girls (13 and 11) at end of August. They look forward to this enormously. There [are] any number of juvenile amusements; Jane wants to ride all the time, and Mary Anne to swim and dive, and of course they will play all kinds of games. For my part, I shall swim, and walk about outside the camp (though I believe Skegness is frightful). . . . I shall drive them there through Cambridge, and stop an hour there to show them a few colleges and the Backs. They are nice intelligent vivacious children. . . .

We have Billy Graham here again. Just now in Scotland, but re-laid into many English churches and (particularly) chapels, and apparently doing good to many people. By the way, what do *you* feel about the Church of South India? Such a fuss going on in *The Tablet* about it! I must tell you later. Nothing now but my love.

R. M.

20, *Hinde House, Hinde St., W.*1
9th *June* (*Corpus Christi*), 1955†

My dear Hamilton,
Turning up a letter of yours posted 5th May, I am reminded, to my vexation, that I meant to write to you for your birthday on 2nd June, but never did, having been circumvented by a number of hindrances in the race set before me, and forgot it

till too late. I am sorry about that. But I now send my belated love for that day; I could wish that you had had a letter from me on it to wish you happy returns and a good year, but better late than never. In your letter you say you are recovered, or nearly, from your illness; I hope that goes on. Thank you for your letter and for saying in it that you keep me in mind in your prayers, which I like to be, and feel it is a great support and encouragement.

I have been, and am, very busy with my book and other things. I am not going abroad this summer, or on any other long holiday, as I must work at this book till it is done. I feel I could approach it with more vivacity if we could have a little summer; but that seems to be a thing of the past in this grey and cold land. This is Fr Henderson's last week here; he is being bishoped[1] on Saturday, 11th June, in St Paul's [Cathedral]. I have been given a seat in a Canon's closet, which I am told gives a good view. I have never seen a consecration. It will be an interesting ceremony. We subscribed to give Fr H. a cope, crozier, rochet and two mitres. All these episcopal garments are terrific in price, and I think it is a shame they aren't officially bestowed; many a poor bishop must be ruined by it, and gaiters too, etc. Fr H. takes his last Mass in our church to-morrow. How we shall miss him! . . . I shall probably go oftener than lately to Grosvenor Chapel. . . .

I met a young German this afternoon outside the Church of the Annunciation, [Bryanston Street,] who asked me when they had their evening Mass there. I said they didn't and asked if what he wanted wasn't a Roman church, and of course it was. He was surprised that the Annunc. church wasn't Roman; he could see no difference. He truly said that it was not at all like St Paul's or the Abbey, which he had lately seen. I had some difficulty in explaining that they were all C. of E. I can't think why the 1928 P[rayer] B[ook] didn't include a service for

[1] Consecrated Suffragan Bishop of Tewkesbury.

Corpus Christi, by the way.[1] One could easily compile one, out of all the many Eucharistic prayers and *Secreta* of the Missal. Or, of course, just take over the service as in the Missal, which is good. I'm not sure, as between the Latin and Eng[lish] versions of Easter 4; both have advantages, don't you think? I like "the unruly wills and affections" rather.[2] I must read that *Life* of Gore.[3] He was a truly venerable man. Did I tell you that in May I went to the funeral of my old cousin W. J. Conybeare, late Provost of Southwell, who died in his Oxfordshire retirement? It was a nice village churchyard funeral and family gathering; full of Conybeares, McCormicks, Macaulays. Now I must go and get my car out. My love always,

R. M.

20, *Hinde House, Hinde St., W.*1
26th June, 1955†

My dear Hamilton,

Your letter posted 7th June did, as you say, cross mine; and now I have the one posted 22nd, so I have *two* good letters in hand, which is lovely. I ought not to write to you this week, however, as you are in Retreat; but you can lay it by unopened till it is over.

To answer first your point about "very"; surely never rightly with a verb, unless the verb (like "tired") has become practically an adjective. Of course there are some border cases (is "hurt" one of these—in its mental, not physical, sense?) but I'm sure never with disappointed, pleased, surprised, occupied, etc., etc. I mean of course people use it all the time, but not

[1] Two Collects and the Epistle and Gospel for the Feast of Corpus Christi are included (inconspicuously) in the 1928 Prayer Book, with those for the "Lesser Feasts and Fasts," under the heading "Thanksgiving for the Institution of Holy Communion."

[2] See Collect for 4th Sunday after Easter.

[3] Presumably G. L. Prestige's *Life of Charles Gore* (1935).

rightly, and it is jarring, don't you think? I don't think one can make hard and fast rules about it; it is a question of what *sounds* wrong to educated ears. One can say "very tired," but not "very exhausted," I suppose because of "tired" having become an adjective. Well, I don't know. I looked up the Latin Trinity collect.[1] I think our English one loses force by "keep us stedfast in this faith and evermore defend us from all adversities"; I prefer "that by stedfastness in the faith we may be defended," and am interested in your idea that it may mean the stability of the faith itself, not our firmness in holding it. I would translate "*ab omnibus adversis*" "from all that is against us," and you suggest "all that conflicts with the faith"; anyhow I don't think "from all adversities" is good; after all, adversities means only misfortunes, and loses the sense of contrary and hostile things which fight against us—a sense which "adversities" didn't carry even in the 16th cent.

Yes, I do like to examine these Latin prayers and get their meaning. It was one of the many good things that you first put me on to. I don't *think* I read Geoffrey Faber's *Oxford Apostles* when it came out, but I may have and forgotten.[2] Anyhow, I will get the Penguin. I know G. F.; he is a red-faced man of business (publishing) externally, but writes excellently, and knows a great deal about the Tractarians, of course.

Since I wrote to you last I had a week-end at Cambridge (in fact, last week-end) and dined at the High Table at King's,[3] which I always like, as I know several of them still, and they all (except the quite young ones) knew and loved my dear uncle the Vice-Provost.[4] . . .

I had such a nice letter from a stranger who wrote to me

[1] Collect for Trinity Sunday.

[2] Geoffrey Faber, *Oxford Apostles* (1933).

[3] "Ladies' Night" is an annual institution at King's College, Cambridge, which was started shortly after World War II. Each Fellow of the College is allowed to invite a lady to dine at the High Table.

[4] W. H. Macaulay (1853-1936).

before about *Ruins*, and has now read *The World My Wilderness* and likes it. I have a few oddments I might send you in a sea envelope, and will put this in (do not return). There are also two letters out of a somewhat odd and acrimonious correspondence in *The Tablet* about Anglicans and R.C.s; Peter Anson (now R.C. of course) writes enclosing quotations from an Anglican Religious friend to him;[1] . . . I wondered if I should cut out and send you a poem by me in the *Times Lit. Sup.* last number,[2] but remembered that you don't care for my poetry, so didn't.

I read David Cecil's Melbourne[3] with great pleasure, but it's less fascinating than *The Young Melbourne*, which he wrote 20 years ago. This is a really superb description of the Whig society of the late 18th century, and of the personalities in it. The new volume hasn't the same charm, I think; perhaps its period hasn't. I didn't feel, though, that he was unjustifiably novelistic about Melbourne. But I don't think I really felt this about his *Stricken Deer*,[4] either, tho' I dare say your grandfathers, who knew Cowper (or anyhow knew all about him from others), would think so. I have just read a very interesting pseudo-memoirs of the Emperor Hadrian;[5] fascinating in its knowledge of the 2nd century Roman Empire, as well as a brilliant reconstruction of Hadrian himself. I think you would be interested in this. It is translated from the French. . . .

By the way, Fr Derry is *such* a nice, human, humorous person.[6] I like him better and better. He came in here for

---

[1] See *The Tablet*, 18th June, 1955.
[2] " Dirge for Trebizond," see *The Times Literary Supplement*, 24th June, 1955.
[3] *Lord M.* (1954).   [4] *The Stricken Deer; or the Life of Cowper* (1929).
[5] Marguérite Yourcenar, *Memoirs of Hadrian* (trans. Grace Frick, 1955).
[6] Rev. W. R. Derry, Curate-in-charge of Grosvenor Chapel and Warden of Liddon House (an Anglican centre for graduates and young professional men and women, founded in Kensington in 1907 and later attached to Grosvenor Chapel).

sherry the other day, alone, and we had an interesting talk about the work he is doing for young people at Liddon House —discussions, debates, addresses, etc. I have promised to speak to them. My love, and thank you for everything. You do uphold me so much.

Yours,
R. M.

20, Hinde House, Hinde St., W.1
27th June, 1955

My dear Hamilton,

Here are the oddments I said I would send you in a sea letter. I have just stuck up the air letter. It is Sunday evening, and I am staying in, writing letters and now going to get on with my novel. It has been a really lovely summer day—most unusual this year—and it seems [a] waste not to be out and about in it, but I can't spare the time. And I won't add to this, except to send my love again. I hope you are having a good Retreat. . . .

My love always,
R. M.

20, Hinde House, Hinde St., W. 1
20th August, 1955†

My dear Hamilton,

Your letter of 15th Aug. filled me with shame that I have omitted to answer the one of 4th July, which has been lying on my writing-table ever since I got it, waiting reply. Again and again I had it in mind to write, but was always prevented. I have been working very hard on my book while at home, and also have done a certain amount of going away, though much less so than usual in the summer; that is, I haven't been abroad, or on any long visit anywhere. On the 27th till 3rd Sept. I go to Butlin's camp at Skegness with my two little girls, and am rather looking forward to it, though it does sound most odd! I will tell you more about it after I have been there. I know we are woken each morning by a reveille and a singing of "Lads and Lasses, get up to play", or something similar, then every one queues up for lavatories, etc., labelled "Lads" or "Lasses" (I mean the lavatories are labelled, not the lads and lasses); but if we like we can plunge into the swimming-pool instead, if weather permits. Then I suppose breakfast, and at 8.30 there seems to be "church", whatever that may mean; if it is Mass, after breakfast would be an odd time for it, one would think; but I believe all these camps have a church and a parson attached; I dare say it is a nice paid holiday for the parson, and really quite a good opening for him to get into touch with the campers. Then follows the day, with not a dull (or quiet) moment, what with bathing, games, physical exercises, riding for those who like it (as my younger charge does), as well as cinemas, television, dancing, concerts, etc. Perhaps there may be an Old Folks' Corner, where I shall sit sometimes and scribble away at my novel and take notes of the camp life, which might turn into an article perhaps. Well, I think a week will be quite enough, but I shall enjoy it, and the children will love it.

Your letter of July 4 was very interesting. What you say about the variety of practices allowed in the C. of E., as compared with the R.C. [Church], brings to my mind a conversation I had the other day with . . . [a Roman Catholic friend of mine]. She (who was till 25 years ago a devout Anglo-Catholic) says that her "cradle Catholic" friends tell her often that they are completely puzzled by the C. of E., which they gather has quite different practices and even beliefs, in different churches; and quite different in many cases from their practices of 60 or 70 years ago. They think this extraordinary, and she can't explain it to them, how it happens, well tho' she understands it herself. I personally think it all to the good, as giving something for every one, however different their minds, backgrounds, and religious temperaments. She and I were comparing our own differences in belief which are very considerable. Then we got on to discussing the question of R.C. "fundamentalism" about the Bible. They do seem committed to this in theory, as much as the Evangelical Grahamites are, but I think the more scholarly and educated ones are trying to extricate themselves without loss of face (I'm so glad we Anglicans don't mind losing "face" about such things) from the impossible position defined in *Providentissimus Deus*[1] and *Lamentabili*,[2] and shown by their expulsion of their Modernist scholars during the early years of this century.[3] This question of fundamentalism is being discussed just now in the *Times* correspondence, apropos of Billy Graham's mission to Cambridge next term, which is got up by C.I.C.C.U.[4] and rather deplored by the University scholars, as "stifling the mind" and alienating many young men and women from religion by presenting absurdities to them. Of course C.I.C.C.U. and O.I.C.C.U., in the two universities, have always been rather of that way of thinking. Did O.I.C.C.U. flourish when you were up?

Another discussion (this time in *The Tablet*) has been raging about the R.C. pronunciation of "Mass," and the way many of them say "Mahss," and why. I think myself it is of Irish derivation; but some R.C. critics complain that it is used sometimes [as] a snob gesture by converts. I find it useful, as I know by that, and by the dropping of "Roman" from

[1] A Papal Encyclical issued in 1893, asserting that the whole of Scripture was written "at the dictation of the Holy Ghost."

[2] A Papal decree issued in 1907 condemning propositions derived from contemporary Modernist teaching.

[3] Clergy who had been identified with Modernism were mostly excommunicated.

[4] The Cambridge Inter-Collegiate Christian Union.

"Roman Catholic," when my acquaintances have suffered conversion. Besides, I rather like these distinctions.

Later. Shocked by news at 1 o'clock of that horrid "Diane"[1] (?) who, it seems, has swept the coast from Virginia to Mass. But how far up Mass.? I wish I knew. Perhaps we shall hear more later. I do hope not near Cambridge, and that the whole thing wasn't terribly disturbing and distressing for you.

To change the subject, did you ever read *Eleanor*, a novel (1906, I think) by Mrs Humphry Ward? I never did till the other day, and I must say I found it unexpectedly interesting. Partly about Italy, the conflict bet[ween] the old Papal Italy and the post-1870 Italy, and the views on this taken by the Englishman who is the chief character and by his Italian acquaintances, all very well done. There is also the human story, about Eleanor, who loved this man and had to fight her jealousy and misery because he fell in love with a young American girl; all her conflict and struggle and final moral victory (Eleanor's, I mean) is very well described; so is the old excommunicated priest-scholar who helped her. I found it all very vivid and good, and even beautiful, and wish you could get hold of it. I must see if I can find a copy in some second-hand bookshop. I think better of Mrs H. W. than I did before.

We are having some more hot weather; I adore it. I bathed in the Serp. this morning after St Paul's Mass, and it was most lovely. I remember beginning this practice, and writing to you of it, in June '51.[2] This is the first hot summer since then (or anyhow when I was in England). I am most anxious to know about the exploits of "Diane," and hope the BBC will be more explicit in its accounts later to-day. I keep thinking about you and her! Much love and anxious thoughts.

Rose.

[1] A hurricane.
[2] See *Letters to a Friend*, p. 134.

My dear Hamilton,

I meant to write before, in answer to yours of 30 Aug. but have been first at Butlin's (!) ... and then in Worcs. for a wedding, and in the spaces in between feverishly writing away at the novel (not *nearly* finished yet, alas).

That devil " Diane," to have flooded your basement and destroyed so much valuable literature, vestments (or were these able to be dried?), and other things; and, worse, to have caused you all that shock and distress. I have been thinking of you with anxiety. The only consolation is that it could have been worse, as it was in those other places, that were flooded and blown to pieces with so much loss of property and lives; it was terrible. I am thankful that " Edith " was comparatively harmless in your parts. And since then there have been others of the dreadful sisterhood; where did " Ione " pass your shores, and what of " Janet "? Alistair Cooke (who gives us a weekly Letter from America on the BBC) says the reason why we used not to hear so much about these creatures is that American news has grown more important since America's growth in world power; but this seems to me to be an improbable reason. Surely they *are* worse?

And now Eisenhower seems in danger.[1] I hope he won't die; it would be sad, I think.

Butlin's was quite fun; rather like a visit to the moon, quite out of this world. Absurd, of course, for an adult, but having the two children made it fun; they loved every minute of it. One unexpected thing was the little camp church, Anglican, with a chaplain of great geniality to one and all; Mass every day at 7.30 and 8.30, to which I went (at 8.30), and it was very well attended. A radio voice announced each morning at 7.29,

---

[1] President Eisenhower had suffered a heart attack on 24th September, 1955.

" In one minute there will be a celebration of Holy Communion in the camp church." Disgusted and sleepy voice from the chalet on my left, " *What* an entertainment! " We all slept in nice little chalets in a row, or rather in many rows, for there were about 500 campers at a time. We had swimming pools (but I bathed in the sea myself) and every kind of game and diversion, and my younger charge, who is pony-mad, rode every day and helped to groom the horses. There was a repertory company, which acted exciting dramas, and television, which I saw for the first time and didn't think much of. Why is it so popular? One programme, which showed a panel of 4 famous people in a game of guessing " Who wrote that? " to my surprise quoted something from me (but I don't know where I said it)—something about "it is to the eccentrics that the world owes most of its knowledge"; no one guessed me; when they were told, they had to discuss its truth or otherwise, and on the whole agreed with me. My two children were delighted by this. . . . By the way, on the way back (in the car) from Skegness, we turned aside to look at Yaxley church and village (Hunts). I wondered if that was *your* Yaxley, or is yours the one in Suffolk?[1] It was a beautiful old church. There was no list of vicars, so I couldn't look for "Johnson." But I expect yours is Suffolk. However, I plucked a little flower from the graveyard and thought of you. . . .

I am still being bombarded with little Catholic Truth pamphlets, and long letters telling how I have no Mass, no sacraments, no priests. How rude they are! Imagine if I started writing in that vein to, say, Methodists. They are so stuck up and arrogant. Of course nothing *could* be so true as they think their Church is. . . . I answered one of these priests who write to me that I thought Christians should tolerate one another's religions, and I was glad *they* had sacraments and thought they ought to be glad that I thought *I* had. The

[1] R. M. has confused Yaxley with Yaxham in Norfolk, where the Johnsons had a family living.

chaplain at Butlin's welcomed everyone to Communion—
Church, Chapel, or whatever—though he was definitely
Anglo-Catholic in his rites. That's the Christian spirit, surely.
Imagine what our Lord would have said. My love always and
I hope you are well and not bothered by hurricanes.

R. M.

20, Hinde House, Hinde St., W.1
18th November, 1955†

My dear Hamilton,

Your letter begun 10th Nov. came to-day, just when I had
it in mind to answer, much too late, the one of 1st Oct. That
one has been lying by me to be answered for some time and
I even took it away with me to Pleshey[1] last week when I went
there for Fr Henderson's very good Retreat,[2] but I didn't get
time there for letters actually. In the free time, which was all
the afternoon from lunch to tea, I walked out and saw the
country, and picked berries in the lanes and fields. Do you
know Pleshey Retreat House, I wonder? You may even have
taken retreats there, I dare say. I was never there before.
Evelyn Underhill used to take retreats there, I think. It is a
nice place; I like its atmosphere. And the addresses couldn't
have been better. . . . But what I was saying was that I really
was about to write to you when your letter came to-day. Only
extreme busy-ness has kept me from it, as from much else.
Yes, I suppose we do have to write rather less often than once;
this doesn't mean that I value your letters, or like to write
myself, any less, but merely that so much else obstructs and
takes one's time. I have kept all your letters from the beginning; and goodness, what I owe to them! No one can ever
have had such letters. Your patience with me, your making

---

[1] The House of Retreat at Pleshey, near Chelmsford.
[2] He was then Bp of Tewkesbury.

clear to me so much that was obscure or that I had never
thought of, your bringing me into touch with the Church, with
the sacraments, with the whole marvel of reconciliation and the
newness of this new life in which I have tried to live, however
faultily, for nearly 5 years now—well, I don't need to tell you
all this, for you know it. It has been the most wonderful
ministry of letters that ever was. And so much else, in the way
of interest you [have] provided—literary, historical, autobiographical, etc. What I want is that both of us should write
whenever we feel like it, and I hope we often shall. I should
miss it terribly if it stopped. One great thing you introduced
me to and made me familiar with was the Roman missal and
its prayers; so many of these have got into my private prayer-
book and are part of my daily prayers at Mass. . . .

[A friend of mine] came to tea to-day, to meet E. M.
Forster, who has always been a great hero of his. E. M. F. was
telling us about Billy Graham's recent mission at Cambridge,
which of course is little to his liking, tho' when he met him
he thought him a nice, simple, friendly person, not "civilised,"
but "a good type". B. G.'s success is largely, of course, among
[members of] C.I.C.C.U., who are a very strong party in the
University. E. M. F. thinks B. G. much nicer and more
tolerant than they are. With his agnostic views, he of course
laments the strong religious trend just now in Cambridge. . . .

Do you know Newman's *Via Media*? I am reading the
3rd edition,[1] which is in one way rather sad; published, I think,
40 years after the first, and long after his conversion, and an-
notated from his present Roman standpoint; *i.e.* every anti-
Roman remark retracted and deplored; even his criticism of
the Inquisition's treatment of Galileo and the new Copernican
theories of the planetary movements is taken back; he says in
a note that of course such new theories, even tho' true, could
not be safely allowed, as they might confuse people's faith, and

[1] J. H. Newman, *The Via Media of the Anglican Church* (3rd ed., 2 vols.,
1877).

the Church was right to forbid them; he adds " I neither know, nor desire to know, by what methods this was done "—which is very insincere, as he knew quite well of course that people who affirmed them were burnt alive.[1] The whole re-issue of this book is pathetic and sad. But I like a lot of the book itself. I never got through the *Glastonbury Romance*,[2] but have always thought I sometimes would, when I have more time. I am just now reading in bed an account by Winifred Peck (born Knox) of her childhood with her brothers and father;[3] the 4 boys were all brilliant: Ronnie (at 4 years old composing remarkable limericks, etc.), E. V., the eldest [and] the wit and leader of the family, then Dillwyn, the King's classical scholar, and Wilfred, the Anglo-Catholic; strange progeny of the Protestant Ulster Bishop. It is a very pleasant account of a childhood in the 80s and 90s. I have just got from Bp David Mathew his new book on Charles I and Scotland;[4] very scholarly and detailed, and dedicated to me, "in memory of a long friendship," which is nice. No room now for more, I see. I am still struggling to finish the novel; shortage of time is acute, and will wreck my life and all my undertakings. I should like to have time for geology and cosmology—perhaps one day I shall. Why *do* we pray that "they [the faithful departed] may have rest?" Rest is *not* what we shall want, surely, but more scope for work and new knowledge.

Much love always.

R. M.

---

[1] Belief in the Heliocentric system was not alone regarded as a heresy to warrant burning.

[2] J. C. Powys, *A Glastonbury Romance* (1933).

[3] Winifred Peck, *Home for the Holidays* (1955).

[4] David Mathew, *Scotland under Charles I* (1955).

20, *Hinde House, Hinde St., W*.1
17th *December*, 1955†

My dear Hamilton,

I am writing to-day and posting to-morrow in the hopes of reaching you by Xmas, but I know this [is] chancey; I meant to write earlier, but have been laid up with prolonged flue, and for the last 10 days bronchitis, which is a bore. I am now getting about again, but not very energetically. . . .

This letter is really to thank you for yours of 1st Dec., and to wish you a happy Xmas. I loved your letter. It reminded me of all the things I have had from you through this rich 5 years. Without your guidance I should not have known all those missal prayers, and found all those riches in them—as you say, progressively, and as mood and occasion suggest. I was thinking how thin and dull and inadequate it would be to have had instead an *evangelical* re-conversion; not, I think, that this would ever have been possible for me, much as I admire our evangelical ancestors. But the material they have to feed on, their literary *entourage*, is so comparatively unsatisfying—except of course for the Bible. Not that they couldn't have access to everything, but they don't seem to much. But how good many of them used to be! And how lucky we have so much more that is attractive and valuable to our imaginations. I am interested in your cosmological and geological readings and thoughts. It is all so extraordinary, it makes me dizzy: goodness yes, *what* a drop-scene behind our animated, just beginning human lives, to be played out against all that gaseous tremendousness, of which our passions and aspirations are such odd and frail reflections. (Though this is not really putting it well, because we are of a higher order. Who would have thought that conscience would evolve from all that?) Are you interested in the discovery of the Dead Sea Scrolls, and have you seen Edmund Wilson's book about them?[1] I don't see,

[1] *The Scrolls from the Dead Sea* (1955).

213

do you, how Christ can have been an Essene; after all, his life was known to the Evangelists, and they must have mentioned it. I am being given Knox's complete Bible for Xmas, which I shall like to have, though it is a pity it should be based on such a comparatively poor text as the Vulgate. But he had the Greek and Hebrew in his mind, of course.[1] I already have the N[ew] T[estament]. The next thing will be the great translation now being worked on here, but we shall have to wait some years for that.[2] I wish we would revise our Gospels for the Day again. I do think it so stupid to have that "begat" Gospel they read on Dec. 12 at Mass. A bad day for it, too, as it is in honour of the B.V.M. and why must we hear at tremendous length of *Joseph's* descent from David?[3] Then I hate all those Gospels about the creatures with wings and eyes. I would much rather have instead some more Wisdom or Ecclesiasticus. I really do hate those fantastic creatures pictured in the heavens in Rev[elation] and in the O[ld] T[estament], they make me feel quite ill, and to bring God into them seems so irreverent. My mother used to tell us that poor St John was obviously feeling ill and delirious. I have been reading *On the Gods and the World*, by the Roman 4th C. pagan Sallustius; something of a Neoplatonist, and very attractive.[4] " When we are good, we are joined to the gods by our likeness to them : when bad, we are separated from them by our unlikeness. When we live according to virtue, we cling to the gods, and when we become evil we make the gods our enemies, not because they are angered against us, but because our sins prevent the light of the gods from shining upon us, and put us into communion with spirits of punishment. . . . To say that God turns away from

[1] R. A. Knox's Bible (1955) is stated, in the sub-title, to be "a translation from the Latin Vulgate in the Light of the Hebrew and Greek originals."

[2] *The New English Bible* (1961).

[3] R. M. probably means the Gospel for 7th December (not 12th), the Vigil of the Conception of the B.V.M., which is Matt. 1. 1-16.

[4] See Gilbert Murray's translation of the treatise of Sallustius "On the Gods and the World" in his *Five Stages of Greek Religion* (1925).

evil men is like saying that the sun hides himself from the blind." Very like William Law, in parts. What he lacks, of course, is redemption, the seeking of man by God. But it is always so good to find the same golden divine thread running back and back through the ages; Christian, pagan, Hebrew, all part of the long gradual revelation, of which one hopes for and expects so much more as time goes on.

Someone has sent me for Xmas a nice little selection from 17th cent. sermons, made by G. Lacey May[1], with a little preface which is unfair to the puritans, though you know how little I like them! But he sees no good in any of their preaching, etc. Whereas Baxter,[2] Samuel Rutherford,[3] Chillingworth (during his puritan phase)[4] had so much that was good to say. He is too much of a Laudian, naturally. Without all these facets of truth, Christianity would be a less rich complex of ideas than it is.

I lunched yesterday with the brothers Mathew—both very interesting. I like David's book very much, and have just been including it in a 300-word contribution to the *Sunday Times* "Books of the Year." I did six books—3 history, 2 autobiography, one *Good Behaviour*, Harold Nicolson's pleasant study of civilizations.

Fr Harris[5] laments that he can't find more servers. What is the reason that women mayn't serve at Mass? If they could, he would have an abundance of willing helpers. It seems silly; women are neater-handed, and would actually serve better than inexperienced young men, surely. But there is a theory that they may not handle the vessels. I wonder why. I suppose it is the oriental basis of Christianity; and one feels that St Paul would not have liked the idea at all! On the other hand, one

[1] *Wings of an Eagle: An Anthology of Caroline Preachers, edited by G. Lacey May* (1955).
[2] Richard Baxter (1615-1691), Puritan divine.
[3] Samuel Rutherford (*c.* 1600-1661), Scottish Presbyterian divine.
[4] See above p. 188*n.*
[5] Rev. D. B. Harris, Vicar of St Paul's, Knightsbridge.

can imagine Our Lord saying that such distinctions were nonsense, and that [there] were neither male nor female in such matters. What a pity He didn't. But obviously there was no chance, and the orientalists had it their own way.

Well, my love for Xmas, and may you be well through it. I hope I shall be by the day, and fit for midnight Mass and Romford next day. This is my sixth Xmas letter to you. Thank you again for those 5 years.

Your affectionate

R. M.

1956

My dear Hamilton,

Now I have *two* good letters from you to answer, that of
31st Dec. written in answer to my Xmas one, and of 21st Jan.
which came to-day, a pleasing sight on my mat as I returned
from Mass at St Paul's. Yes, thank you, I am now quite
recovered from both pre-Xmas flue and post-Xmas bronchitis,
which detained me for a little while. I only now have the
slightest of coughs remaining, and am very vigorous in
pleasures and chores. Not even badly affected by our 5 days
of arctic weather which it seems was the coldest since 1895 and
which froze everyone's pipes and cars; but fortunately here
such visitations are usually short, and a blessed thaw arrived
last Saturday to melt us again. I do hope you didn't suffer
badly from it, but of course in your parts it is common form
each winter. Though I don't know that that makes it much
more bearable to the poor Anglican priests with licences to
practise their professions in a cold land.

Among what you describe as the "unordinary, time-taking
things" that occupied me lately was the finishing and despatching of my novel; Collins now have it, and are retyping it.
Mark Bonham Carter, the director there who is my friend . . .
likes it, I am glad to say. He read the beginning of it to his
mother (Lady Violet B. C.) and he said it made her laugh, also
him; he says he was also moved, so that is a good combination,
I suppose—laughter and being moved, I mean. I think some
people won't care about it much. I do *hope* you will! Its name
is *The Towers of Trebizond,* and Trebizond stands for not
merely the actual city (tho' this comes in, and a lovely place it
is) but for the ideal and romantic and nostalgic vision of the
Church which haunts the person who narrates the story. I
won't tell you more about it now, but shall send it you when
it comes, which probably won't be till September, as it takes

six months to print a book now, and July and August aren't good months. I am now catching up on arrears of articles, etc., and letters and much else, before starting to think about another novel; I think I shall write only novels in future, it seems less trouble, and if one stays out of novels for some years it is bad for one's sales. Yes, I saw that review of *Books for Schools*, I don't know who Norman Culpan is, or what his qualifications; I suppose he didn't think my novels suitable for the young, or perhaps just didn't think of them, owing to my not having written many lately.[1] Perhaps it's time I got on the fiction map again! As a matter of fact *They Were Defeated* used to [be] (perhaps is) recommended to Eng. Lit. students at Cambridge, I believe. I am reading some interesting books: James MacKinnon's *Historic Jesus*[2] (he was Regius Professor of Ecc[lesiastical] Hist[ory] at Edinburgh). It is v. learned, and interests me so far. Also I read a book by an Italian professor (trans.) about the "Cult of the Virgin Mary,"[3] tracing its gradual growth after the first few centuries, its sources (largely apocryphal gospels, of course), the resistance to it from various early Fathers, its extraordinary claims, based on no Gospel evidence of any kind, the reception by the different doctors of the Church of the Immac[ulate] Conception and Assumption—Aquinas very much against the I.C., also, I think, St Bernard. The Roman doctrine of the evolution of revealed truth is very dangerous; it means they can dispense with evidence and simply declare revelation to the Church whenever they choose. It is feared (by conservative R.C.s) that the next thing will be the declaration of Mary as sole mediatrix. If it is, they will have either to take it, or to leave the Church. I am very sorry for them. The Pope gets very unreliable. Gerard

[1] Norman Culpan (Lecturer and Librarian, County of Stafford Training College), in his booklet *Modern Adult Fiction for School and College Libraries* (School Library Assoc., 1955) does not mention any novels by R. M.

[2] James MacKinnon, *The Historic Jesus* (1931).

[3] Giovanni Miegge, *The Virgin Mary: The Roman Catholic Marian Doctrine* (trans. W. Smith, 1955).

Irvine was saying that two things hinder Anglicans going to Rome more than anything else—these fantastic pronouncements, made or feared, and the intolerant manners of R.C.s towards Anglicans, refusal to pray with us, etc. I certainly could never myself join a Church which wouldn't pray with other Christians.

I have been reading the Liturgy of South India, and a commentary on it, also an article about it by a French R.C. in *Theology*.[1] I might send you this number of *Theology*; I think it would interest you. The liturgy itself seems very good. Another thing I will send you is *Latin in Church*, which I got to send you before, but see it is still lying about.[2] I will try and post it in the next day or two. . . .

Fr Harris is the most cheerful and affable and sociable of people; he holds salons in the porch on Sunday evenings after church; getting to know people. . . . He seems to have arranged a busy Lent programme for us, too. To-morrow he is coming to lunch with me at my Club to meet a few friends of mine who are all anxious to induce the Church BBC Advisory Committee (headed by Cantuar)[3] to allow the television of High Anglican Masses in some of the times allotted to the C. of E. At present the R.C.s always put on a High Mass during their times, and the effect is enormous; many seem to be converted outright to Rome, having never seen anything like these services before. So John Betjeman and I think our Church too should be in on it, and we are persuading Sir G[eorge] Barnes, the Television head at present, and a very able King's man, to work for this. . . . Fr Harris is also coming, as I am hoping St Paul's may be one of the churches chosen, if we succeed. It has a very beautiful Mass and choir, and I don't see that it wouldn't convert as many people as Downside Mass

[1] Louis Bouyer, "A Roman Catholic View of the Church of South India," *Theology*, January 1956.

[2] F. Brittain, *Latin in Church* (1934; 2nd ed., 1955).

[3] The Chairman of the BBC's Central Religious Adv. Com. was then the Bp of Bristol (Rt. Rev. F. A. Cockin) not Archbishop Fisher.

does; it has what is to the large majority the advantage of being in a language they understand. Televiewers in this country are not on the whole an intellectual type. None of my friends have a set, but nearly all my sister's patients at Romford do, also my nice window-cleaner, in fact nearly everyone. Much love. I see there is no room for anything else! But what a lucky chance that you turned into that bookshop in 1950 and got my publisher's address!

Your affectionate

R. M.

20, *Hinde House, Hinde St., W.*1

7th May, 1956†

My dear Hamilton,

Your letter of 1st May came to-day, and I am shocked to learn that my last was as long ago as 6th Feb. I have [been] meaning to write, and have had yours of 5th March lying among my letters waiting to be answered. But, being much taken up with jobs, writing and others, I suppose I didn't answer it. And now I have another. I did indeed mean to write long ago, and don't know how it happened that I didn't. . . . Have you had Fr Huddleston's *Naught for Your Comfort*? I know he was touring America speaking about South Africa, so no doubt his book has also done well there. He is a delightful person; I have heard him more than once, and did so to-day at the Caxton Hall. He is certainly rousing the nation's conscience about South Africa, and is also much annoying the S.A. government. To-day the Community [of the Resurrection's] feast began with a High Mass at the Annunciation church, [Bryanston Street,] to which I went, invited by my C.R. cousin,[1] who is home on leave from South Africa, and knows Fr Huddleston well. He introduced me to him after Mass.

[1] Rev. C. Reginald Smith, c.r.

Then this evening there was this meeting. It is a tragic situation; people seem to think the C.R. missionaries will be all expelled from South Africa within a year or two. At present, the[ir] Johannesburg schools being all closed (I think), they are fighting to keep their Rhodesian ones going, and trying to raise enough money for this.

Don't think I am ill when I don't write. If I was dead, my sister would write and tell you; I have asked her to. But I shan't be dead! I have not had flu since March, and have been well and active, missing few morning Masses. I alternate for these between G. Chapel and St Paul's. . . . I like to know that you remember me at Mass; I feel I need it in these days.

I shall get Wilfred Knox's book from the library.[1] I used to see him sometimes at Cambridge, when he ran the Oratory (at least I think he was [Warden then]). He was a great influence among undergraduates.[2] I knew all the Knoxes: E. V., who is charming always, Wilfred, Dillwyn, of King's, who died long ago, and Ronald. Over 30 years ago, when Wilfred wrote that book, I suppose "the Catholic movement in the Church" was much less advanced than now. I see people in the C[hurch] Times are complaining that there are fewer confessions now, which surprises me rather.[3] I want to read W. Ward's *Life of Newman*.[4] The fact is there are so many books I want to read and can't get time to; but I will make a note of that one to ask for at the London Library next time I am in. I am reviewing for the *Times Literary Supplement* a little book called *The Saints and Ourselves* (series 2).[5] Not much

[1] *The Catholic Movement in the Church of England* (1923).

[2] Wilfred Knox (1887-1950) came to Cambridge in 1924 as Warden of the Oratory of the Good Shepherd, a society of prayer. In 1941 he became Chaplain of Pembroke College.

[3] See correspondence in the *Church Times*, " Fewer Penitents? " (13th April—4th May, 1956).

[4] Wilfrid Ward, *The Life of John Henry Newman* (2 vols., 1912).

[5] *Saints and Ourselves: Personal Studies*, edited by P. Caraman (2nd series, 1955).

in it; and I find these little studies of saints rather boring on the whole. They ought to have more *faults*. The Bible saints had plenty, and their historians don't try to smooth them over. The Apostles were all full of faults. But these medieval saints wear an air of pious perfection which makes them unreal. One always is told of their remarkable and invariable humility, till one longs for some of them to be stuck up for a change, or grasping and impertinent like John and James trying to grab the best seats in heaven, which was so natural, or cross and crotchety and impatient like St Paul, or disagreeable and bullying like St Jerome with his matrons, virgins and widows. A touch of original sin would certainly help to make these later saints more real.

I expect the proofs of my novel in a day or two; it is to come out in September. Meanwhile I am reading lots of books about the Greek islands, as I am probably going to some of them in August, together with Archbp and Fr Gervase Mathew, o.p., Sir Maurice Bowra, the Bp of Exeter,[1] etc. But if things get worse with the Greeks over Cyprus, I shan't go.

I shall be writing again about 25th May, so till then, my love. Do remain well, strong, young, and read a lot of interesting books to tell me about.

Your affectionate
R. M.

20, Hinde House, Hinde St., W.1
[Postmark: 26 May, 1956]†

My dear Hamilton,

This is the letter I said in my last that I meant shortly to write, in time for 2nd June, that auspicious day. Isn't it, besides your birthday (don't tell me *which* birthday, I don't want to know how the people I love are getting on, as I hope they will

[1] Rt. Rev. R. C. Mortimer.

live for ever here; anyhow, I know you, unlike some of my friends, such as dear Gilbert Murray, and Max Beerbohm who died the other day, are [one of the] happy and young septuagenarians, which to-day is nothing)—this sentence has now got a little lost, but what I was saying was, isn't it also the day you became a S.S.J.E. Father?[1] If so you have been one for well over half a century, I know. Anyhow, this is a birthday letter, to send my love and greetings. I keep on looking for *Eleanor*, that book of Mrs H. Ward's that I like, but it hasn't yet been unearthed by any bookshop. I think perhaps I'll send you a novel I have by L. P. Hartley, which I think his best, a rather moving story about the involvement of a boy in the affairs of adults.[2]

I have just finished doing the proofs of my own novel. . . . Later (when it comes out in Sept.) I shall want to know what [you] . . . think of it. Bits of it you may take exception to, as too critical of the Church; but you will see that the real point of the story is a great nostalgia for the Church, on the part of the central character, who is lapsed from it. They go to Turkey on an Anglican mission to Turks. This all sounds like a rather odd book, I fear, and perhaps it is. It has a camel in it, also an ape.

I don't think Becket (I learn that it was his doing) ought to have hurried us on so quickly from Whitsun to Trinity, do you?[3] Only a week to remember the Holy Spirit, then we start brooding over the Trinity for some 26 weeks, which is absurdly monotonous and unimaginative. I could have done with at least six weeks of Whitsun. About the Trinity, I haven't much to think, actually. However, Corpus Christi comes on Thursday, and about *that* one would gladly think for months, not just for one day. Some of us from St Paul's are

[1] Father Johnson was professed on 2nd June, 1909.

[2] L. P. Hartley, *The Go-Between* (1955).

[3] The observance of the Sunday following Pentecost as a Feast in honour of the Holy Trinity became popular in England in the Middle Ages, partly because St Thomas Becket had been consecrated Bishop on that day.

going down to Nashdom (Burnham) on C.C., to see (or take part in) the Nashdom monks'[1] procession through the Beeches. I hope it will be warmer than to-day! I always remember our Varazze C.C. procession through the town, from one church to another, people throwing down roses from their windows all the way, the blue sea rustling on one side of the town, the hills climbing back with their pines and olive terraces on the other; and in between the little town with all its bells ringing and the harsh singing of the procession as it wound along bearing its crucifix and banners and incense. It is a lovely memory to have. The beeches round Burnham won't be so good.

Now I must write to an aged schoolmistress of mine[2] who writes to me that she is very nearly blind now and can scarcely read print, but relies on some library where they read aloud; I don't know if she also reads Braille. Thank goodness for the wireless, on which she relies for News and many other things. She used to be a grand person, whom I adored when I was a little High School girl and wrote essays for her.

Did I mention in my last how much I liked Fr Waggett's *Heart of Jesus* (Holy Week addresses of 1904)?[3] I wish I could get hold of another copy: my sister and I have only one between us. This must stop: again, my love. . . .

By the way, why does the Lower House of Convocation reject women's lay ministry? It seems so stupid.

[1] Anglican Benedictine monks of the community at Nashdom Abbey, near Burnham, Bucks.

[2] Bertha L. Browne, who taught History at Oxford High School, 1892-1897.

[3] P. N. Waggett, *The Heart of Jesus* (1902).

My dear Hamilton,

Thank you so much for your letter posted on 13th. It is ages since either of us wrote, I know. I too have thought of it many times, like you, after I had sent you *The Go-Between*, but I was frightfully busy, finishing off my proofs, catching up on arrears of reviews, etc., and the time hurried by. I do hope you won't ever feel it on your mind that you ought to write; I know you are always there, and that I am too, and so securely that letters don't matter much after all, though it is nice to exchange news sometimes. I was glad to get yours. Mine isn't very sensational. My book is coming out on Sept. 3, and I already have some advance copies, so am sending you one almost at once. I do wonder if you'll like it. Don't think my jokes, comments, speculations on religion, etc., flippant, will you. They aren't actually, of course, mine, but those of my protagonist, who is the narrator of the story, for it is in the first person, a method I have never used before. This has both advantages and disadvantages. It is fundamentally a serious book, particularly the religious side of it; but the narrator and the other characters may be thought by some readers to be discussing things in too sceptical a spirit. I *hope* you won't. When I reflect that but for you I should probably still be straying beyond the verges of the Christian Church, I remember that you are at least in part responsible for a novel which you mayn't really much like, in all its parts. Still, you may. Let me know candidly sometime, if you will; no hurry.

I hope you are taking things easy in August, after your retreat period. If you read the *T[imes] Lit. Sup.* for 17th August, you will see it has a huge special supplement about " The Frontiers of Literature"; one of the many articles is called " Religious Writing," and is by me. Not v.g., as I didn't quite know exactly what we were supposed to be writing about; what, I mean, was the theme. Nor, I think, did most of my colleagues.

I am reading a v. interesting large book on *English Pulpit Oratory from Andrewes to Tillotson*, by W. Fraser Mitchell (1932). All 17th century, naturally. There is a long section on " The Anglo-Catholic Preachers," a good many besides Andrewes and Donne, who are less familiar than these. This morning I sat under Fr Ross at All Saints', [Margaret Street,]. . . . I like All Saints' (though I avoided it on Aug. 15, thinking I should be worried by Assumption fuss). G[rosvenor] Chapel is shut for August, and I go often to All Saints' on week days.

We are having a wet chilly August. I go away for short times, but am mainly here, partly because [while] my sister's holiday was on she wanted to stay at home as her eyes are bothering her rather (cataract ripening slowly, and she won't see so well till after she can have the operation, but she can read all right, and do her work). I'm glad you enjoyed *The Go-Between*; I like it best of Hartley's books myself. I saw something of him during the July P.E.N. conference in London, when we had the foreign writers over here and entertained them. He is a nice, modest, quiet person. . . . Full, I mean, of good and kindly feelings. I thought you would like the Norfolk setting of that novel. I don't mind these Americanisms as much as you do, I think; some of them, of course, are 16th and 17th century English, which they took over there. I have noticed lately that some Americans use *"presently"* in its old sense of *now*, instead of its modern sense of *soon*. Is this common? I mean, e.g. " He is presently in New York." I have my enchanting godchild Emily[1] over here from Mass., where she lives, with the Harvard Glee [Club] singers, she being a friend of the conductor's daughter,[2] so she has been travelling about Europe with them. She is just 21, and delightful.

[1] Emily Smith.
[2] Harriet Woodworth, daughter of G. Wallace Woodworth.

I will get hold of Bede Frost's book from the Library and read it. By the way, my novel (*The Towers of Trebizond*) is coming out later in America under another name, I think *A Strange Wild Power*,[1] which words are taken from the epigraph I wrote for the title page.[2] They thought the other sounded like a travel book! Besides, what Americans have heard of Trebizond? I can't wait for you to read it. But don't feel you must write. This business of letters gets me down too; unanswered letters pile up like an unscaled mountain on my desk, daunting me and giving me faint nausea. I think you should be firm, and not give in to them. Have you read L. E. Jones's *Edwardian Youth*? Mainly about the Balliol of 50 years ago. Not quite so charming as his *Victorian Childhood*[3] (mainly Eton), but very interesting. But he is wrong about the relations of the sexes; girls weren't at all in the segregated state he suggests.

My love always,
R. M.

20, *Hinde House, Hinde St., W.*1
24*th September*, 1956†

My dear Hamilton,

Yours begun 16th Sept. came this morning, telling me my *Towers* had arrived; they took a long time en route. I do hope you will like the book, when you have finished it. Most people do, I think, and it has had a very good kind press, with a few exceptions. I think all *Anglicans* (including many clergy) like it. John Betjeman gave it a v. good review in the [*Daily*] *Telegraph*. The *Church Times* hasn't yet done it; I hope they'll approve! On the other hand, it doesn't go so well with R.C.s and

---

[1] See below p. 234.
[2] *Dialogues of Mortality.*
[3] L. E. Jones, *A Victorian Boyhood* (1955).

dissenters. I had a letter to-day which pleased me, from a friend who is agnostic, but wistfully religious. She writes: " That a person of your distinction and your entourage should affirm publicly, in August 1956, that she believes there is such a thing as sin, and that she is agin it, must hearten many also-rans who have had a suspicion all along that this might indeed be so. It will enliven their endeavours to stick to their notion that 'what we have to gain, Is not one battle, but a weary life's campaign', and that it is better to wear our lives away in a doubtful attempt to see the job in hand through to the finish." I was touched and moved by this; I know the kind of thing she has in mind—a life with a difficult husband. And [another friend] . . . who has had a storm-tossed emotional life, with several successive husbands and lovers, wrote me a long letter, saying she loves the book, which "henceforth shall be my Bible. It is the most *improving* novel in my lifetime." That is nonsense, of course, and I only repeat it because I thought you might like to hear it said of a book by your daughter-in-God, for that I really am, you know, even though I feel that much of the way I have to look at things isn't the way you look at them, owing to different backgrounds, different temperaments, different minds. I don't mean that what I have, through six years, learnt from you, has any of it been rejected; it is all there, but planted, perhaps, in another soil and growing up therefore a little differently—I fear not so much *seges* some-times as just grass and things. But oh yes, there is the *seges* too, as you know. Anyhow, I do hope that you won't see any irreverent flippancy, or unseemly religious speculations, in this book of mine, even when it does seem to show levity on serious subjects. All I have said about the tensions set up by being separated by sin from God and the Church, are, as you will know, very personal.

The *seges* quotation is Ovid, the *Heroides*—I now forget which book. I don't know if he ever visited Troy's site, then a Roman city of course; lots of Romans did. Nor does one know if *seges* ever flourished there; when I saw it, it was far from looking like corn land.[1]

Fr Chantry-Pigg was old-world, and had his own whims about pronunciation, such as *woof* for wolf, and *hool* for howl. It does seem to me that *ow* was *oo* in most English words till I'm not sure when; it has been retained in names, such as Cowper. And a good deal in Scotland, as *doon* for down, *hoo* for how. O[ld] E[nglish] for owl was *ula*, Old German something similar, Latin *ulula* (hence *ululate,* and howl). Dunbar makes *fule* rhyme with *oule*. I say *Cooley* for the poet, but not for the Fathers, until I have their leave. Nor, I think, is it used for Cowley in Oxford.

Hugh Ross Williamson, lately seceded to Rome on account of the Church of South India, has written his autobiography,[2] which I am reviewing for the *T[imes] L[iterary] S[upplement]*. He has some surprising opinions about Anglican churches; he says there are now only two that he would call Anglo-Catholic: St Magnus the Martyr's, and the Annunciation, Bryanston Square [*sic*]. Not All Saints', [Margaret Street,] nor St Mary's, Graham St., nor St Matthew's, Westminster, nor any other—these are only " High Church". It has also come to seem to him that Cranmer composed more of the P[rayer] B[ook] than he can have thought when an Anglican; e.g. the Prayer of Oblation, which he says is a Cranmer composition, to stress the idea of the sacrifice of ourselves as against offering the sacrifice of our Lord. But this prayer surely is a pre-Reformation one; my American P.B. [commentary] ascribes it to "ancient liturgies". Also he has since his conversion read only "true Catholic sources" of history so now he knows that the Gunpowder Plot was a Protestant one. How odd

[1] See *The Towers of Trebizond*, p. 36, where " Fr Chantry-Pigg" quotes from Ovid (*Heroides* 1.53), *Iam seges est ubi Troia fuit* ("There is corn now where Troy was once").

[2] Hugh Ross Williamson, *The Walled Garden; an Autobiography* (1956).

it must be to have one's whole intellectual outlook so coloured anew.[1]

I expect you perhaps by now may have read a little more of *Trebizond* and I long to know what you think of it; I do hope not too badly. You probably also by now know the sex of Laurie. I saw no need to stress it, since so much of life is common to both sexes; but of course I mention it near the end, and most people discerned it early. I adopted for Laurie a rather goofy, rambling prose style, to put the story at one remove from myself. I find that many readers and reviewers like this style, and some say they have caught it. I hope you laugh at the jokes, such as they are. The *Queen* reviewer, a woman, only saw one joke, the name Chantry-Pigg, and thought that a poor one.[2] I thought there were more than that. The camel and ape are popular with those who don't make much of the religious theme, so there is something for everyone. But I do know it is very faulty and imperfect. Farrar, Straus & Co.[3] are publishing it in America in the spring. My love; I hope you are well. I am. We are now all assembling after our summer holidays. Grosvenor Chapel is open again for daily Mass.

Always,
R. M.

[1] Hugh Ross Williamson points out that his book *The Gunpowder Plot* (1951) was published four years before his conversion.

[2] *The Towers of Trebizond* was given an unfavourable (unsigned) review in *The Queen* (18th September, 1956), but the name "Chantry-Pigg" was not mentioned.

[3] Farrar, Straus, & Cudahy, Inc.

20, *Hinde House, Hinde St., W.*1
1*st October,* 1956†

My dear Hamilton,
    How lovely to get your letter postmarked Sept. 24. You
will know by now that I also got the one before, that you
feared was mis-posted. I think letters are, on the whole, pretty
tough and clever, and usually wing their way to their destina-
tion, tho' there is an occasional annoying mishap of course.
Anyhow, yours came, and I answered it, and I think in my
letter I tried to explain that my book might perhaps in some
parts make you feel not quite in accord with it, in some of its
criticisms of the Church in history, and perhaps some of its
jests. But now I have your letter written after you had read it,
which much relieves me and delights me, because you do like
it. I am so very glad. I looked up the pages you mentioned,
and felt particularly glad that you had liked them (they are
about the Church, and Laurie's vision of it), in spite of your
being aware that some people might not. I should have been
very very sad if you had disliked those pages or felt jarred by
them. I suppose I was trying to set down some of the things
I felt myself about it all.
    I too, you know, felt Laurie's half-stunned insensibility,
and even aversion, towards the Church, for some time after the
man I had loved for so long died. I don't take Laurie far enough
in her life to get to where she, as I did, encounters some
influence that brings her church-ward. But of course it came:
feeling as she always had about the Church and about separation
from God, she would not for very long be outside it. I like the
Knox version of II Corin: 4. [3, 4,] which you mention: "our
Gospel is only a mystery to those who are on the road to
perdition, those whose unbelieving minds have been blinded
...so that the glorious Gospel of Christ cannot reach them
with the rays of its illumination ...". The whole rendering of
that splendid chapter is admirable. Oh dear, I often feel well

on the road to perdition myself, and that my mind is so blinded as to be incapable of prayer and access to God, so often. Perhaps I am permanently blinded and deafened, by all those years away from it all.

I have long had that prayer on Ember Friday, about *gratiae tuae lumen ostende*, written out in my MS prayers, and often use it.[1] *Ember days.*[2] You might be right in your etymological guess, for, says the O[xford] D[ictionary], " It seems however not wholly impossible that the word may have been due to popular etymology working upon some Vul[gar] Lat[in] corruption of *quatuor tempora*; (cf. German *quatember*, ember-tide)." But how odd that such a popular corruption should have got into the written missals made by the clergy. First example in O.D. is [A.D.] 1000, *Laws of Alfred*, "*ymbren-wican*", ember week.

I think the Latin in my American edition will be carefully checked over there. I am glad to say that Farrar, Straus have accepted my English title; it is much the best. The firm seems to like the book v. much. I wonder what the critics there will make of it. Here they have been wonderfully nice; many understand what it's all about, many are amused, some edified (this comes out in private letters more than in reviews), and the low-brows find in it a camel and an ape, which they enjoy. If you were at hand, I would show you the reviews; they might interest you. Only 3 reviewers haven't liked it. I was told that Christopher Hollis has done a good review for *The Tablet* (not yet out), which pleases me, as R.C.s don't all like it, and I'm not surprised. It amused Archbp Mathew, and apparently Evelyn Waugh, tho' I expect it made him cross too, he is so jealous about his own Church. One friend told me she had been considering poping, but, reading in my book about the

---

[1] "(Graciously hear us, O merciful God: and) shew forth (in our hearts) the light of thy grace"; see Collect for Ember Friday in Lent.

[2] Three days of fasting and prayer occurring in each of the four seasons of the Church year. Traditionally associated with the crops, now almost entirely with ordinations.

C. of E. and its glories, she is now going in for that instead! So perhaps it really is, as John Betjeman claims, Anglican propaganda, I hope so. And I am asked where "the great O's" are to be found.[1] I am getting to feel a little like an Anglican missionary to the heathen! . . . Did I tell you I had been seeing my American cousin and godchild, now just 21? . . . An enchanting child. I wish she would go and see you. She is at Radcliffe.

Much love always.

R. M.

20, *Hinde House, Hinde St., W.*1
14th October, 1956†

My dear Hamilton,

How good you are. Two letters, one posted 4th, the other 9th, and both so full of good things, and both answering mine. What you say about the Prayer of Oblation sent me to the *American Prayer Book* [*Commentary*] that Father Pedersen so kindly presented me with some four or five years ago.[2] I see it is, as you point out, much fuller than ours (the Prayer of Oblation, I mean). I had noticed that before, and marked the parts we don't use. I see the Invocation was in the 1549 book but left out of the 1552; what a pity. At least, it was, in 1549, stronger than it became in the American version. As to the oblation part, I can't think why Cranmer left out those words; they in no way imply re-sacrifice.[3] I shall remember to say

[1] The Greater Antiphons (or Great Advent Antiphons) are to be found in the Roman Breviary and translations are included in *The English Hymnal* ("Introits and Anthems" 734). See *The Towers of Trebizond*, p. 208.

[2] See *Letters to a Friend*, p. 170.

[3] The words here italicized in the 1549 "prayer of oblation" were omitted from the Prayer Book of 1552: " Humbly beseeching Thee that whosoever shall be partakers of this holy communion may *worthily receive the most precious Body and Blood of Thy Son Jesus Christ*; *and* be fulfilled with

them myself during that prayer in future. I do add in a good deal of extraneous matter to the Mass prayers, actually. . . . Hugh Ross Williamson . . . whose autobiography I am reviewing for the *Times Literary Supplement* implies that Cranmer *invented* this prayer. . . . With it I am doing a little book by the Red Dean of Canterbury[1] [who says] . . ., talking of the feeding of the 5000, that Christ ordered the food to be distributed "equally, to each according to his need." Well, it couldn't have been *both*. . . .

Yes, I like my grandfather's translations of the Epistles, and of 2 Corinthians 4. I have been comparing it with Knox's; both are good. Those verses would indeed grace the *Towers of T.* I suppose that in grandfilial loyalty I ought to use my grandfather's. I have a very nice copy of that book—leather bound, 2 vols., 1881.[2] Has your 1892 edition got all those beautiful plates? Mine has. I wish books still went in for those lovely soft pencil drawings; there is nothing like them now. I always wish—so did she—that my mother could remember her father; he died when she was a year old.

Thank you for speaking so well from behind your side of the grating. A pity, I always feel, that I have no access to that grating; I should acquire many good things through it. But perhaps letters are as good. You invariably supply my mind with such various food both for thought and spirit. So I won't bother any more about perdition, but shall concentrate on grace. We have just been having a Church Week, in the Rural Deaconry[3] of Westminster; I am not quite sure what it was in aid of, but designed to put the C. of E. on the map in some way more than it was before. I didn't walk in a torchlight procession from St Stephen's, Rochester Row to the Abbey,

---

Thy grace and heavenly benediction, *and made one Body with Thy Son Jesus Christ*, that He may dwell in them and they in Him."

[1] Very Rev. Dr Hewlett Johnson, *Christians and Communism* (1956).
[2] W. J. Conybeare and J. S. Howson, *Life and Epistles of St Paul* (1852).
[3] Probably a slip for "Rural Deanery."

but some people did, including my friend Susan Lister. I don't know what effect such things really have, nor the rather dull addresses given at St Paul's Knightsbridge by five clergy from Monday to Friday. We had the Bp of ——, and him also of ——, besides 3 lesser divines. I only heard three of them, but they weren't interesting, not even the bishops. Much too earthen, many of these vessels.

Did I tell you I had a very nice review in *The Tablet*, from Christopher Hollis? I somehow wasn't expecting that. He no doubt thought that Laurie said some rather erroneous things about the Church, its past history, etc., but kindly provided me with a nice alibi, pointing out that her intellect had been somewhat corrupted by sin, and that her views were not to be identified with mine, as this would be most unfair. I thought rather generous in one of his communion; and as a review, it couldn't have been kinder. This *Towers* seems to be by some way the best received of any I have written, which I am glad of, for many reasons.

Next Sunday I discuss with C. S. Lewis (before the St Francis Society in Cambridge; Fr Lothian Sumner[1] is its head), with Dr Chadwick[2] in the chair, "Some Difficulties which keep people out of the Christian Church." I put the difficulties; C.S.L., who is full of resource, supplies some answers. I have grabbed the easier role, as he says; but I obviously couldn't take the other. There will be a discussion after it, in which the undergraduate audience takes part. Dr Lewis says, "I can't fight Logical Positivists, and that is what we shall get." So think of us on Sunday next, 21st, undergoing this from 4.30 to 5.30. I shall have time too to call on my Conybeare cousins, and perhaps see E. M. Forster. . . .

Here come in by the 2nd post two more letters [about the *Towers*], one from a stranger, one from an old friend, who says:

[1] Fr Lothian, s.s.f., Friar-in-charge of the Cambridge house of the Society of St Francis.

[2] Dr Owen Chadwick, later Professor of Ecclesiastical History.

" It moved me more than [any] modern book I have read."
The stranger (in the Highlands) says something similar. All this
kind of thing makes me feel extremely small, it is *so* undeserved.
But something in the book which was part of my own most
poignant experience has somehow got across to people and
moved them, and of course I am glad of that. No room to
comment on your *"Nunc autem mihi forsan vaces*[1] . . ." but it
seemed to me flawless.

My love always.

R. M.

20, *Hinde House, Hinde St., W.*1
14*th November,* 1956†

My dear Hamilton,

I am not typing this, so I will try and write as well as you
do, so that you mayn't have to bother at guessing any words.
Ever since I had your last letter (posted 25th Oct.) ending with
your just having had a visit from Constance B[abington]
Smith, I have been longing to write, but time was more than
usually elusive, and I never did. And the other day Constance
telephoned, on her way through to Cambridge (Eng.), and this
morning I drove her to Mass at 8.30 at St Paul's, Knightsbridge,
and we had a delightful talk about her doings, and about how
lovely it was seeing you, and how charming you had been, and
all you had talked about. I wished I had made a third. I had
asked her to visit you if she could, but hadn't warned you, in
case she found it impossible. She is a great dear, isn't she,
and did a very good job in America, I think. . . . I *must* tell
you of someone who likes [*Trebizond*] . . . Princess Margaret!
It seems she read it, to herself and to her companions, on her
voyage to Africa, and liked it so much that she wants to meet
me! So Mark Bonham Carter, a friend of hers and of mine,
is having me to dine to-morrow night to meet her. I am

[1] " But now however you may perhaps have time to attend to me."

delighted that she likes it. What with Royalty, and the Anglican Hierarchy—who next, I wonder? Perhaps it will be the Pope, or Nasser; you never can tell. I hope my head won't get turned! (By the way, you ask who *Dialogues of Mortality* are by. By me, they are—I usually have to compose my own epigraphs. Do you like it? It says what I feel is the book's real theme.)

Yes, the *Times Literary Supplement* reviewer (don't know who) took me to be more "in the dark" than I am. Laurie *was*, of course, still, when the book ends. So, once, was I. Laurie will come later on to where I am now, give her time. As to "the Rev. Chantry-Pigg," it rather surprised me that the well-informed editor (Alan Pryce-Jones), or his colleagues, didn't put that right. Some people who should know better do say it, in these days. Lord Kinross put it in some book, and I rebuked him in a review. But *he* was bred a Presbyterian, and is now nothing.[1] It used to be a complete vulgarism, of course.

It was quite interesting meeting C. S. Lewis at St Francis House. He is very good and quick and witty in public speech, and I enjoyed him. It was my part to stimulate him with questions, and the evening went quite well. He is a great influence among undergraduates. I wish I knew what century had the first pictorial representation of God the Father. Nothing B.C., I think, owing to the Jewish inhibitions about art. Perhaps the catacombs. *How* pleased I feel that Constance saw you! But she said you looked very "frail", which disturbs me rather. How are you? I send much love.

R. M.

---

[1] Lord Kinross (who was an Episcopalian) recalls that when he wrote to R. M. explaining that his "solecism" had been meant facetiously, she replied apologizing for not having seen his "joak."

1957

My dear Hamilton,

I have a feeling that it is more than time I heard from you again. Your last letter that I got was posted October 25; you had just been seeing Constance Babington Smith, you said in your very last lines at the end of the letter. I answered that, and wrote for Christmas, and sent you my Christmas card (self-composed) by surface mail, which I expect reached you after Christmas, or even may not have yet done so. But I am a little anxious about not having had a word for over two months, and no line of Christmas or New Year's greeting, and have been fearing that perhaps you haven't been well. Do send me a word to say how you are. I hope it was merely that you were rather tired, and not writing letters; but sometimes I reflect, if you are ill, should I know it? And [I] probably shouldn't, which disturbs me at times. But I do hope all is well.

We had a rather uneasy Christmas, with the Suez disturbance, and petrol rationing, and everything. One's activities are rather hampered by petrol shortage; e.g. early weekday Mass, to which I can't drive every day now. I sometimes go to St James's, Spanish Place, just across the street, but of course can't make my communion there, owing to these absurd walls that churches put up round themselves (how unChristian it is); sometimes to All Saints', Margaret St., which is slightly nearer than Grosvenor Chapel, and to which there is a bus if I can get it; to St Paul's, Knightsbridge, on the mornings I take the car (about twice a week, so far). The Annunciation, [Bryanston Street,] (nearer than these) I find tiresome and self-conscious. In St Paul's, Portman Square, just round the corner, nothing at all seems to occur on weekdays, and very little on Sundays. They have the 10 Commandments printed large outside, but the service list contains remarkably little. I suppose having my car has spoilt me; plenty of people have to do without this.

All Saints' is only 12 minutes' walk, actually. To-morrow they have one at 9, a very nice hour! No one knows when rationing will end; perhaps not at all, even after the Canal is opened again, as oil costs dollars. Alas, what a sad mess Sir Anthony has made of things. . . .

My book has been doing quite well, and has been received with almost universal kindness, which pleases me more than the money, though I am very glad to have the money just now, with so many things needing it—refugees, South African causes, personal needs such as that of my sister who is just retiring from her life-long job of nursing, and has tied up most of her money in covenant subscriptions. . . . Luckily I have plenty for us both, and can take over her covenants, so far as she will let me. She has never spent a penny on herself, scarcely. I am glad she is now retiring, as she isn't anything like strong enough to go on. She means to do a little relief work, unpaid, but needn't do anything she doesn't feel able for.

This should be a New Year's letter, but 1957 begins to-morrow, and I am late for it. Constance did so enjoy seeing you—but I think I told you that before. Didn't you find her charming? She is such a lovable, delightful person. I think her book on Air Photography, which she went to America to interview people on, is going to be v.g.[1]

Did you read Fr Huddleston's *Naught for Your Comfort*? . . . He is such a very nice person: we meet sometimes, and he likes my book. He is now much troubled about these S. African trials of alleged "traitors", most of whom he knows. "Christian Action" (Canon Collins's movement) is getting up a fund for their defence, and I am on a panel for this appeal. The world grows more and more dreadful and illiberal and unChristian. What kind of a year begins this midnight? One can't get one's thoughts off that poor boy of 21 who was

[1] C. Babington Smith, *Evidence in Camera: The Story of Photographic Intelligence in World War II* (1958).

244

deliberately gagged and suffocated in a box by the Egyptians, and his poor parents.[1] What *is* this awful substance of which human beings are so bestially made? It is hard to face.

Much love for 1957. I hope for a letter soon. Perhaps one may cross mine. Meanwhile, I think of you often, and hope you are well.

Yours always,

R. M.

20, *Hinde House, Hinde St., W.*1

12*th February,* 1957†

My dear Hamilton,

Your letter posted Feb. 8 arrived yesterday, a coal of fire, because it is your 3rd since my last to you, and that last was one of anxiety because it was longer than I liked since I [had] heard, and I was rather anxious lest you might not be well. You can imagine my relief when I got yours of 31st Dec. I didn't reply to it at once, nor to the next, partly because very much occupied, and partly because I didn't want to burden you with the feeling that it was again your turn to write. I myself know so well that inhibition caused by preoccupations, demands for immediate replies to other letters, reluctance to write at all, in my case laziness and the mere hurrying by of time, so relentlessly fugitive. Don't think that when I don't write I don't enjoy and peruse and think about every line you send me; they are always so full of interesting and suggestive and delightful matter. The two I have before me (I seem to have mislaid for the moment the one posted Jan. 11, but it will turn up) are both most interesting. I didn't know I hadn't told you of my dinner to meet Princess Margaret. I enjoyed it v.

---

[1] Lt Anthony Moorhouse, of the West Yorkshire Regiment, was abducted by Egyptians in Port Said on 11th December, 1956, and died a few days later from suffocation in a large steel box.

much. She is a charming person. . . . There were, besides my hosts (Mark Bonham Carter and wife), Lady Elizabeth Cavendish, a great friend of the Princess, and of John Betjeman and other people I know, a very nice girl . . . and two men . . . I had a conversation with her; she first read the *Towers* at Balmoral, and laughed so much, alone in a room, that the Queen her sister came down to know what was the matter. Then the Queen read it, and also laughed. She took it on her African trip and read it aloud to people. . . . Her talk is very largely about records and gramophones and Covent Garden opera; one of the men at dinner was concerned with this. We heard some records during the evening and also discussed the pronunciation of words a little, which is much more up my own street. She is a very bright, high-spirited girl. One calls her " Ma'am " at intervals, just to show one remembers who she is; but conversation with her is quite easy and natural. Yes, it was a great thing that she made that decision;[1] I think she would have felt very unhappy and out of things if she had made that marriage, besides feeling wrong. It would have been a tragic situation, and no life for her. . . . I hope some one she can love and marry will turn up before long. And that she will always stay within the " heavenly mystery", whoever she marries. . . . Mr Phipps, the very influential Chaplain of Trinity, Cambridge, of whom she is very fond . . . gave last week a series of broadcast 5-minute talks at 7.50 a.m. (a series I always listen to as I get ready to sally out to Mass) and was admirable.[2] This week the talks are anonymous, and called " I was an atheist " or ("an agnostic") and are by an Anglican Franciscan, a doctor, a journalist, a headmistress, a housewife, and an electrical fitter (who calls his talk " I was a pagan." I don't expect he knows what a pagan is, or about the number of

[1] Princess Margaret's decision (in October 1955) not to marry Group Captain Peter Townsend.
[2] A series of talks, "Jesus Lives," in the BBC programme " Lift up Your Hearts."

strange gods in fields and hills and woods that pagans worshipped; but illiterates, including, alas, many of our clerical, even episcopal, earthen vessels often use the word as meaning atheist, so I expect this fitter does too). I wish they would have also a writer, as this might have been interesting. The general subject is how they became Christians. A psychologically fascinating theme. I agree with you about the under-statement usual in novels about religious belief, and that there *must* be far more prayer and awareness of God than is generally allowed in fiction. Many reviewers share this blind spot; reviewers of the *Towers* were divided into those who apprehended its religious theme and discussed it, and those who didn't really take it in at all, but found the book merely amusing, and perhaps a good travel tale. Its readers are also thus divided; many of them tell me how much they enjoyed it, but lots of these say " I never laughed so much at a novel. The camel! " etc. I'm glad to find, tho', that very many others liked the serious theme, including, to my surprise, known unbelievers such as Julian Huxley, who told me he "much liked the religious parts. One realises that there must be an institution like the Church, to enshrine people's religious and moral values." I feel particularly glad that most clerical readers and reviewers have liked it. I will send you a copy of Gerard Irvine's review in the monthly *London Magazine*. He describes my Anglicans as being " High, and also regrettably broad"; he means, of course, Laurie and me, not Fr Chantry-Pigg!

I am interested in your reading my earlier novels, especially *And No Man's Wit*. I'm glad you like the way they converse. I haven't, so far as I remember, got much religion in that; but some discussion of it may have seeped in; it is difficult for any of my family to keep it out, whatever our beliefs! An end seems to have come to this. I do hope you are fairly well. . . . I keep well, and get to Mass somehow most mornings. I've just heard that the *Towers* has been awarded the James Tait Black annual prize by Edinburgh University, which pleases me.[1] No more now but my love. I hope you'll get some nice Valentines on 14th.

Your affectionate
R. M.

20, Hinde House, Hinde St., W.1
29th March, 1957[†]

My dear Hamilton,

Thank you for yours of 25th March, *and* for that of 17th Feb., which I have left far too long in answering; but you know how time rushes by. One is delighted to have a letter, reads it more than once, and lays it by in the place where to-be-answered-presently letters lie and pile up. "To-be-answered-at-once,-or-as-near-as-I-can" is a more urgent pile, consisting of bills, invitations, questions which demand reply, etc., etc. Both piles grow much too high, I needn't say, while one pursues one's other labours. Mine have partly consisted lately in a contribution to a book to be presented to T. S. Eliot on his 70th birthday. I am trying to recall what I felt about his poetry when first I read it, or some of it, in the early 1920s. The impact was enormously exciting, and I have been trying to put it into words.[2] Also, I have other literary jobs to try and finish before I go to Venice in early May.

The Towers of Treb. is coming out in America this month, I think; I am shocked at the vulgarity of the paper jacket, which is covered with absurd figures, meant, so far as one can judge, to represent the people in the book, absurdly caricatured. I asked to have the jacket sent me to see beforehand, but the

[1] The annual choice of books for the James Tait Black Memorial Prizes is made by the Professor of English Literature at Edinburgh University.

[2] See R. M.'s essay " The First Impression of the Waste Land " in *T. S. Eliot; a Symposium for his Seventieth Birthday edited by Neville Braybrooke* (1958).

publishers didn't send it. So now I expect it will be reviewed as a vulgar comic book!

I am sorry you find that I am not well considered in the American press. I certainly don't complain of the attitude towards me of the English press, which is revealed in my press cuttings, and in the periodicals I see. Perhaps if the Americans neglect me (they didn't use to) it is because I haven't published anything there much lately, and one gets forgotten. Nothing between 1940 and 1950, and nothing since then till now, as they didn't do my Ruin book. I was interviewed the other day by an American called Webster (the same that did the one on Ivy Compton-Burnett that you mention, probably). He is engaged on a survey of contemporary fiction, and is including me. He said he had at first decided not to include me, on the grounds that I was "frivolous"; but he had, on second thoughts, and on taking advice, decided to do so, as he discovered that I was "thought good", tho' perhaps still rather "frivolous". But serious too, he thought. He isn't a very weighty thinker, I imagine. But I don't mean to be depressed by your reports of American neglect; I really do get some very nice attention from there; all I merit, I feel. One day I will send you some English reviews of the *Towers*—spares, that I don't want back. I don't know what more one could want. I have to-day from Germany an article which, quite untruly, calls me "*seit dem Tode Virginia Woolf's Englands klügste, wenn nicht bedeutendste Schrifstellerin. Ihre Bücher sind getragen von Shawschem Witz, Swiftscher Phantasie und Ironie . . .*"[1] etc., etc., if you can make all that out; I can't quite, but I see it is kindly meant! (I expect your German isn't as good as your Latin!)

More than enough about my reputation. Don't be anxious when I don't write. I am seldom ill, and have had no ailment

[1] " England's most intelligent or even most prominent authoress since the death of Virginia Woolf. Her books are sustained with the wit of Shaw, the fantasy and irony of Swift."

for ages but a touch of flue. I have more reason to worry about your health, I feel. I was interested in your point about the childishness of many of my young female characters. I expect it is that I was young for my age myself, what is called a tomboy, and liked to do all those things you mention. But I don't think girls and women in general do, so much as boys and men. I used to find that most of my adventures were more shared by my brothers than my sisters, on the whole, though we all liked adventure. And when I was at Oxford, at 18, I had a reputation for liking roof-climbing, etc., which wasn't shared by any of my friends. Surely men do far more uncomfortable things than women do; camping out in snow, exploring tropical jungles, etc. I think women are much less fitted for and fond of such rigours. As to their clothes—well, I suppose high heels are pretty comfortless for walking, and I never wear them myself. Nor do I like cold or draughts. But I too am puzzled by some of the uncomfortable things some women wear. But, as to that, look at men in hot weather in heavy suits. But I agree that men like comfort in clothes and chairs, etc., before appearance and that many women don't. Food, too. But I should die in an Arctic blizzard. Just look what men voluntarily go through. No, I don't think you have anything there.

Marry come up. Derived (see O[xford] D[ictionary]) from St Mary of Egypt, by whom people used to swear. Became " Mary Gipsy ", then " Mary Gip ", [then] "Gup" (what you say to horses when driving them), [and then] got (by association with this) to be " Mary come up." This seems a natural enough development, I suppose. Language is queer. I've never seen the 1636 P[rayer] B[ook] meant for Scotland, but always thought it was only a little different from the B[ook of] C[ommon] P[rayer], and, as you say, the source of the American one. Isn't it also what the Scotch Episcopals use now? The Scotch thought it was "the Mass"—but they thought ours was too, of course.[1] Very odd about that word " Mass", why it is so hated by extreme Protestants, when all it is is (as the 1549 book says) "the Holy Communion or the Lord's Supper, commonly called the Mass". St Paul's (Knights.) is sometimes picketed on Sunday mornings by sandwich-board men saying " The Mass is a blasphemous fable" (see article [31]) and other Kensitite[2] utterances. It seems all a question of the name you give it. I am just now following High Mass with the 1549 book, rather confusing, as we've chopped it about so. So much of the service *followed* the consecration and administration then. I must say I like it as we now have it (*not*, of course B.C.P.). Oh dear, so much more I meant to say, but here is the end, as usual.

Yes, surely: *Benedictus benedicat*, and *Benedicto benedicatur*. Has it gone wrong? I correct proofs shockingly.[3] Your letter is full of interest; e.g. about reasons for non-religious novels in America. I meant to tell you about an R.C. novel I am reading. I will, later.

Till then, my love.

R. M.

---

[1] The first Scottish Prayer Book (approved in 1636, but usually known as the Scottish Prayer Book of 1637, the year of its publication, or as "Laud's Liturgy") was based largely on the Book of Common Prayer of 1549. The first American Prayer Book (of 1789) was based partly upon the subsequent "Scottish Communion Office" of 1764, and partly upon the English Prayer Book of 1662. The Prayer Book currently used by the Scottish Episcopal Church is a twice revised version of the "Scottish Communion Office."

[2] Reminiscent of the Protestant propagandist John Kensit (1853-1902).

[3] Presumably R. M. had misquoted the Graces *"Benedictus benedicat"* (" May the Blessed one bless"), said at the beginning of a meal, and *"Benedicto benedicatur"* (" Blessing on the Blessed one"), said at the conclusion.

My dear Hamilton,

I put off writing till I was back from Venice, as there are no air letters there, so I think I have not yet answered your last letter, which I have before me now; it came to Venice with me, and I thought of writing, but decided to wait till I was back, as you suggested. Venice was delightful, as always. *What* a place it is! A unique mixture of physical beauty and magnificent works of art, both architecture and painting. St Mark's always wholly captivates me, tho' I know some people don't care for the shape of its façade; but I agree with Ruskin about the beauty of this. And how marvellous inside, with its great cruciform shape and golden mosaicked apses. It has very beautiful singing, and we often dropped in for vespers or some Mass. In all the Venice churches there are evening Masses now, as well as in the mornings. (Our little C. of E. church is rather bleak; I went there at 8.30 on Sundays for communion, as these fanatic and intolerant Romans won't let us communicate in theirs.) Then the Piazza, and the Doge's Palace, as beautiful Gothic as St Mark's is Byzantine, and the little streets winding along by the little canals, and the wonderful, mainly baroque, churches all about, some most beautiful, and the charming little campos, or squares, with their market stalls and stone fountains in the middle, and the Grand Canal with all its splendid palazzos. We stayed in a small and pleasant *pensione* on the Giudecca Canal, with a wonderful view of the Giudecca opposite, and the island of San Giorgio with its Palladian church. Quite near us was the magnificent Salute church. Near also was the Accadèmia gallery, with its wonderful pictures. The weather was, in the main, warm and sunny and delightful, and coming away was sad. But more and more I am struck by the follies of the R.C. church—the sheer childish nonsense. [A friend of mine] . . . a convert thro' marriage, who was in

Venice, says that he just by-passes the follies (e.g. indulgences and miracles), which he says are only meant for the simple. I don't think I would like to belong to a church which deliberately taught nonsense to children, and "simple" people, which the more educated priests don't believe themselves. Can this be right?

The Towers of T. has had an excellent reception in America. *Time* only gave it a snippet, after asking me for a photograph and saying it was giving it a full-page review. . . . I got a quite kind review, however, from an R.C. Religious, who had been interested by it, and thought it revealed "a new facet of the Protestant mind." But, he said, the feeling left by it in Catholics must be sorrow that so much faith and earnestness in religion was based on nothing (i.e. on false premises and false teaching). It amounted to saying that God was "nothing", but of course he didn't mean that. What a strange and sad point of view theirs is—I mean, discounting all other faiths but their own narrow one. I'm afraid there is rather an unseemly rivalry and even war being waged now between the two Catholic churches in this country. The Archbishop of C[anterbury] spoke strongly about the Roman propaganda campaign,[1] and about the boast they make of converts, which [sic] he says are less in number than the other way round. They are starting a Church Enquiry Centre, to offset the "Catholic Enquiry Centre", which has launched a huge campaign for converts. Yet, feeling as R.C.s are taught to do about their exclusive rightness, I suppose they must try for converts. The really unChristian thing is to forbid their members to join in prayer with other Christians; goodness, what *would* Our Lord have said to that? They have certainly taken a very wrong turning. But then I suppose all Christian churches have, being human as well as divine. . . .

I should like to show you also another kind review, this time from the Nonconformist angle, in the *British Weekly*. It

[1] Archbishop Fisher, reported in the *Church Times*, 31st May, 1957.

said how few novels depicted *Nonconformity* in action, compared with those which dealt with R.Cism and Anglicanism, and what a different standpoint it was, with its emphasis on the Word, Bible reading, and preaching, and its comparative neglect of the sacramental life that means so much to Rom[an] and Anglican Catholics. " The sin of Anglicanism is to make sacraments more and more central but to neglect preaching. The sin of Nonconformity is to treat sacraments often as little more than optional embellishments," etc. It is an interesting, fair, and thoughtful review; the writer thought I have no knowledge or understanding of Nonconformity, and probably would not like it if I had. Of the book he says he laughed all through it, but takes it also very seriously. It all makes one feel how many mansions there are, and must be, inside the Christian Church, each contributing its facet of light and truth. How angry R.C.s are at this point of view, however!

I do hope you are well. Write to me sometime and say how you fare. Meanwhile, my love.

R. M.

20, *Hinde House, Hinde St., W.*1
2nd August, 1957†

My dear Hamilton,

Yours of 22nd July came the other day, rather to my remorse, as I hadn't yet answered the one of 22nd June, which was really an answer to mine. I now have both letters before me, and very nice too. Thank you so much. I do know how troublesome writing is, and I do take it as a mark of great kindness and affection, and value it much. I myself have been pretty busy finishing one or two things I had on hand, such as a long article on the Mediterranean for a book of photographs which is to be published early next year, also in America.[1]

[1] Roloff Beny, *The Thrones of Earth and Heaven* (1958).

The photographs are beautiful, the text is by four different writers; me, Freya Stark, Stephen Spender, and Bernard Berenson.[1] And now I am free to turn to other writings, such as my coming novel (not yet begun). . . .

Talking of "markets" for books, I too was surprised that *The Towers* got on to the American best-selling list. I was interested in an article in (I think) the N[ew] Y[ork] *Times* (or was it the *Saturday Review*?) a little while back, on these lists. The writer, a very intelligent young man, said that on every such list there seemed to be two or three samples of what he called "minority literature", which were forced into best-sellers by good reviews, but would never be naturally so. Those he mentioned in this class were *The Towers of T.*, *The Fountain Overflows* by Rebecca West, and I think one by Aldous Huxley. He was talking of the most recent best-seller lists, and of what he called "intellectual" novels that got into them. What the great mass of readers make of them when they read them is another matter. As to *The Towers*, those who didn't care about the 39 Articles perhaps quite liked the camel, and one or two of the jokes. I wonder how E. Waugh's *Mr Pinfold* is liked in America. It has had a mixed reception here. It's not amusing at all, and deals with hallucinations, which is rather a boring subject, but it is very clever in parts. As to the *Towers*, I find they have introduced me to a number of priests who like it, and who accost me about it, and whom I am glad to meet. One is Simon Phipps, the Dean[2] of Trinity, Cambridge . . . whom I met the other day at a *Spectator* sherry party, and found delightful. I believe he has a great church influence in Cambridge, among undergraduates, and is a counter influence to C.I.C.C.U. But an Oxonian told me that the most numerous conversions at Oxford just now were to Islam. I said that this seemed to me very odd, and what was the attraction? He replied that so many men liked women to be behind grilles and in galleries when at church, and not taking up the seats on the

[1] Also by a fifth, Jean Cocteau.   [2] R. M. means Chaplain.

255

floor, which annoyed them. This seems rather unfair! If they get to church in time, they can get seats all right. But they don't, it seems, like the *idea* of a church full of females. Even Pusey House is now invaded by women undergraduates. Well, I suppose Moslemism is better than no religion at all, tho' to me it is very unattractive. Did you over there get the reports of the claim of a priest to have converted Gilbert Murray to the R.C. Church on his deathbed? It sounds most unlikely to us who knew him well, and even his R.C. daughter, Mrs Toynbee, made no claim for it, as she said her father had been practically unconscious, except for moments, for 5 or 6 weeks before he died.[1] His son Stephen was indignant, and firmly repudiated such an idea, in letters to *The Times*, saying his father had died as he had lived, "a reverent agnostic"[2]. . . . I went to the memorial service at the Abbey, where the ashes (after cremation by his own desire) were buried; it was a fine, rather austere service; the Dean[3] composed it, I think. He put emphasis on the words " Not every one who saith Lord, Lord, shall enter into heaven, but rather whoso doeth the will . . ."[4] which G. M. certainly did. Some distinguished agnostics here were rather alarmed lest their convert relatives should intrude a priest to *their* deathbeds and make the same claim. I hope to protect myself with Anglican rites. . . . Not that one would make a distinction between two forms of Christian rite, but one would want what one is used to and loves. The differences are, of course, really things of this world, things of the flesh, and we should not mind them. Are you quite fair in classing Maugham . . . with Aldous Huxley and Lawrence, who both have spiritual vision, I should say? D. H. L. isn't cynical; he

[1] Rosalind Toynbee comments that R. M.'s account of her attitude appears to be based on indirect information which she regards as inaccurate.

[2] This statement by Stephen Murray was first made in a letter to the *New Statesman* (29th June, 1957), not to *The Times*.

[3] Very Rev. A. C. Don.

[4] See Matt. 7. 21.

has great and earnest enthusiasm for what he believes of life . . . [sic] but I see I can't expatiate on this as space has run out. I wonder if you are still almost alone in your House. How good that your novices are so promising. I like to think of you deep in Terence and Plautus. What a nice study! Do read a book on Crashaw, by an American Austin Warren—it is v.g.[1] Much love, and my thanks always,

R. M.

20, *Hinde House, Hinde St., W.*1
3rd December, 1957†

My dear Hamilton,

Thank you so much for your welcome letter dated Nov. 12-15. I was so glad to get it. I knew it was a long time since I wrote, but not that it was as long ago as August! Time goes by so quickly, in such a rush, one can't keep pace. And now Xmas makes it worse than ever. But you have been much and often in my thoughts and prayers, and always in my affections. I have been quite well, not even had the Asian flue, which has afflicted so many of my friends and non-friends but has not come nigh me, perhaps because I got myself inoculated against it, as I usually do get any flue that is going about. I have been very much cluttered up with work, mainly articles and reviews, which after Xmas I hope to shed, as I want to get down to my next novel, not yet begun. Now here we are in Advent, which I find a very exciting and rather disturbing season, and [it] makes one think more than ever of the hourly judgment of God on every thing one thinks, says, or does; I suppose the advent of God in this way becomes closer and more apparent the more one lives, unless one goes on ignoring it entirely till it fades into unrecognizability. This, to me, seems

[1] Austin Warren, *Richard Crashaw; a Study in Baroque Sensibility* (1957).

to be the Judgment, not any unspecified and dateless Great Day, *Dies Irae*, etc., in which people used to believe with such apprehension and looking forward. Judgment; coming each morning at Communion, coming whenever one turns one's mind that way, which one ought to do more often. I like Advent and the great O's. I have printed four of them, *Radix, Clavis, Oriens* and *Sapientia*,[1] to work into the verse I have composed for my Xmas card this year, and which I shall send you by surface mail to-day, I hope.

You mention Constance Babington Smith's book. Bits of it are even now being serialised in the *Sunday Times*, and she is very busy arranging these, and very happy. The book comes out here in January. I hear it is selling well in America;[2] I don't quite know why, but I never quite understand why all these books about the last war and its doings have such a sale. I never read them myself, and shouldn't read this one if it wasn't by my dear Constance, whom I love. She . . . has put the story together in a very efficient way, and her publishers are pleased with it. She is a great dear. Not intellectual, like some of the Babington Smiths, but capable, and very charming. She began by making smart hats, then fell in love with planes and once designed a hat made like a bomber, which she wore at an aeronautic garden party. I saw her this very morning, when she was up for 2 days, and I drove her to 8.15 Mass at Grosvenor Chapel. You would like her very much if you knew her, and she you; in fact, she did.

Please keep this under the seal, so to speak (*really* under),[3] as it isn't the thing to mention it beforehand, and I should simply hate it to get about America, or London, as it is really private. I have been officially offered the rank of Dame, of which there [are] very few just now, and only Edith Sitwell

[1] "O Root (of Jesse)"; "O Key (of David)"; "O Day-spring"; "O Wisdom."

[2] *Air Spy*, the U.S. edition of *Evidence in Camera*, was published in 1957.

[3] R. M. does not mean this "literally" (Father Johnson had not been her confessor since 1916).

to represent letters, though several actresses. I am considering whether to accept it or not. It might make me feel rather foolish, and I should prefer a C.B.E., which a lot of writers do get, it is less conspicuous. But I am told that perhaps one can't commute for this! So I am still undecided. What would you do? But don't bother to answer this, as I have to decide by next Monday, before you even get this letter. I have only told my sister, who of course is for the Dame, but her advice is not impartial.

I am glad you occupy yourself with Plautus and book-covering. I was reading the other day in the *Latin Hymns* you sent me once (nicely covered by you),[1] and in which you enclosed separately part of St Bernard's great hymn, the part beginning *Hora novissima* and translated by Neale.[2] It strikes me that Neale made rather a noisy business out of "*agminis et sonus est epulantis*"; "the shout of them that feast" suggests rather a pagan banquet than a feast of saints. But it goes well; I remember liking it, and the picture it evoked, when I was a child.[3]

Someone said to me the other day that my next novel was bound to be a let-down, to some extent, to those who liked very much the last, which a good many people did. I dare say the next won't be liked so much, and I shall miss the appreciation of so many clergy; but I don't feel one should be daunted by this. I shall write it as it comes, and keep its readers as far out of my mind as I can. Oh dear, how well I know all you say about putting off things one has to do. It is a disease with me, and letters pile up like snowdrifts, accusing me all the time. So do books I ought to have reviewed, etc., etc. I will send you the Xmas *Spectator*, with an article I wrote in it about

[1] *The Hundred Best Latin Hymns; selected by J. S. Phillimore* (1926); see *Letters to a Friend*, p. 261.

[2] John Mason Neale (1818-1866) translated several parts of the long poem *De Contemptu Mundi* by Bernard of Cluny (not by St Bernard of Clairvaux) including the passage which begins *Hora Novissima*.

[3] See *The English Hymnal*, Hymn 412, "Jerusalem the Golden."

Xmas.[1] There seems to be more and more a general revolt against the racket we have made of it. I suppose really it should be a time for giving to the most needy, not exchanging presents and cards with one another. I am glad to say that Fr Harris preached very well about this on Advent Sunday. I must stop this and do up my card for you now, and sally out to the post. I do hope you will keep well over Xmas, and not get unwritten letters on your mind as you cover books and read Plautus. I have been reading a lot of Tractarian-age books, all interesting. How terribly the Articles bothered most of them! But Newman wrote (*Tract 90*) didn't he, that R.C.s could sign all of them except the one about the Pope?[2] R.C.s now write in *The Tablet*, "Catholic toleration" (of Anglo-Catholics) "has been carried to its very limits". But what do they propose to do about it? I pass Smithfield with apprehension![3] My love and greetings for Xmas and New Year.

Your affectionate

R. M.

---

[1] "Saturnalia," see *The Spectator*, 22nd November, 1957.

[2] This is a free interpretation, not a literal one, of Newman's *Tract 90*.

[3] It was at Smithfield that about 300 Protestants were burned during Mary Tudor's reign.

1958

20, Hinde House, Hinde St., W.1
12th June, 1958†

My dear Hamilton,

It *was* nice to see your handwriting on a U.S. air letter yesterday morning on my return from Mass at G[rosvenor] C[hapel]. It is indeed far too long since we wrote. Not either of our faults really, I think, for we were both hampered and let by circumstances. Of course I should have written ages ago, to tell you all my news and comment on yours. But I was attacked soon after Xmas (you did, I hope, get my Xmas card —the one with tumbling towers and my version of some of the great O's; perhaps you have written since then, yes, I think you did) by rather bad and repeated onslaughts of what we call here fluemonia, the kind that goes to the lungs, and when you think you are recovered returns and strikes you again. I was in and out of bed for some time; [then] went to the Palace to be damed on 11th Feb., a rather nice occasion, for I knew most of the five Knights in my category (the K.C.B.E.s),[1] I being a D.C.B.E.[2] (but for short we are K.B.E.s and D.B.E.). And most were Cambridge, such as Julian Huxley, Jim Butler, and others,[3] and we had a friendly get-together beforehand while we were coached in how to deport ourselves when receiving our decorations from H.M. She does those things very charmingly, pinning on the decorations and saying a few pleasant words to each recipient. I felt rather ill, however, and after that went down to Dorset to Raymond Mortimer's house to rest and recover. Soon after my return I lunched with Patrick McLaughlin in Dean Street, and, coming out, turned to speak to Fr Denis Marsh[4] behind me, stepped into space down the steps and crashed into the street, breaking my right

[1] Knights Commander of the British Empire.

[2] Dame Commander of the British Empire.

[3] J. R. M. Butler, as well as Claude Elliott, S. C. Roberts, and Steven Runciman had been at Cambridge; Julian Huxley at Oxford.

[4] Fr Denis, S.S.F.

263

wrist and thigh. I was ambulanced to Charing Cross Hospital, where the fractures were set (very expertly) and I was put to bed in the public fracture ward, where I lay for a fortnight, tended by pleasant nurses and surrounded by other fractures. It was rather noisy and restless of course; I liked my seven fellow-fracturees, but they never stopped talking. We were brought H[oly] C[ommunion] on Sunday morning from St Martin-in-the-Fields ; I was the only one in the ward to "take it", so my bed was curtained off, including a young man from the men's ward, and we had it. The others were very nice and quiet during the short service. One of them said to me sympathetically afterwards, " It makes a nice change, doesn't it ?" She herself had been brought up R.C.—" but there, you can't *believe* it, can you," she added philosophically. There was another R.C., an Irish girl who told us about Our Lady's statue at Lourdes weeping "real tears"; we were all quite polite about this. But after a fortnight I was moved to a private room at the Univ[ersity] Coll[ege] Hospital in Gower St., where I could have my typewriter and type with my left hand, the other being encased in plaster, and have all my kind friends to see me and adorn my room with lovely flowers. Two chaplains used to drop in, the Anglican, a cheerful and gossipy young man who entertained me, and the Roman, v. nice, tho' quieter. There was a third, from the Whitefield Tabernacle close by,[1] but he didn't call in the Private Wing, as he had no adherents there. What a snob business church life is, to be sure. Reading a book by Peter Kirk lately,[2] I learnt that his father, the late Bish. of Oxford, had been brought up a Methodist, and that Peter never knew this till after his death when he was going thro' his papers. Isn't that odd. So difficult, one would think, to conceal it from one's children. I suppose the grandparents were dead. But children ask questions of their parents, how

[1] The Whitefield Memorial Church (Congregationalist church in Tottenham Court Road).
[2] Peter Kirk, *One Army Strong?* (1958).

many times did they have to go to church on Sundays, etc.; we certainly knew, from my father and uncles *all* about Hodnet church where my grandfather[1] was rector, in fact we have often been there. Dr Kirk must have found it a job to keep his childhood so dark from his enquiring young. I wonder if his wife knew. One can only suppose this was a form of snobbery, tho' P[eter] K. says he can't imagine why it was. Well, I was hospitalized for 6 weeks, and came out a few weeks ago, since when I have been desperately trying to catch up on my life. My hand is still n.g. for writing more than a very short time, but I can type. My leg is almost all right. I can now drive my car again. But it was all a great interruption, and I am very much behind. Yes, you address me quite correctly as "Dame R. M." The simple call me often "Dame Macaulay", which is like "Rev. Jones", or "Sir Churchill"; I think they are rather shy of Christian names. A letter in *The Observer* lately spoke of "The Venerable Higgins and the Rev. Wilson". Lady Juliet Duff, whom I have been visiting in hospital lately (St Saviour's, Osnaburgh St.) was called by all the nuns except the Mother "Lady Duff". This letter seems all about me; I meant to write for your birthday, and wish I had. I am glad you are stronger now, and *very* glad you are retiring early, and generally being looked after. The "shattering Reformation" in your cell is one I need in my flat! I would love to see you as "no small dandy" in your shortened habit. Brother Paul[2] writes to me, to ask me if he may use in his devotional magazine[3] some verses of mine from the Xmas cards I have sent you, and which he says you have passed to him. Of course he may; I am writing to him. I haven't got L. P. Hartley's book,[4] and am not reviewing it; but I think I shall get it for you as a belated birthday gift if you would like it, so expect its

[1] Rev. S. H. Macaulay (1807–c. 1873).
[2] Brother Paul, Oblate, s.s.j.e.
[3] *Many Mansions*, a privately circulated devotional magazine.
[4] Probably *The Hireling* (1957).

arrival soon. I have now got on to my new novel (after finishing a number of other literary chores) but work slowly and erratically without a serviceable writing hand.[1] I was glad that the American reviewers and public took so kindly to *Trebizond*. I am going to the Black Sea again in late August . . . on a cruise. I like being back at Mass again. I seldom am there without thoughts of you—and love and gratitude. Now I must write, if I can, to Brother Paul; a short note only, and I think by surface mail. His letter to me began " Your old friend Fr Johnson has . . ." and for a moment my heart jolted in fear. But all was well.[2]

My love always, and take care of yourself.

R. M.

[1] R. M.'s new novel had reached the stage of some rough notes and a roughly drafted first chapter before her death on 30th October, 1958, aged 77.

[2] Fr Johnson survived R. M. for 2½ years. He died on 17th March, 1961, aged 84.

Index

Index

277

142, 189; in Cyprus, 75, 97, 100; in Isle of Wight, 166; in central London, 198-9

Mowbray, booksellers and publishers, 49, 54, 60, 77n, 82, 173

Muir, Edwin, 175

Murray, Gilbert, 176, 179, 214n, 225, 256

Murray, John, publisher, 16

Murray, Rosalind, *see* Tonybee, Rosalind

Murray, Stephen, 256

Musophilus (S. Daniel), 120, 121, 122-3, 124-5

My Host the World (G. Santayana), 116

Mystery, in religion, 127, 128, 138-9, 152

Myths, 147, 187

My Way of Faith (M. D. Petre), 106

Nashe, Thomas, 125

Naught for your Comfort (T. Huddleston), 222, 244

Neale, John Mason, 259

New and Contrite Hearts (A. Pardue), 195

New Commentary on Holy Scripture (C. Gore, H. L. Goudge & A. Guillaume), 34, 38, 52

Newman, J. H., Cardinal, 72, 81, 103, 119, 211-12; *Letters and Correspondence* (A. Mozley), 103; *Life* (Wilfrid Ward), 223; his '*Tract 90*', 260

Newman's Way (S. O'Faolain), 72

New Statesman, 79, 125, 130, 265n

Nicholas, St, 55

Nicolson, Harold, 30, 215

Nicolson, Nigel, 105

Niebuhr, Reinhold, 188

Nonconformist Churches, 21, 86, 152, 254

Non-jurors, 49, 107, 119, 164

Norms for the Novel (H. C. Gardiner), 144

North, Sir Thomas, 124-5

Notestein, Wallace, 182-3, 188

Nothing is Quite Enough (G. MacEoin), 175-6

Noughts and Crosses (J. Hichens), 30, 32-3, 40-1, 172

Nova et Vetera (G. Tyrrell), 106, 109

Novels, 144; depicting Roman Catholicism, 106, 251, 254; depict-

ing Nonconformity, 143, 254; and "alien worlds", 146; lack of "supra-mundane communications", 158; American (early 20th c.), 164; for school libraries, 220; understatement of religious belief in, 247; survey of contemporary fiction, 249; non-religious, 251; depicting Anglicanism, 254; "intellectual", 255; and best-seller lists, 255

Observer, The, 130, 176n, 265

O'Donovan, Jane, 118, 121-2, 126-7, 129, 130, 132, 137; R. M. holiday with, 205, 208-9

O'Donovan, Mary Anne, 22, 118-19, 121-2, 126-7, 129, 130, 132, 137; R.M. holiday with, 199, 205, 208-9

O'Faolain, Sean, 72

Oldenbourg, Zoë, 177

Olivier, family of, 43

On the Gods and the World (Sallustius), 214-15

One Army Strong? (P. Kirk), 264, 265

One Poor Scruple (Mrs W. Ward), 110, 112

Oratory of the Good Shepherd, 223

O Sapientia, see Liturgies: the Greater Antiphons

Ordeal of Gilbert Pinfold, The (E. Waugh), 255

Ordinations, 149, 234n

Orthodox Church, The, 96, 99, 127

Out of the Silent Planet (C. S. Lewis), 37, 40, 44

Overton, J., 192, 193

Ovid, 155-6, 161, 230-1

Oxford American Prayer Book Commentary (M. H. Shepherd), 33, 231, 235

Oxford Apostles (G. Faber), 202

Oxford High School, 15, 226

Oxford Inter-Collegiate Christian Union, 206

Oxford University, 177, 263n; Somerville College, 16, 33, 140, 250; Lady Margaret Hall, 33, 42; Literary Society, 44, 50; Oriel College, 72; religious revival in, 171; Balliol College, 229; reported conversions to Moslemism, 255, 256; women undergraduates, 256

Raby, F. J. E., 130n
Radcliffe College, 235
Raleigh, Sir Walter, 81
Raverat, Gwendolen (*née* Darwin), 40, 41, 140
Raymond, John, 125
Recovery of Belief, The (C. E. M. Joad), 41, 42, 45-6, 47n, 48
Reformation, the, 52-3, 60, 61, 74, 82, 83, 85, 113, 123, 125, 128; psychological origins of, 78, 91
Reformation and the Contemplative Life, The (D. and G. Mathew), 120n, 121
Refugees, 80, 100, 244
Renouncement (A. Meynell), 165
Reserved Sacrament, the, 52n, 92
Retreat Addresses (E. K. Talbot), 173
Retreats: attended by R.M., 17, 22, 24, 210; attended by Fr Johnson, 74, 159, 160, 201, 204, 227
Richardson, Samuel, 96
Rieu, E. V., 85, 117
Roberts, S. C., 263n
Rolle, Richard, 85
Roman Catholic Church, The, 41, 116, 234; and birth control, 37; and St Mary Magdalene, 39; and Assumption of the B.V.M., 46-7, 79, 86; election of Cardinals, 56; R.M. on, 58, 107, 108, 111, 113, 115, 128, 139, 163, 195, 209, 221, 252-3; and death-bed dispositions, 59; and Reason, 81; "Bible *v.* Church" in, 86; and fasting rules, 88, 92; and "vague non-Catholics", 106; and "central point" of Faith, 112; and anti-Anglican propaganda 115-16, 176; teachings of, 127, 128, 138-9, 220; and Passion-tide, 152; and variety of practice, 205; "fundamentalism" of, 206; and modernism, 206; 'enquiry centre' in London, 253
Roman Catholicism, 118, 125; R.M. and, 21; in the U.S.A., 35; Irish, 35; appeal to the simple, 42, 253; potential converts to, 56, 120, 122, 129, 221; converts to, 79, 106, 109, 111, 113, 117, 163-4, 172, 175, 177-8, 192, 203, 205, 206-7, 211, 221, 231, 252-3
Roman Catholics: "refusal to worship with other Christians", 15, 32, 73, 163-4, 221, 253; nuns, 15,
127, 140, 265; and other faiths, 41, 73, 163, 190-1, 253, 254; and Anglicans, 42, 47, 49, 78, 203, 209, 221, 252, 260; in the U.S.A., 42; and prayers, 43; Jesuits, 51, 64, 65, 72n, 105-6; undergraduates, 55n; Dominicans, 56, 72n; writers, 72, 80-1, 83, 106, 110; historians, 78, 132-3; English Recusants, 80, 81, 128, 137; and persecution of heretics, 81, 82, 84, 85; priests, 86, 89, 122, 127, 165, 209, 253, 256, 264; R. Murray on, 89; devotional manuals of, 92; Irish, 175-6; critics of A. Toynbee history, 179; and "authority", 190, 197; broadminded, 191, 197; scholarly, 39, 206; "conservative", 220; and indulgences, 253; and miracles, 253. *See also*, Letters, from Roman Catholics to R.M.
Rose, family of, 14, 43, 119-20
Ross, Rev. K. N., 42, 46-7, 228
Ross Williamson, H., 51, 190, 231-2, 236
Rothley Temple, 153
Royalty: extravagance of, 56, 61; "royalty-worship", 92, 158
Rugby School, 14, 15
Ruins, 18; at Rhodes, 64; Bantu, 74; in Cyprus, 75, 93, 97, 99; mosques, 90; of Salamis (Cyprus), 99; in Syria, Lebanon and Jordan, 100, 101, 103; at Capernaum, 102; Greek, 127; R.M.'s passion for, 142; Roman, 149; Theodosian Wall (Istanbul), 156; at Trebizond, 159; Temple of Artemis (Ephesus), 160; Quarr Abbey, 166
Runciman, Steven, 87, 149, 263
Ruskin, John, 252
Russell, Bertrand, 117
Rutherford, Samuel, 215

Sackville-West, Edward, 172
Sackville-West, Lionel, 172
Sackville-West, Mrs Lionel, *see* Hichens, Jacobine
St Anne's House, Soho, 51
Saints, the, 44, 45, 49, 130, 139, 224. *Individual saints are indexed by name*
Saints and Ourselves, ed. P. Caraman, 223-4
Saints in Politics (E. M. House), 108
Sallustius, 214-15

Thomas à Kempis, 85
Thomas Aquinas, St, 177, 220
Thomas Becket, St, 225
Thrones of Earth and Heaven, The
(R. Beny), 254-5
Time (journal), 253
Times, The, 92, 130, 194, 206, 256
Times Literary Supplement, The, 79,
145, 162, 194, 203, 223, 227-8, 231,
236; review of *The Towers of
Trebizond*, 23, 239
Tomis, 155n, 156, 161
Tom Jones (H. Fielding), 96
Tortosa, 100, 103
To the Lighthouse (V. Woolf), 141
Toynbee, Arnold, 176, 178-9, 182
Toynbee, Philip, 176
Toynbee, Rosalind, 89, 256
Tractarians, 89n, 108, 164, 202, 260
Travel, R. M. and: by air, 95, 97,
101, 103, 156; in Cyprus, 97, 98-9,
100; in Lebanon, 100; in Syria,
100; in Jordan, 100, 101, 102; in
Israel, 101, 102, 103; reactions to
Middle East, 103; in the U.S.S.R.
(attempted), 147, 148-9, 150; in
the U.S.A., 148-9; in Turkey, 159-
60, 161, 176; enthusiasm for, 150;
expenses, 150. *See also* Holidays,
R.M.'s
"Treacle wells", 113, 190
Trebizond, 23, 159, 160, 219
Trevelyan, family of, 14
Trevelyan, G. M., 167
Trilling, Lionel, 146
Troy, 160, 230-1
"Tulliver, Maggie" (*The Mill on the
Floss*), 158
Turks, 149, 159-60
Tutin, Dorothy, 123
Two Studies in Virtue (C. Sykes), 111
Tyndale, William, 83, 124-5
Tyrrell, Rev. George, 109, 120, 197;
works of, 105, 106, 149; *Auto-
biography and Life* (M. D. Petre),
105-6

Understanding Europe (C. Dawson),
57
Underhill, Evelyn, 210
United Nations, 100, 101
Unity, of the Churches: Christian
Unity week, 73: Bp of Bristol on,
87
University College Hospital, 264

Varazze, 15, 76, 118, 137, 226; con-
vent school at, 15, 92, 127
Vaughan, C. J., Dean of Llandaff,
163
Vaughan, Canon Edward, 163n
Vaughan, Henry, 76
Vaux of Harrowden (C. Anstruther),
128n
Venice, 23, 24, 248, 252
Vesuvius, Mt, 126
Via Media of the Anglican Church, The
(J. H. Newman), 211-12
Victorian Boyhood, A (L. E. Jones),
229
Victorian England (G. M. Young),
194-5, 196
Vidler, Rev. A. R., 151n
View-Review (journal), 71
Viper of Milan, The (M. Bowen), 180
Virgin Mary, *The* (G. Miegge), 220
Vision of God, The (K. E. Kirk), 165
Visits, by R.M.: to Oxford, 29, 44,
50; to Dorset (Long Crichel
House), 111, 112, 114, 171-2, 263;
to Mottisfont Abbey, 153; to
Cambridge, 202, 237, 238; to
Worcestershire, 208; to Nashdom
Abbey, 226
See also Holidays, R.M.'s *and*
Macaulay, Jean, R.M.'s visits to
Von Hügel, Baron, *see* Hügel,
Baron Friedrich von

*W. G. Ward and the Oxford Move-
ment* (W. Ward), 112-13
Waggett, Rev. P. N., 16, 116, 226
Walled Garden, The (H. Ross
Williamson), 231, 236
Ward, Mrs Humphry, 207, 225
Ward, Maisie, 72n, 111n, 120
Ward, W. G., 112-13, 120n
Ward, Wilfrid, 112, 120, 223
Ward, Mrs Wilfrid, 110
Warren, Austin, 257
Waugh, Evelyn, 30, 197, 234, 255
Webster,—249
Wedgwood, C. V., 183, 188
Weidenfeld, George, 149, 151, 152
Weidenfeld & Nicolson, publishers,
112, 125, 133, 142, 144, 147, 149,
151-2
Weil, Simone, 35
Wells, H. G., 168
Wesley, Charles, 180

287

Dame Rose Macaulay

ROSE MACAULAY, who died in 1958, was born in England in 1881. During much of her childhood she lived with her parents and five brothers and sisters in Italy. Her father, G. C. Macaulay, who lectured in English literature at Cambridge University, was the first in generations of his family not to become a member of the clergy. Miss Macaulay herself grew away from the Anglican Church in her middle years, but in later life, through her correspondence with Father Johnson, returned to the Church's sacraments. After her first novel *Abbots Verney* was published in 1906, she produced over the next forty years a succession of novels, verse, essays and criticism. Her last book, a satirical novel, was *The Towers of Trebizond*, published in 1956. In 1951 Cambridge University bestowed upon her an honorary Litt.D. and in 1958 she was created Dame Commander of the British Empire.

Constance Babington-Smith

A cousin of Rose Macaulay, CONSTANCE BABINGTON-SMITH is the author of *Evidence in Camera* and *Testing Time*. She was born in 1912, and joined the W.A.A.F. in 1940. For her work as a photographic interpreter during the war, she was awarded the Medal of the British Empire and the American Legion of Merit (the first time this had been awarded to a British woman). After the war she stayed on in the United States, but now lives again in England.

111
116
129
131
145
158 - for lectures
190 - image at 74, 192
197 - for lectures
219 recommend
   attitude toward R.C. reflects not only her
opinion but gives index to the thawing produced
by John XXIV. 221

222

239 Mention to C.E.L. when writing